ON THE ROAD

Frank Skinner performed his first stand-up gig in December 1987, and four years later went on to win the prestigious Perrier Award. During the 1990s, Frank established himself as a major name in entertainment – both in live comedy and on television. In 1994 and 1997 he sold-out two UK tours, the second of which culminated in a performance at London's Battersea Power Station – what was then the largest ever audience for stand-up comedy in the UK. On television, Frank has created and starred in a succession of hit comedy shows, including nine series of *The Frank Skinner Show*, from 1995 to 2005; and with his comedy partner David Baddiel *Fantasy Football* (1994–2004) and *Baddiel and Skinner Unplanned* (2000–2005).

As well as live stand-up and television, Frank has attained three number one hits with the iconic football anthem *Three Lions* alongside David Baddiel and the Lightning Seeds. He has starred in the West End in both *Art* and Lee Hall's *Cooking with Elvis*; and his critically acclaimed first book *Frank Skinner* was the bestselling autobiography of 2002, spending a total of 46 weeks in the *Sunday Times* bestsellers' list. In 2006, *Baddiel and Skinner's World Cup Podcasts* caused an online sensation with over one million downloads, leading to yet another Number One chart hit.

In 2007 Frank Skinner returned to stand-up with another sell-out tour of the UK.

Frank currently splits his time between London and Birmingham – and of

Also available by Frank Skinner

Frank Skinner

FRANK SKINNER
ON THE ROAD

arrow books

Published in the United Kingdom by Arrow Books in 2009

1 3 5 7 9 10 8 6 4 2

First published in the United Kingdom in 2008 by Century

Arrow Books
The Random House Group Limited
20 Vauxhall Bridge Road, London, SW1V 2SA

Addresses for companies within The Random House Group Limited can be found at:
www.randomhouse.co.uk/offices.htm

The Random House Group Limited Reg. No. 954009

www.rbooks.co.uk

A CIP catalogue record for this book
is available from the British Library

ISBN9780099458036

The Random House Group Limited supports The Forest Stewardship Council (FSC), the leading international forest certification organisation. All our titles that are printed on Greenpeace approved FSC certified paper carry the FSC logo. Our paper procurement policy can be found at:
www.rbooks.co.uk/environment

PART ONE

EDINBURGH

SUNDAY 12 AUGUST 2007

I'm sitting on the midday train from London to Edinburgh. Tomorrow night I start a two-week run at the Pleasance Cabaret Bar. It's the first time I've done stand-up comedy at the Festival for ten years. In truth, apart from the odd corporate gig – with an audience of business-people whooping at jokes about Paul from Marketing's dodgy haircut – and a cluster of hit-and-miss warm-up shows earlier this year, it's the first time I've done stand-up anywhere for a decade.

It's fitting that my official return to this job should be at the Edinburgh Festival. I was onstage there, one night in 1988, when I first found my comedy voice; first felt at home with a microphone in my hand, bantering with a mouthy crowd and spitting out punchlines that hit and hit and kept hitting till I, at last, goodnighted them into one big roar. Over the next nine years, there were many nights like that in Edinburgh. I won awards, got knockout reviews and played to packed houses, night after night. But then ten years of television caused me to put stand-up on the back burner. All through that period, people would come up to me in bars, at football matches or just in the street, and say, 'When you gonna do stand-up again?' and they'd follow the question with reminiscences from a show they saw in the nineties, in Worthing, Wolverhampton or Hull. 'It was brilliant,' they'd say. And now I'm back to either reinforce that opinion or piss all over it. And I really don't know if I'm good enough, if I can do it any more, if I've lost it.

The train is busy. I'm scribbling in my journal, cautiously shielding the page with my left hand. I like writing in public; fresh and hot. Thoughts are liable to go cold if you leave them sitting on the work surface. These last few years, I've very much taken to keeping a journal. Each year I buy a bigger book, keen to note ever more detail. I'm not sure why, but a day doesn't seem to have happened until I've written it up.

All around me, English voices are charged with expectation. There are a lot of English voices at the Festival, onstage and off. Sometimes, in an audience of two hundred, there'll be just three or four Scots. I was thinking of a line I might try:

> I probably speak to more Scottish people in London than I do in Edinburgh. Sadly, I don't always HAVE spare change.

I scribble it in my notebook, with additional thoughts: 'Emphasis on "have"' and then, in brackets, 'not too early'. This latter note is based on the old comedy rule that an audience will tolerate all sorts of dark subjects, bad language and downright abuse as long as it's a) funny, and b) not too early in the act. a) is impossible to guarantee, but all b) needs is a wristwatch. The idea is that you take time to establish the audience's love before you put that love to the test.

I like train journeys. In the past, when everyone FLEW to Edinburgh, I always got the train. My carbon footprint was like that delicate scratch a sparrow might leave on a snowbank. Of course, back then I didn't know I was saving the planet. In those days the only news the weather made was '*Phew! What a scorcher*', accompanied by shots of bikini blondes on beach towels in

Torquay. That headline has lost a lot of its zing since it started appearing above pictures of dead polar bears.

I like to hear a train at night, as I lie in the darkness of my room. I know it's not everyone's cup of tea. I got a text from a friend in Melbourne, Australia, last night, asking me if I was already at the Festival. *I'm getting the train from King's Cross tomorrow*, I texted back.

The train? How Harry Potter! she replied.

Now what did she mean by that? Do Australians see trains as old-fashioned and quirky? She, I think, envisioned a mighty steam engine, thundering through the glens; her imagination cutting to the interior of an oak-panelled carriage, where my right hand reached around an enormous newspaper to grope for a buttered crumpet. Mind you, just as the Hogwarts Express is crammed with wand-wavers and mystics of all levels – a fat kid, desperately searching a top hat for a missing rabbit, might sit next to a gaunt and grey-haired man who has duelled with Lucifer – this train too, this COMEDY Express, is carrying passengers with a whole range of experience. Jon Plowman, Head of Comedy at the BBC, just said hello as he headed for his seat. I once read an interview with him where he said that comedy is about character, not jokes. To me, that's like saying a cup of tea is about hot water, not tea. This opinion might be influenced by the fact that I have a list of 226 jokes in my bag. Plus a paedophile routine that I've only tried a couple of times and am still unsure about. (Definitely not too early.) I consider discussing this definition of what constitutes comedy with Mr Plowman, but my thoughts are halted by a woman who comes over to tell me we were on the same bill at the King's Head Comedy Club in Crouch End one Thursday night, a few months back. As Thursday is essentially a new comedians' night, with the odd veteran feeling his way back into the spotlight, I would say she probably has her hand on the rabbit but it's still hatbound at the moment.

I don't remember meeting her at the King's Head so I say, 'Oh . . . right. Right. Yeah.' This is what I always say when I can't remember people. It might not look much on the page, but when I accompany it with a range of expressions from 'I'm completely baffled' through to 'Oh, wait a minute' and then follow up with a slowly emerging smile that could possibly suggest actual remembrance-stroke-recognition, the overall effect is pretty good.

I'm not sure she falls for it, but she goes on to say that she runs a little comedy club in Leytonstone. Such statements are usually followed by an invitation to perform. When a well-known comic is doing little clubs, trying out new material, he is usually unpaid. The comic gets the benefit of learning whether his new stuff is funny or not, and the club gets a free booking and a few more bums on seats because people like to see a 'name'.

But being a name will only get you so far. There's a great documentary about Jerry Seinfeld called *Comedian*. When I was doing those warm-up gigs earlier in the year, a club owner said to me, 'There's a film about Jerry Seinfeld doing new-material gigs in clubs and dying on his arse. I think you should watch it.' It was a comment I felt like workshopping but I decided to let it go. I also decided to watch the film. In it, Seinfeld says that being well-known will help you for the first few minutes of a gig but the magic soon wears off and, if you're not funny, you're dead; just like everyone else. I think this is generally true, but being the well-known comic on the bill can actually have disadvantages. I did one warm-up gig where a guy in the crowd shouted, 'You're not on telly any more.' It was a generalisation but I knew what he meant. It wasn't a response to the new material because, by that stage, I'd only used 'Thank you very much' and 'Good evening' – two old standbys that never get big laughs anyway.

I completely respected his right to say what he said. There are many ways to enjoy a comedy gig. When *I* walked out in front of an audience of fifty people – some drunk, some still returning from the toilet – to do ten minutes, unpaid, he decided to enjoy it in the way one enjoys watching King Lear on the heath, or Teddy Sheringham playing for Colchester United – the mighty have fallen; let's watch them struggle. The heckler didn't qualify his remark in any way; he didn't offer any explicit value judgement; he just stated the facts, baldly. Nevertheless, I felt an obligation to comment.

'The thing is,' I said, 'whereas my television career does, indeed, seem to be in the doldrums, you, as far as I can tell, have never had a television career at all. Therefore, in a game of Human Being Top Trumps, I still win.' It didn't get an enormous laugh but *I* enjoyed it. The old gunslinger was back in the saddle; hand still steady, eye still true.

Of course, those who generally do like to see a name in a little club might not always like the name in question. While browsing myself on MySpace (always a risky business and also perhaps a little vain), I read a bit where a woman was saying to a friend that she'd gone to a comedy club because there was a 'special guest' billed and she'd heard it was the Scottish comic Frankie Boyle. 'Imagine my disappointment,' she wrote, 'when it turned out to be Frank Skinner.' I decided against imagining her disappointment and decided, instead, to imagine her brutal murder.

Anyway, the woman on the train doesn't ask me to do her club in Leytonstone. We are interrupted by the man with the complimentary newspapers. In truth, newspapers are rarely complimentary so I decide to avoid the Edinburgh Highlights page. Nor will I be reading stuff about my show while I'm up there. There are two things I always try and avoid at the Edinburgh Festival: reviews and revues. Neither is as easy to sidestep as you might think. Revues, especially if they aren't selling well, have a habit of going alfresco. Groups of students will roam the streets in full costume and make-up, shouting stuff and handing out leaflets. In those circumstances, you can always be sure of one thing. Regardless of the show's theme, be it Charles Dickens, ancient Rome or *The Tibetan Book of the Dead*, there will always be girls in stockings and suspenders. That, in Edinburgh at least, is the way to market a revue. How many men who should know better have sat through an hour of tedious songs and sketches in a draughty Presbyterian Church hall, lured much too close to revue's ragged rocks by six inches of white thigh?

Avoiding reviews is even harder. People just love to tell you about them, especially bad ones. Earlier this year I did a corporate gig for Birmingham City Council. For some reason, it was in Cannes, in the South of France. This combination of moonlit beaches and mushy peas proved irresistible. Six weeks before the gig, and many miles from Cannes, as I sat in my usual seat at The Hawthorns, home of West Bromwich Albion Football Club, a nearby Albion fan leaned across and said, 'I read, in the *Birmingham Post*, you're doing a show in Cannes. They described you as "the ghastly Frank Skinner".' It was, I felt, about time we revised the accepted wisdom on shootings and messengers.

The gig wasn't open to the public. It wasn't even in the United Kingdom. What's more, I hadn't actually done it yet. There could be no review, only an unpleasant aside, but duly noted and passed on. Still, it only nagged at me for a week or so. I must be getting more resilient.

The *Sunday Times'* Culture supplement recently had a big feature on Edinburgh. I couldn't resist a peek. I flick back through my journal to see what I wrote in it that day. 'The Culture had a Top One Hundred Edinburgh Shows. I wasn't in it. It bothered me for about fifteen minutes.' That was two weeks ago and I'm still talking about it. One could argue, I suppose, that there's a difference between remembering and being bothered.

So, no Edinburgh Highlights page for me. I arrive at five o'clock and I intend spending the rest of the day avoiding anything that might put a dampener on tomorrow night's opening. It's positive vibes all the way.

I'm met off the train by Adam, who'll be looking after me in Edinburgh and on the sixty-odd date national tour that follows. He was a late replacement – my original tour manager, Steve, pulled out at the last minute, to tour with Morrissey instead. I imagine Steve, when he was still undecided, standing before the masks of tragedy and comedy, about to flip a coin.

Adam has tour-managed other comics – Russell Brand, Reeves and Mortimer – but he usually does music, from Motörhead to James Blunt. We've only met twice before and conversation is still a bit pedestrian. During the course of our last meeting, he used the phrase 'suited and booted'. I took this to be a very bad sign.

We are going to be spending many hours, and many miles, together over the next four months, often in quite stressful situations; just him and me in a car. No support act. No sound or lighting man travelling with us. What if we don't get on? It will be a nightmare.

Anyway, this same Adam, six feet tall, with short, dark, greying hair and a countenance that suggests he's spent a lot of his life walking across a barren landscape into a raging hailstorm, sticks my bag across his broad shoulders and, with his slightly staggering gait, heads off towards Frederick Street to show me the flat that's my home for the next two weeks. I follow on, clutching my banjo in its slightly battered black carrying case. It is raining. I can actually hear a piper in the distance.

It's a twenty-minute walk to the flat, up along Princes Street, Edinburgh's main thoroughfare – shops on one side, park and castle on the other – and I haven't seen a single stocking top. I guess all that was ten years ago. I'm out of touch.

As we turn into Frederick Street, I see an approaching couple; she, I'd guess, in her late thirties and quite attractive, he a little older and grumpy-looking. As we pass, she says, 'Oooo! Hello, Frank.' I make it my business to be polite and friendly in these situations, even when I'm carrying a banjo and it's raining. I smile, say hello and move on towards my new front door.

'Why should I know you?' asks the grumpy guy, suddenly enraged. 'Why should I know you if you don't know me?'

I turn. 'She said hello; I said hello back,' I explain, in a 'what's the problem?' tone.

'Yes, but why should I know you, if you don't know me?' he says again, his accent getting more Scottish with each repetition.

'Mate, I don't need you to know . . .' I begin, but am soon interrupted.

'But why should I know you if you don't know me?' he growls, by now sounding like an extra from *Whisky Galore*.

The woman is telling him to hush. As we are about fifteen feet apart and he isn't advancing, I smile and turn away. Adam just looks fed up with carrying the bag. I check my watch. I've been in Edinburgh seventeen minutes.

Sylvester Stallone should be glad they didn't film *Rocky* at this house in Frederick Street; if he'd run to the top of these fucking stairs there would not have been a sequel. As we approach my top-floor flat, Adam is looking like the hailstorm has whipped up into a hurricane. But when we finally arrive, it's a nice place; what I'd call a typical Edinburgh flat – sort of stately, with high ceilings that you feel must have absorbed the intellectual energy of generations of early-hours, undergraduate philosophers; wild-eyed young men with moustaches who would occasionally walk to the sash window to shout, 'Leave it by the bins' to Burke and Hare. What's more, there's a roof terrace with a hot tub.

Adam leaves and I decide to unpack before heading out. My former personal assistant, Sarah, now lives with her partner in Royal Crescent and I've been invited round for dinner. I thought it would be a nice, relaxing way to spend my only non-gig night in Edinburgh. I'll have a shave, watch a bit of telly and then stroll across town to Sarah's. My current PA, Jenny, is down in London, likewise my cleaner, and I'm thinking it will do me good to be up here, shopping at the supermarket, doing the ironing, generally fending for myself. Within fifteen minutes I'm on the phone to Adam, telling him there's no Sky Sports and I can't get the plug out of the sink. He calms me down and says he'll sort things out tomorrow.

Sarah lives in a beautiful big house with a beautiful big garden that has a sort of communal swing which seats six. I share the swing with her and her partner Fran and two sweet old guys, one a relative of Sarah's, the other an old army friend of Fran's dad. It's stopped raining now and the evening is cool but pleasant. Good food, good company and beautiful surroundings, but, three hours later, as I stand, post-ascent, gasping for breath at the door of my flat, I can't help thinking I wasn't really funny enough tonight. For me, four other people constitute an audience, and I don't think I went that well. There were a couple of old anecdotes that worked, but I feel my improvising was a bit flat. The swingers joke just seemed a bit inappropriate. It's not a BIG deal, but it is a deal. I can imagine the reviews: 'He's a nice enough chap, but you'd never guess he was a comedian.' Oh, the horror.

This is the lot of the performer. I'm not as bad as I used to be but . . . No, actually, I AM as bad as I used to be. About a year ago, I read a bedtime story for a five-year-old girl called Dolly, the daughter of my sometime comedy partner, David Baddiel. I'd never read anyone a bedtime story before and, though I was, no kidding, a bit nervous beforehand, I quite enjoyed it and left Dolly's bedroom feeling it had gone pretty well. A couple of months later, I was round Dave's again and I did another bedtime story. Later, Dave's partner, Morwenna, asked me how it had gone. 'Well,' I said, 'not that good, to be honest. I'm not sure the story itself was as strong as the last one and I . . . Oh, I don't know, I felt a bit flat. It was OK; it just wasn't quite what I'd hoped for.' Many mothers would have laughed me out of the house, but Morwenna, who is a performer herself, put her hand on my shoulder and seemed to understand.

I still can't get this fuckin' plug out.

MONDAY 13 AUGUST 2007

I had a restless night. I tell myself it was the unfamiliar bed, but it probably had something to do with tonight's show. I've always thought of myself as a very un-nervous performer. No pre-show shakes or vomiting; just focussed and ready to go. Then, about three months ago, I got myself a new watch. It's got a button on the front which, if held down for a few seconds, tells you your current heart-rate in beats per minute (bpm). The average male heartbeat, at rest, is 70 bpm. Anything over a 100, at rest, is a worry. Your maximum heart-rate (come on – stick with it) give or take 10 bpm, is 220 minus your age. In other words, as a fifty-year-old man, my maximum heart-rate is between 160 and 180 bpm. Anything higher than that and I'm liable to start getting dizzy and eventually black out. Obviously, the heart-rate is increased by physical effort and/or anxiety. Well, now, my stand-up is not terribly energetic. It basically involves walking, talking and holding a microphone that weighs around ten ounces. Some comedians use a microphone stand but, hey, I like to work that upper body. My point is: any increase in my heart-rate during a gig is going to be largely down to anxiety. If that anxiety takes me over 180 bpm . . . well, we could be talking Tommy Cooper.

Shit, in the old days, my only gig-based worries were, in order of importance, will they laugh and will I get a shag afterwards? Now, at fifty, it's will they laugh and will I have a heart attack? And yes, that's still in order of importance.

A few days after I got the watch I had a warm-up gig in Windsor. Just before I went onstage I measured my heart-rate at 73 bpm. The gig lasted about an hour and a quarter. Immediately afterwards my heart-rate was 81. I figured that was pretty good for a new-material gig. Two days after Windsor, I did a similar-length gig in Aldershot. Pre-gig, Mr Consistency, my bpm was a smooth 74. Post gig? 170!

So what happened? Well, my set was different but not drastically different. It's just that Windsor was a good gig and Aldershot was a bad one. In Windsor, I knew it was going to be good as soon as I walked onstage. The applause was warm and welcoming; they were ready to laugh should I give them the opportunity to do so. There was love in the room and it brought out the best in me. In Aldershot, the opening applause sounded like half-a-dozen unsynchronised dripping taps. They laughed like Hitler laughed: not very often and for all the wrong reasons.

Even so, 170, that's scary; and, presumably, a worse gig than Aldershot will push it even higher. I have eighty-three gigs till the end of the tour. I'm playing the heart-attack lottery. And I've just remembered those fucking stairs. They've got to count as a bonus ball.

Just to round off all these cardiac calculations, I now recall that I actually have quite a slow average heartbeat, about 58, at rest. That means I was a bit more anxious before both those gigs than I thought. Also, my watch tells me that as I lie in this unfamiliar bed, ten and a half hours before tonight's show, my heart-rate is 63; 5 bpm above my usual average. Not much of an increase, but just enough to make me feel marginally different. Right down in the depths of me, a small fire is burning – small, but the crackle of it, the smell of the smoke, lets me know it's a gig-day.

I'm off to the Pleasance Cabaret Bar, about thirty minutes' walk from my flat. It's raining again, but only lightly, and Princes Street is bustling in a very Festival kind of a way. I can hear the piper playing 'Scotland the Brave', a fat, bare-chested man sits between shops, playing a didgeridoo and, next to the statue of the Duke of Wellington, Native Americans (you know, feathers, tepees and tomahawks) dance and sing to the primal rhythm of rattle-type-things on sticks.

I arrive at the Pleasance theatre complex – every lean-to, lobby and walk-in wardrobe seems to constitute a venue – just before eleven and am greeted by a slightly damp Adam. He shuffles towards the Cabaret Bar and I follow, smiling at old memories. My Perrier Award-winning show was in the Pleasance Cabaret Bar, but it's changed a lot since then, refurbishment making it bigger and squarer. Now, it's a black box of a room with a piano on a low stage in one corner, and a bar, to be closed during the performance, in the corner opposite. It's still pretty cosy, with a capacity of 175, and smells, inevitably, of stale beer. When it's sold out, which it is for these coming two weeks, the doors at the back of the room are slammed shut, and the air get hot and syrupy.

'If it gets too hot,' says Aaron, the chunky, black-bearded venue manager, 'you can switch that fan on.' He gestures towards a small electric fan at the rear of the stage. I make a mental note to some-how incorporate all this into tonight's performance. This mid-morning trip to the venue is what they call a technical rehearsal. As my show is essentially one man and a microphone, it doesn't take very long. The soundman plays my walk-on music, 'The Container Drivers' by The Fall, and I walk on and talk into the microphone. I'm not a big fan of one-two, one-two, so I generally recite William Wordsworth's 'She Dwelt Among the Untrodden Ways'. This morning it's the first two stanzas into the stage mic, and the third and final one into the reserve mic that stands in the wings. I generally find if a sound system will take a Lucy poem, it'll take most stuff. Then the soundman plays my post-gig music, 'Back in the Saddle Again' by Gene Autry, and I tell everyone I'll see them at 7.45.

The tech, as they call it, seems to have given me a confidence boost; probably because the Cabaret Bar crew laughed at most of my impromptu comic asides. Crew members, in theatres and television studios; sound engineers, lighting people, camera people – basically anyone in a headset – are usually, it seems to me, grimly determined not to be impressed, amused or even mildly distracted by anyone who's standing on a stage. This, of course, may just be my own paranoia. Reassuring producers and tour managers, over the years, have suggested to me that I shouldn't expect a crew to behave like an audience because they are busy doing their jobs and concentrating on a dozen different things. The thing is, they never LOOK very busy. They just look bored, and riddled with hatred.

Of course, it's possible that I might not be funny or entertaining enough to actually make a crew laugh; that a proper audience, who generally have bought a seat, hired a babysitter, paid for a parking space and are, all in all, making a night of it, might be laughing because they have invested time and money and are going to damn well laugh whether it's funny or not; or because they are slightly hysterical with the sheer excitement of getting out of the house. Maybe all those theatre and TV crews represent an HONEST assessment of my work and I should thank each one of them, individually, for making me aware of my utter worthlessness, for making me feel humble and small. Perhaps I should turn to that unshaven chap in the *Men Behaving Badly* fleece, or that fat woman wearing red spectacles and a *Mamma Mia!* tour t-shirt and say, 'You're right, I'm shit, and thanks for acknowledging that fact in all your dealings with me.'

Anyway, as I say, the Pleasance Cabaret Bar crew seem rather nice. Their crumbs of encouragement have made me feel suddenly confident, invincible even. In fact, I feel so invincible I tell Adam that I'll deal with the sink plug myself. I march back to Frederick Street with a spring in my step that almost upgrades into dancing when I pass the Native Americans.

I decide to have a restful afternoon at the flat, going through my set for tonight, playing the banjo, nice and relaxed; but first I have to deal with this plug. It's one of those that are anchored to the plug hole. There'll be a lever somewhere, a thing to pull or turn; it's about staying calm and thinking logically. There's probably a manual in one of the drawers.

One and a half hours later, I'm watching last night's shaving water slowly disappear. I stand, hands on hips, head held high, as Isambard Kingdom Brunel must have stood when watching one of his mighty steamships slide down the ramp. I've prised the plug upward with a spoon and wedged the small gap open with the plastic cover from a disposable razor. I rub my hands together, gleefully. 'Lunchtime, I think.'

Sooner than seems right, show-time looms. Still, even allowing for a certain amount of trepidation, it's always nice to be able to walk to work. I close the front door behind me and step out into the early evening Edinburgh air. I look at my watch. Its digital display says 18.15. How apt, I think. It's 18.15 and I'm heading to my Waterloo.

Stand-up comics are often inclined towards melodramatic analogies with other, much more hazardous professions. I'm an explorer crossing an arid desert, a wizened old gunslinger strapping on his six-guns after a ten-year break or, tonight, Napoleon, the haemorrhoidal emperor, marching towards humiliation and exile. I've sat in dressing rooms and heard the turns comparing themselves to a boxer entering a ring to take on a brutal opponent, a test batsman striding out, mid innings-collapse, to face a barrage of bouncers, and even a gladiator, hiding his terror behind a devil-may-care exterior and trying to avoid the lion shit as he pouts and poses his way into the arena of death. My journal for 28 August 2006 tells how, that day, I bought a small notebook – the same one I used on the train yesterday – and, scribbling excitedly, blasted out my first stand-up routine for years. That night I watched a documentary about Scott of the Antarctic. Afterwards I wrote, 'Seems like I'm off on a bit of an expedition myself. Hope it's an Amundsen and not a Scott.' All I'd done was written nine gags about having sex from behind. I mean, even if it didn't get laughs I was never going to have to eat my dogs.

Sometimes, I'll deliberately avoid these historical analogies, and adopt a topical approach. Thus, I've recently taken to likening my arrival onstage to a middle-aged man, stepping edgily from his front door to remonstrate with a group of hooded youths. There'll be plenty more melodramatic analogies to come, I'm sure. But tonight it's Napoleon and I give Princes Street's statue of the Duke of Wellington a Gallic sneer as I pass.

The didgeridoo bloke has moved to the other side of the road. Do people actually play tunes on didgeridoos? If I leaned over him and asked, raising my voice above the aboriginal vibrations, 'Do you know "All by Myself" by Eric Carmen?' would he be able to knock up a recognisable version? Or would it just be 'arum-rum-rummmmm-arum' like it always is?

By the time I reach the Pleasance that small fire in the depths of me is beginning to swirl and spit a little. However, I've resolved to stop checking my heart-rate at gigs. It only adds to the anxiety. There is a big queue outside, stretching across the courtyard. Some of them smile as I pass. Hands in pockets, eyes forward, I smile back but don't really want to speak. What if I said something that wasn't funny? They'd be soiled with doubt before they'd even crossed the threshold. It'd be an uphill struggle from the start.

Then I smile to myself as I remember the last *Celebrity Big Brother* series. The stars were arriving, one after the other, in their limos, and Dirk Benedict, the former *A-Team* star, appeared. The previous celebrities had all given it large, hands raised in celebration, keen to co-ordinate their own welcome. Benedict instead moved edgily forward, grabbed the upper arm of a random young woman from the crowd, and said, bleakly, 'Pray for me.' I decide against doing that. I wouldn't want the person I grab to realise I'm not joking.

Adam, wearing a smart black dress-shirt for opening night, is at the door and ushers me into the venue. There is a tiny dressing room, separated from the stage by only a thick black curtain. There's no room for pacing. I sit amidst the racks of costumes and boxes of props from a dozen other shows that are on before or after me. The walls are covered in old posters and publicity shots, including a fat-faced me from sixteen years ago.

Adam comes in to see if I need anything. 'Only a very funny hour of stand-up comedy,' I say.

'No,' he says, 'you've already got one of those.'

'Well, we'll soon find out,' I say.

'It's gonna be great,' he says, sitting down. 'Did you fix the sink?'

'Yes.'

'And have you got Sky Sports now? I phoned the . . .'

'Look, Adam,' I say, 'I'm not very good at conversation just before a gig. I don't mean to be . . .'

'No. No problem. I'll go and er . . .' He leaves. Poor Adam. I wonder if Marshal Ney had to endure similar tetchiness from Napoleon, pre-battle.

'Emperor, how are zee piles?'

'Oh, not *trop* bad.'

'By the way, your fringe . . . it eez not as pointy as you usually . . .'

'Look, Michel, I've got Blucher on one side and Wellington on zee other. I just don't feel chatty.'

I can hear the buzz of the audience, from the other side of the curtain. What are they thinking? Ten years is a long time. Some will have seen me in the old days, that same cheeky chappie that grins from the wall above me. Will they be expecting more of the same, another big dollop of bawdy Birmingham, Jack-the-Lad fuck-fuck-fuck 'em all and fucking football fuckness? Does that work with a fifty-year-old man? Is that what I've got for them tonight? Am I out of date? What do modern comedy fans like? Is it too late to get a catchphrase? 'Container Drivers' suddenly kicks in. That's my cue.

I push the curtain and I'm out there. Big cheer. Music fades. 'Thank you very much. It's great to be back in Edinburgh.' Another big cheer. 'Oh, have we got some Edinburgh people in?' Even bigger cheer. They all seem to be from Edinburgh. 'I wasn't expecting that. I usually speak to more Scottish people in London than I do in Edinburgh. Sadly, I don't always HAVE spare . . .' Way too fucking early but they laughed anyway. I got brave.

It's hot in here, isn't it? I did a gig at a big music festival in the summer. It was so hot I saw a dog loosening its neckerchief.

Small laugh. This is a gag I've now tried about six times and it's never really worked. I don't normally give a gag that many chances, but I seem to have a misplaced affection for this one. Anyway, now that the second gag of the night has died, or, at least, sustained a life-threatening injury, I need to hit them with a sure-fire winner, get their confidence back, let them know they're in safe hands. But while I'm thinking this I've already started the next bit. I'm like a kid running down a hill. I just keep going: '. . . and I said to him, "Do you know 'All by Myself' by Eric Carmen?"'

In that Jerry Seinfeld movie, he talks about the dangers of doing new material at the top of the set. The comedy rule is: save the new stuff until they've already laughed a lot, till they trust you, till you're on a roll and they're enjoying the ride. But the temptations are terrible. A new joke is like a new child: Daddy wants everyone to know about it as soon as possible. But, as I said before, you have to break them in gently, at the start of the show; nothing new and nothing too rude. Shit. Where am I going now?

. . . he said, 'if it gets too hot you can put that electric fan on!' I used to be quite big, you know. Now I'm doing my own ventilation. Then I thought, 'Maybe I could do a prop-joke.' And I was gonna put a little plate of chopped, raw liver behind the fan, and when I switched it on, with my back to you, I was gonna put my hand near the fan, scream and make a grating noise, and throw the chopped liver over my shoulder, all over the front three rows. And you'd have thought . . . (I TRAIL OFF INTO A FARAWAY LOOK AND A SIGH.) But I decided against it. I just didn't want a headline in tomorrow's paper that said, '*Frank Skinner puts three fingers in a fan*'. (BIG LAUGH) It's an image I'm trying to shrug off.

That last sentence added post-punchline, delivered as a throwaway line, barely discernible above the laugh, is a technique I rarely employ. It's a thing that Jay Leno, the American stand-up and chat-show host, uses a lot. He'll do a punchline like 'Maybe someone should tell George Bush' and then, during the laugh, he'll mumble, 'Give him a call. He's always home.' I think Leno's trying to suggest that his punchline wasn't actually a punchline. It's a sort of anti-vaudeville approach; like he's saying, 'Hey, I'm just chewing the fat here. If you happen to find something funny, that's OK, but there's no joke-pause-joke-pause thing going on. I'm just talking.'

The technique itself certainly pre-dates Leno. I suspect it came about as a result of some old comic trying to disguise failed gags. If you fill the post-punchline silence with more talk, the audience might not notice that the punchline happened at all. Suddenly you're not a comic with some shit jokes and some good jokes, you're a comic who chats quite a lot in between his good jokes.

Is that why I used this technique tonight? Was it a safety net in case the laugh didn't come? I'm not sure. Stand-up comedy, like all human discourse, is part-deliberate and part-mystery. If I had to guess, I'd say I hid the punchline in this way because I was slightly ashamed of the joke, thought it was a bit too easy. Still, maybe I should save the analysis till after the gig.

I move on to material that I've done a few times before, material that I've worked a little, material that I've started to find my way around. They laugh. In fact, they laugh quite a lot. I'm happy in the black box.

At one point, in the midst of a routine about patriotic songs, I start talking to a teenager in the front row. 'Have you heard of Vera Lynn?' I ask.

'Yeah, of course,' he replies. I'm pleased. One worry for me as a fifty-year-old comic is that I'm likely to refer to people and things that half my audience have never heard of. 'She's that abortion woman,' he adds. He's thinking Vera Drake.

'No,' I say, 'Vera Lynn was the Forces' sweetheart! I don't mean she was a slut; I mean she was much-admired by soldiers and stuff, in the war.' He shakes his head. I only brought her up because when she was ninety I heard her being interviewed on daytime telly, discussing her career. She talked about her big hits, 'We'll Meet Again' and 'White Cliffs of Dover', and then she said, 'A modern singer wouldn't be able to have a career like mine because wars nowadays . . . they're just not long enough.' The presenters nodded at this wisdom. You have to admit; it's not a sentiment you hear expressed every day.

These lines and fragments in isolation don't sound rip-roaring, but it was good; I rocked and I felt that post-good-gig glow that is the best feeling in the world. The courtyard was still busy, despite the fact it was raining again. I saw Sarah. She'd told me last night that she'd bought four tickets for the opening show. She smiled as the departing audience members filed past her, and said, 'You're going to have a lot of fun on tour.' With this she dashed off to the other three in her party, who waited for her under a distant awning. They included one of the sweet old guys from last night. I may have imagined it, it may have been the rain or my own near-sightedness, but it looked to me like there was great disappointment in his face; maybe a sense of having been let down.

This is the cross that the dirty comic must bear. Some of my stuff is quite near the knuckle; not too near, but near. But at the same time, I've been worried that I'm cleaner nowadays and my old fans will feel I've gone soft. Anyway, some people, probably most people, don't even want to be in the same postcode as the knuckle.

They're embarrassed and disgusted to hear things like masturbation and granny porn discussed anywhere, let alone as a form of public entertainment. I've always defended this stuff in a freedom-of-speech kind of a way. Dirty jokes, good dirty jokes, make me laugh. They always have done. They make a lot of people laugh – heartily. The granny porn stuff stormed it tonight:

> The video starts. I see a woman in her late seventies, lying on her sofa wearing only stockings and suspenders, and I think to myself, 'How marvellous; how marvellous that an old-age pensioner can afford to have her heating on that high.'
>
> There are all sorts of plusses in granny porn that you'd never expect. For example, in normal pornography, it's almost impossible to get a close-up shot that includes the vagina AND nipples. (AND THEN, THROUGH THE LAUGH, IN A JAY LENO MUMBLE) In granny porn they're much more adjacent.

'Much more adjacent' . . . that's what I love, when a routine becomes a sort of filth-poem. Like the bit where I talk about an actual incident from one of these movies: a young guy getting oral sex from a very old lady. The contrasting ages of the two protagonists gives me the opportunity to consider how we view sex differently as we get older: him deadly serious; her light-hearted. I tell how the old lady, mid blow-job, suddenly puffs out her cheeks, runs her fingers up and down his penis and makes like she's playing a clarinet, even reproducing its sound.

And what I loved was that I actually recognised the tune she was playing. It was 'American Patrol' by the Glenn Miller Orchestra. At that moment, I had an image of her as a beautiful young girl, jitterbugging with a handsome GI who never came back from the war.

The routine, having soared upwards; a moment of golden nostalgia amidst the clammy smell of sex; then dives back down to earth again.

The young guy didn't even smile at her musical interlude. He was too worried about how he was gonna get the smell of mint humbugs off his helmet.

You know, if they'd let me write my own reviews, I'd read them avidly. Anyway, I accept that this dirty-mouth material isn't everyone's cup of tea, but I do come with a warning. 'Not for the faint-hearted,' it says on the poster; not a phrase I would've chosen myself; it's only knob-jokes, not Alton Towers. Still, the old guy did look disappointed, maybe even contaminated. In normal circumstances that would have nagged at me for the rest of the evening, but it got superseded.

What did Sarah mean, 'You're going to have a lot of fun on tour'? I hate it when post-gig remarks are slightly cryptic; just 'slightly', but enough to keep me awake for the rest of the week. I'd just seen Carol Sarler, the newspaper columnist. She nipped backstage and said, 'Frank, I loved it!' and that was that. She's an experienced journalist; she knows a lot of performers and she knows what they need.

A friend of mine was in a show at the National Theatre in London. It was a big production with a large cast. I'd arranged to see him in the bar afterwards. Twenty minutes before the show began, he sent me a text that said *Don't forget to say I'm best.* It's not often an audience member gets their own prompt. I knew it was a joke but he wasn't joking. I saw him after the show and said, 'It's ironic that you sent me that text message because you actually WERE best.' He grinned, proudly. My job was done.

I'm back at Frederick Street, gazing up at my moonlit bedroom ceiling. You'll have a lot of fun trying to turn that pile of shit into a decent tour show . . . is THAT what she meant?

TUESDAY 14 AUGUST 2007

It's nearly lunchtime and I'm sitting on the settee, playing the banjo. When I say 'playing', I mean 'learning to play'. I could leave it vague and have you imagining me with my fingers a bluegrass blur; but that would be inaccurate. I'm playing 'Shortnin' Bread' over and over, badly. I did a documentary for the BBC last year in which I learnt the banjo; or, at least, began learning it. It culminated in me playing in the National Banjo Championships in Kansas, up against an array of brilliant banjo-men (they WERE all men. I don't know why). Many of them had been playing for twenty years or more. I'd been playing for three months. I was profoundly out of my depth. I didn't even get the sympathy vote because the audience were never told I was a beginner. When I walked onstage, they were expecting to hear genius; instead they heard only nervous, fumbling shitness. They would have realised I was new to the instrument a few seconds into my performance had I not confused the issue by injecting my stage presence with a hint of stroke victim. Whereas a beginner would have just got a 'Why are you wasting our time?' glare, I think the vague suggestion that I was a once-great picker, reduced to this state by cruel circumstance, slightly softened their response.

At the time, it seemed to be a valuable experience. It came only a few months before I started doing stand-up again and it made me feel thick-skinned and empowered. If I could face that humiliation, that pathetic failure, and come out smiling, any stand-up gig would be a stroll. Utter bollocks, of course. The reason I coped with Kansas was that I knew I was shit, I had every right to be shit, and the thing I was shit at was a new hobby not a long-time obsession that I used to be fucking good at. If the stand-up proved to be shit, I'd be that fumbling embarrassment of a once-great banjo player without the stroke for an excuse.

And that is still a real possibility. The eight months of try-out gigs leading up to last night were not without their disappointments. I'd say they were about 70 per cent good and 30 per cent shit. It's the kind of average I'd happily accept in any other area of life except my work. Sorry, I'm saying 'shit' a lot. So would you if you could hear my version of 'Shortnin' Bread'.

Maybe I should give you a few facts. As preparation for these Edinburgh shows and the impending tour, I did thirty-four new-material slots, varying in length between ten minutes to half an hour, at various small comedy clubs all over London. I wrote all the stuff myself and, after each gig, I went through the night's set ticking the jokes that worked, crossing the jokes that failed and question-marking the ones that did neither. Sometimes, a bit of re-jigging promotes these latter gags into the ticks column, but they don't get many chances. They are on a yellow card. I would say that 80 per cent of question marks end up taking an early bath. On the plus-side, my post-gig analysis usually reminds me of a few ad-libs that went well and which now can be added to the list. These jokes arrive with the tick already attached.

Oh, and if you want maths, I'll give you maths. I reckon that, according to my own experience, twelve ticks (i.e. punchlines that get a good laugh) constitute about five minutes of material. The Edinburgh shows are an hour in duration so that's 144 ticks required. I'm planning on the tour show being ninety minutes in duration. That's 216 ticks.

I started writing, in earnest, last October. By 19 January I had 285 jokes. At this stage they were all untried. The little egomaniac comedian on my right shoulder whispered that they were all solid gold and all I had to do now was soak up the adulation. The insecure little comedian on my left shoulder told me there wasn't a decent laugh in there and this whole return-to-stand-up thing would turn out to be a terrible error.

My first gig was 22 January. By the time I'd completed my check-list after the thirty-fourth try-out gig, on 19 April, I was left with 340 ticks; nearly two and a half hours of material. Yeah, I wrote a lot of gags along the way. I was still worried. Stand-up ticks are rarely written in stone. Sometimes a whole routine will just collapse under you like Devon Loch. (Oh, fucking Google it!)

For each of the thirty-four gigs, I appeared on a normal club-night, as a surprise guest, sharing the bill with anything from four to fifteen other comics. Then, at the beginning of May, I set out on a series of twelve one-hour gigs in arts centres across the country. There were no other comics to soften the blow. These performances were billed as warm-up gigs and the tickets were a fiver each, but my name was on the poster. They knew who they were getting.

After these twelve gigs, the 340 ticks had shrunk to 226. And that includes the dog's neckerchief. As I say, I need 216 for the tour. It's tight.

Then a thought strikes me that causes me to stop 'Shortnin' Bread' mid-verse: I'm sure it's still possible to have a lot of fun on tour, even though your show is clearly unsalvageable. Is THAT what she meant?

On the toilet, I browse the Fringe Programme; seeing if there are any interesting shows I might check out. I concentrate on the Pleasance venues because, if you're doing a show at the Pleasance, you can usually get into their other offerings for free. When I was a drinking man, my social life didn't involve a lot of decision-making other than, Shall I get pissed or shall I get very pissed? Nowadays, I cram the void that alcohol left behind with movies, exhibitions, music gigs, sports events, lectures, theatre shows; my thirst for booze has been replaced by a thirst for endless stimulation. I live in Central London because, if you keep a regular eye on the What's Ons and newspaper preview pages, London can be like a giant Fisher-Price activity centre. Edinburgh, at Festival time, is another box of delights.

There's a one-man show about Charlie Chaplin, at the Pleasance Dome at three o'clock. I'd be out at four so I'd still have plenty of time to chill before my own show. I figure a play about a great comedian might be inspirational, might help me to see myself in heroic terms. One of the things that keep me going as a comic is the romance of it. When you've done a crap gig, all your new material has fallen on stony ground and you're heading home alone, you can feel pretty empty. This happened to me back in February, when I did twenty minutes at a club on a boat, called the *Tattershall Castle*, permanently moored near Waterloo Bridge. As I wrote in my journal, 'I felt like there was a lot of hate in the room.'

I walked back home along the dark river, hands in pockets, with my overcoat-collar turned up against the icy wind. A dark overcoat is a boon for any struggling creative type. It conjures up those black-and-white pictures of James Dean in a New York winter, looking troubled but cool. Mind you, aged fifty, even with my imagination fired up by a traumatic gig, I struggle to see myself as James Dean any more, so I've switched to Samuel Beckett. He was another dark-overcoat man.

Anyway, I was walking along the Embankment, trying to feel angst-ridden and misunderstood instead of just feeling like a shit comic. Why didn't they laugh?

When we got back to the hotel, it turned out she had anal warts; or, as I call them, speed-bumps.

It was, if nothing else, accessible.

By now, I was absolutely wallowing in it but I hadn't quite got the balance right. I was still more shit comic that tragic hero. Then, just as my self-dramatisation looked like it was failing, I plucked an obscure quote from the past that made the whole *Tattershall Castle* experience seem suddenly glorious: 'There's a certain beauty in defeat.' Yes, the pain, the humiliation, was strangely beautiful. I savoured it, bathed in its cruel radiance. 'A certain beauty in defeat'; it's what Terry Griffiths said when he got knocked out in the first round of the World Snooker Championships in 1980. I'll take my tragic consolation wherever I can get it.

When it got too warm for the overcoat, I had to start smoking again. The cigarette is another classic prop in my post-crap-gig romanticising. I hold it right down where my index and middle fingers join. When I take a drag, the whole hand wraps around my jaw. It's how Dean Martin used to smoke. I'm mysterious in tobacco clouds; the wounded veteran, just trying to get along.

Anyway, back in the toilet, I'm thinking a play about Chaplin is likely to throw up a few images I can replay when I'm trying to see myself as part of a great British comic tradition, stretching right back to the court jesters and wandering minstrels. This is another of my aides-de-self-esteem.

I once went to see a Chaplin double-bill, *The Rink* and *Modern Times*, with live accompaniment by the Royal Philharmonic Orchestra, conducted by Carl Davis. At the end, Davis came out to take his applause and then gestured towards the now-empty screen. A still image of Charlie Chaplin appeared there. The crowd clapped and cheered, not only with admiration, but also with real love. I was very moved by it. To be honest, it's hard to imagine a similar response to a picture of me, after a double bill of granny porn and the anal warts joke, but I do sometimes feel real affection – love, even – from an audience. You don't have to be a legend; you just need to have been around for a bit, be associated with happy times, nights-out or nights-in. It's a beautiful feeling and it keeps you going back for more or, at least, the chance of more.

At the Pleasance Dome, Chaplin is being played by an actor called Pip Utton. He seems to specialise in one-man biographical plays, because he's also doing one earlier in the day at another venue. That one is called *Adolf.* I start to wonder how Hitler's picture would've gone down after a *Dad's Army/'Allo 'Allo* double bill. Oh, maybe I'll just play some more banjo.

I meet Adam for dinner at six. We're still struggling with each other a bit, but he likes football so that keeps our restaurant conversation ticking over. I notice a new, up-and-coming comic I met during my recent club try-out period at a nearby table, so I nip over to say hello. He is doing a late-night show here and his whole family have come up to see him perform. There's about seven of them at the table. Seven, to me, easily constitutes an audience, so I start fooling around, riffing on themes; I'm on fire. It's like a hot ten-minute warm-up for tonight's show. The new comic seems alarmed. I sense he is thinking, 'Oh, no. My act isn't anywhere near as funny as this. My family have come all the way to Edinburgh to see a show I have been writing and rewriting, pruning and polishing for months, and they will go home with only one lasting memory, one glorious anecdote to thrill and delight their stay-at-home friends – ten minutes at a restaurant table with Frank Skinner.' Of course, he might NOT be thinking that but he looks to me as if he is. As I walk away from the still-giggling family, I half expect to hear 'Back in the Saddle Again'.

Tonight it's raining worse than ever. We stop at a newsagent's on the Royal Mile so I can buy a tartan brolly. It'll keep me dry and also give me something to hide under during the scary late-night piss-head slaloms that I'll no doubt be zigzagging through on my way back to Frederick Street. In the newsagent's I meet two middle-aged women from West Bromwich, my home town, so I have my photo taken with them and, like Elvis dishing out Cadillacs to complete strangers, I buy each of them a plastic poncho. That's me: big-hearted. I actually start singing the old British comedian Arthur Askey's theme song, 'Big-Hearted Arthur', as we head for the Pleasance.

A friend of mine once told me that he'd seen Arthur Askey on a chat show. He skipped on, five feet two, horn-rimmed spectacles, as the band played 'Big-Hearted Arthur', and then, during the course of the interview, suggested the return of National Service and the death penalty and an end to immigration. As he left the stage, my friend explained, the band once more played the now extremely inappropriate 'Big-Hearted Arthur'. I pointed out that maybe 'Bigoted Arthur' would have been a more suitable choice.

As we head to the Pleasance, I feel funny, munificent and dry. I can't wait to get on stage.

The show wasn't that great. I made my new-material-at-the-top mistake again. I began by telling them about meeting the young comic and his family in the restaurant, but I think it just came over as arrogant – cruel even. I'm not sure they ever quite forgave me. Some of the other new stuff went OK:

Every day I pass those Native Americans, dancing and singing at the bottom of Princes Street, and every night it pisses down with rain. Are you gonna fuckin' tell them or shall I?'

. . . He's also doing another show in which he plays Hitler. He's obviously thought, 'Fuck it! I've bought the moustache. Might as well get my money's worth.'

Apart from those bits, I basically did the same show I did last night, but none of it went quite as well. Because I wasn't changing anything in the body of the show I decided I didn't need to go through my material again today. I figured I'd be better just forgetting about it and relaxing. Now I realise that was me taking my foot off the pedal, and I'm pissed off about it. I fluffed a few lines and faltered a bit and it's inexcusable.

Still, I'm not exactly beating myself up about this. It's midnight and I'm in the hot tub. I am smoking a clay pipe. It gives me a sore throat and makes me feel nauseous but I like the idea of it. It suits Edinburgh. It makes me feel like a thinker; a David Hume or a

Walter Scott. I've turned it upside-down to keep the rain out, but the tobacco is staying put.

It's dark on the roof, except for the blue glow of the hot tub, and it's cold and windy this high above the street. I sit with my shoulders beneath the rain-dappled surface of the steaming water and feel cosy. I'm disappointed by the gig, choked by the pipe; but the hot tub is good. I can see the castle, silhouetted against the ink-blue sky. Dancing spotlights, some Festival celebration or other, carve up the dark clouds. Their bat-signal beams emanate from the beautiful city that twinkles below.

I really wanted to come here and be the talk of the town – the master of his art returns, better than ever – but I don't think it's going to happen. I'm getting better; my performance is sharper; my material is benefiting from repetition; I'm finding its rhythms and stresses; it's organically growing with each performance. But I'm not THERE; and by Edinburgh I intended to be THERE. These gigs aren't billed as warm-ups, but that's exactly what they are: work in progress. I start to feel bad that people are paying twelve quid to watch me practise. I seem to hear their outraged hissing. Then I realise a hunk of red-hot tobacco has dropped into the water.

You know, it's very hard to do the post-crap-gig tragic-hero thing when you're in a hot tub. You just can't mix heartache and hydrotherapy.

WEDNESDAY 15 AUGUST 2007

I got up at ten and now I'm at the Andy Warhol exhibition at the nearby National Gallery of Scotland. I'm slightly obsessed by art galleries. Back home in London, I'm usually in one at least once a week. One of my best-ever celebrity perks was to get invited to an exhibition of paintings by the seventeenth-century Spanish artist Velázquez at the National Gallery in London. I was told to turn up at 6 p.m. As I walked across Trafalgar Square that night, I realised the gallery was closing and the crowd was filing out. A woman from the gallery beckoned me in through a side door and led me to the entrance of the exhibition. It was empty. 'If you need anything, give me a shout,' she said, and wandered off to talk to a colleague. Usually, a high-profile exhibition like this is crammed. I spend a lot of time waiting for people to finish looking at a painting, sculpture or whatever, so I can step into their spot. Even as I do, there'll be someone at my elbow waiting for me to move on. In twenty-first-century Britain, where, according to the papers, everybody's drunk, illiterate and carrying a knife, people still queue up to look at beautiful things.

I walked around the exhibition remembering childhood dreams in which I was, after hours, completely alone in a toyshop. I stopped at a painting and stared. In it, some sort of supernatural being – celestial glow and flowing robes – had appeared in a blacksmith's workshop. The four or five workmen around the forge were wearing just little toga-skirt things, so I figured it could possibly be ancient Rome. At this stage I always hold back from reading the little card at the side that tells you what the painting's called and what it's about. I've got a sort of a three-stage approach to looking at paintings, self-taught and simple, and the little card doesn't come till stage two. I like to see what I can find in the painting on my own, before I start getting official information.

The workers looked like workers – ancient Rome or Kwik-Fit, it doesn't make any difference – a bunch of blokes who never miss an opportunity to get their shirts off and show the upside of manual labour: a toned torso, given extra definition by sweat and grime. There was an older guy with a grey-flecked beard, that older guy you always get in a bunch of workmen, and he was looking particularly taken aback at the celestial's talk. I liked the feel of it; the idea of the supernatural suddenly happening amidst the workaday; the smell of incense mixed with axle-grease. One thing I like about the Bible is that it's packed with those juxtapositions. For us, nowadays, it's a phenomenon you only really get on *Britain's Most Haunted*.

Anyway, that's what I was getting from the painting. And I loved the way the workmen were deliberately staying cool, like workmen do; not letting the others see their terror. Even the older guy, while definitely disturbed, was still managing to keep it together; still somehow playing it down; get a grip; not in front of the lads; reacting like it was just the sandwich-man turning up and saying he's only got brown bread. Then I moved to stage two.

The little card said:

VELÁZQUEZ: 'APOLLO AT THE FORGE OF VULCAN': Vulcan, blacksmith to the gods, being told by Apollo that his wife, Venus, is having an affair with his brother, Mars, the God of War.

One thing I've had to get used to with this three-stage approach is being wrong. It wasn't ancient Rome, it was ancient Greece; and he wasn't just some older workman, he was the brother of Mars, so, presumably a god himself. But you have to keep your nerve. Rome . . . Greece . . . does it really change anything? More importantly, had I known, from the off, the old guy was a god, I think I would have viewed him differently, seen the other workers as familiar with god-ness, known that they chatted to celestials on a regular basis. I might have overlooked the non-godlike realness of the painting, the Kwik-Fit timelessness of the workmen in their workplace. This way, I get my own painting: a painting of a god who smells of Swarfega, who's got a Twix and his *Daily Mirror* waiting for him in the tea-break. Besides, if Velázquez just wanted us to see them as gods and associates of gods, behaving goddishly in a goddish world, why didn't he give EVERYONE in the picture a celestial glow?

Anyway, at stage two, I combine my gut-reaction to the picture with the official opinions on the little card and come out with an informed response that's still got some me in it. Some initial thoughts discarded; those remaining integrated into the official mix. An older workman, probably already troubled by the insecurities that age-amidst-youth brings, not unlike an older comedian (like I said, 'some me in it'), finds out his wife is having an affair with his brother. Not only that, but he gets told in front of his workmates. He's a god – a fact which gives the moment potentially planet-shaking consequences – but if he's JUST a god, I know his god-ness ultimately removes him from my reality. If he's a Kwik-Fit god, he's humiliated and suddenly lonely and I can feel his pain. It's like Jesus: if it's God on the cross it's like Superman in a car-crash – nothing really bad can happen. If it's man-god on the cross, those cries for help are from the gut.

Incidentally, one last point on the little card: if it's a Velázquez exhibition, it's a safe bet that the paintings will be by Velázquez; although you do sometimes get an influencer or influncee of the artist chucked in as background. But if I'm just wandering around a gallery, with lots of different artists' work on the walls, I avoid the artist's name until I've had a good gawp, because it's easy to get star-struck and like the painting because it's by somebody famous.

This is a doubt that occasionally haunts me in my stand-up life. I know Jerry Seinfeld said being a comedy name only helps for the first few minutes of your act, but this is only a general rule and not an absolute. I did two or three try-out gigs, earlier in the year, when I got a sense that the audience were just pleased to see me and stayed pleased to see me till the end of the gig. I worried they were laughing because they didn't want to let me down. I found myself thinking, 'That joke didn't deserve that volume of laughter'; a seven was getting a nine. Sometimes there'd be laughs on the way to a punchline – I think, to be fair to them, because my as yet unrefined delivery gave a punchline emphasis on a non-punchline word – but they still shouldn't have laughed. I have to earn it, not with a stockpile of affection built up over the years, but here and now, at this particular gig, with this particular gag. Whenever I walk onstage, to me it's year-zero.

The third stage in my art-appreciation method doesn't always happen. It entails going away and finding out more; reading about the painting, the artist; maybe looking at some of their other stuff; getting in deeper. On that night, one of the women who worked at the National Gallery joined me for part of the tour and I got stage three right there and then, from the expert's mouth; usually it comes courtesy of the Internet, a few hours later.

Anyway, trust me, being in an empty art gallery is a special experience. I just wandered around in the company of greatness, hoping I didn't get murdered by an albino monk.

Mind you, an empty art exhibition is the last thing some gallery goers want. More than one person – actually, now I come to think of it, they've all been men – has told me that art galleries are great places to pull. I suppose I have gazed at those gallery-goer girls, dressed like Jackie Kennedy but with nouveau-beatnik horn-rims, geometrically carved crimson hair and Tokyo eight-inch platforms, looking at three orange oblongs and nodding significantly, and I've thought, 'Wow! She looks interesting.' But that thought is always followed by another: 'I bet she's neurotic'; and then an image of that same woman, standing on my doorstep at three in the morning, wrists oozing blood, shouting something like, 'I have cut deep as our love cuts deep. Drink my pain.' And that always seems to put me off.

I was once at a Gilbert and George exhibition at the Tate Modern, when a beautiful Oriental woman approached me and asked what I thought of the pictures. The pressure was on. Where, on the scale between philistine and pseud, would my comments register? I decided to just tell the truth. I'd always suspected that Gilbert and George were a lot of old nonsense, but, having seen this exhibition, I'd been completely converted to their cause. 'I think their art is like your comedy,' she suddenly said. I was quite keen to hear the next adjective, especially as Gilbert and George have been known to use their own shit in some of their pictures. She continued: 'When you first experience it, it seems like it's just filth and obscenity, but when you dig deeper you realise it's about truth, and about challenging our avoidance of truth.' There was a pause while I considered what I might say next. Rather lamely, I opted for, 'Would you like to go for a coffee?'

'No,' she said, and moved on – a hit-and-run compliment – leaving me standing in the middle of the enormous gallery, dwarfed by the yellows and reds, the glossy grandeur of Gilbert and George's great truth. Had I just tried to 'pull' in an art gallery, or was I merely trying to prolong a flattering analysis of my work? Either way, the attempt was short-lived. Her 'no' was not rude or aggressive; it was just final. Anyway, romance was never an option. I couldn't cope with the stares and whispering. The moment a Caucasian male grows one grey hair on his head, it becomes impossible for him to date any Oriental woman without people assuming he got her on the Internet.

I'm loving Andy Warhol. He seemed to find art hiding in everyday stuff. Instead of de-godding gods and making them ordinary, he reversed the process and consecrated everyday items. I like the idea that he sat eating soup one day and suddenly fell in love with the can; or saw a car-crash aftermath, windscreen cubes against black-rubber skid-lines, and thought, 'Hey, this is beautiful.' There is one picture, hanging in a downstairs room, where a man eases a hypodermic needle into his own arm; it's funny how needle-drugs still seem shocking. I notice a smartly dressed, stately old lady in a hat staring disapprovingly at the picture. In a fabulously posh Edinburgh accent she says, under her breath, 'Oh, no, no, noooo!' I thought it would make a perfect slogan for Scotland's anti-drug campaign: 'Just Say, Oh, no, no, noooo!'

From the Warhol exhibition, I walk to Edinburgh's Old Town for 12.30 Mass at St Patrick's Roman Catholic church. Yes, I'm a practising Roman Catholic. In fact, last March, *The Tablet*, the Catholic weekly journal, had me down as the sixty-ninth most influential lay Catholic in the country; only one place behind Princess Michael of Kent. Of course, it had to be sixty-nine, didn't it? Even a public rating of my religiousness had to be stained by double entendre.

I wouldn't normally go to Mass on a Wednesday, but today is what Catholics call a Holy Day of Obligation, when, as the name suggests, you are obligated to attend. There used to be quite a few of these days when I was a kid, but they have gradually been reduced, often by moving them to the nearest Sunday. Catholics are obliged to go to church on Sundays anyway, so it's like a two-for-one offer. Each Holy Day of Obligation is tied to a specific event, but it's hard to see why some qualify and some don't. For example, Christmas Day, the feast of Jesus's birth, is one, but Good Friday, the feast of Jesus's death, isn't. They also differ from country to country. In Germany, Easter Monday is a Holy Day of Obligation, as is Boxing Day, which they call Second Christmas Day. They actually have ten separate Holy Days of Obligation; England and Wales only have four. But, keen as the German Church is on messing up people's Bank Holidays, it still does not oblige German Catholics to attend church on Good Friday. This was especially good news in the nineteenth century because no German Catholic wanted to walk back from Good Friday Mass having to endure 'I told you so' looks from Friedrich Nietzsche.

Today is the Feast of the Assumption. I'll be brief. The idea is that Mary, because of her special status as mother of Jesus, instead of dying and rotting in the ground, was assumed, body and soul, into Heaven. It kind of makes sense. If Jesus is going to get an Access All Areas pass for anyone, it's going to be his mother. And remember, this is a JEWISH mother: 'So I'm expected to wait in the dirt with everyone else? Forget about it. I'll be ready at eight. Send a car.'

Now, I can understand atheists thinking all this is ridiculous. What I don't get are the people who say stuff like, 'I believe in God but I don't believe in the virgin birth.' Surely if you believe in God, anything is possible. The sky's the limit. No, actually the sky ISN'T the limit. That's the point.

I read that Richard Dawkins's book *The God Delusion*. It's a kind of beginner's guide to atheism. It was hyped so much I got slightly spooked at the prospect of starting it. I remember holding it in my hand and thinking, 'By the time I finish this book, I might not believe in God any more.' I'll admit old Dawko had me going a couple of times, but I came through fairly intact. I kept thinking of that old saying 'Those who dance are thought mad by those who cannot hear the music.' Obviously it's a metaphor. When I actually do dance, I've often been thought mad by people who CAN hear the music. In truth, that old saying is a bit smug. It's got a 'we know something you don't know' feel to it that I don't like. I think Dawkins can hear the music; he just doesn't like the tune.

I suppose it's illogical that a stand-up comedian who doesn't read reviews is also a Roman Catholic who DOES read Dawkins. You either avoid criticism or you don't. The difference is that, with stand-up, I've got a room full of people telling me whether it's worthless or not. With religion it's easy to get cosy in your own certainty, so I read lots of anti-religious stuff to guard against complacency. If I'm wrong, I'd quite like to find out. It would certainly free up my Sunday mornings.

I know religious people slag Dawko off for concentrating on negative religious types, so he puts the spotlight on Osama bin Laden and not Martin Luther King, but I think that's fair enough. If you're going to punch holes in something, you want to be hitting where it's rotten, not where it's strong. Believe me, if I wrote an anti-science book I'd be concentrating on Dr Mengele, not Marie Curie.

One of the things that can wind me up about atheists is that they often come over a bit snobbish. The way they see it, they're in their leather-Chesterfield book-lined private members' club with George Bernard Shaw and Bertrand Russell, while I'm in Julie's Pantry with Cliff Richard. David Baddiel once said to me, 'Doesn't it worry you that the other people who share your views seem to be either stupid or mad or both?' I asked him whether HE felt like that at Chelsea matches.

It's a cliché to say that football is like religion, but it's a cliché with a lot of truth in it. Maybe the best way to understand religion is to understand football. Those who hear football's music place it at the centre of their lives; those who don't often think it just promotes violence, idolatry and tribalism. Those criticisms have validity, but they really aren't the whole picture. The problem is that it's impossible to explain why football is magical, because the place where it touches you is some highly charged emotional mystery zone where words feel a bit pedestrian. I'm aware of the bad stuff, but its significance seems to dissolve when I'm in that zone. It's probably all to do with the unfathomability of love. Anyway, I still don't see why critics of football, and certainly of religion, have to be so relentlessly hoity-toity.

The funniest bit in *The God Delusion* is when Dawko says that, on two different occasions, he sat and listened while his wife read the whole book aloud to him. He then recommends this method to other authors, but is quick to point out that not any old reader-outer will do. They need to be a trained actor like his wife, 'with voice and ear sensitively tuned to the music of language'. Hoity-toity! She was in *Dr Who*, for goodness' sake. I like to think she did the first reading in her normal voice, and then did the second one as a Dalek.

Still, there's something sweet about Dawko, cross-legged on the floor, with a large tub of popcorn and a regular cola, hanging on his own every word, getting all excited when he knows a really good bit is coming up, and eventually, as the book is dramatically slammed shut, rising to his feet for a one-man ovation. Then, seven minutes into this ovation, the wife gestures him to be quiet and says, 'Right, now I'll sit while you read Episode three of "The Horns of Nimon". And this time, let's have a bit more volume on the Tardis impression.'

It's when Dawko sets himself up as a member of some sort of atheist gang that I really go off him. I read a thing about him in the paper where he said, 'My advice to any religious person who considers having a debate with Christopher Hitchens – don't!' It sounded like two posh boys had got into a Christian disco and decided that suddenly, in the context of this new environment, they were tough guys.

However, there is one way in which Dawko could be my saviour. Twenty-first-century Britain was a pretty godless place to start off with. Dawko, with his writings, has probably trimmed down the number of casual believers by about 20 per cent. In my darker moments, I wonder if this atheist cloud could have a silver lining. Being part of a much smaller catchment area makes me a big fish in a little pool. It's like that feeling, nagging at me over the years, that, if I'd been born in, say, the Faroe Islands, I could well have been an international footballer. Likewise, come the Judgement Day, I'll be able to endorse my application for Heaven by saying, 'Look, surely you want at least a handful of believers to represent twenty-first-century Britain in your glorious kingdom? Not just Cannon and Ball.'

And God will probably say, 'Sorry, lad. If I really need believers to represent twenty-first-century Britain, I'll play safe and use the Poles.' And I'll be dragged off, shouting, 'But you don't under-stand! I'm the sixty-ninth most influential . . .'

Anyway, Mass at St Patrick's is lovely and, like those black-smiths, who ceased hammering so they could hear the celestial voice, I don't really think about work for the fifty minutes I'm in there.

Having paid homage to Warhol and the Blessed Virgin, I'm now back at the flat, working out changes for tonight's show. Whereas my patriotic-songs bit has been storming, the section on misplaced patriotism that follows has been going less well. I think it might be time to pluck it out. It's always sad to say goodbye to a routine, partly because that's eight or nine gags lost from an already reduced squad, and partly because, particularly in this case, I have an emotional attachment to the piece.

The misplaced patriotism routine is special to me because most of my stuff is written at home on a notepad but this routine was more or less completely created onstage, spontaneous and free-form. I was doing a try-out gig at the Comedy Café in East London, a garish, glitzy spot like Jessica Rabbit might have played. The swaggering, sweaty audience get drunk and eat giant burger-and-chips dinners; their laughter mum-mumble-umming as it filters through a sesame bun.

The comic on before me was Canadian and funny. He did a bit about Harold Shipman. Said his chosen modus operandi, killing by injection, must make him the most boring serial-killer of all time. He riffed on this theme and he was good, but, standing at the back of the room, lost in shadow, I was noticing something about my own reaction to the routine, something I decided to run by the audience when I got on stage, something I interpreted as misplaced patriotism.

The compere did a short link, so, when I walked on, the Shipman routine was still fresh in the air, swirling amidst the smell of ketchup and fried onions. I swan-dived right into it:

Can you believe it . . . fucking foreign comedians, coming over here and having a go at our serial killers?

Never mind the methods, Harold Shipman killed 215 people. They're like goals; they all count.

When it comes to serial killers it's not quality, it's quantity.

He's the second most prolific serial-killer of all time. The MOST prolific, you probably know, is a Peruvian bloke called Pedro 'Monster of the Andes' Lopez. He killed 300 people. EXACTLY 300 people. What kind of person kills EXACTLY 300 people? He must have been some kind of weirdo.

I bet he's the kind of guy who, when he's putting petrol in the car, starts doing that click-click-clicking thing to get the cash-meter EXACTLY on the pound.

That's if he did kill 300 people. I've got my doubts. I reckon the Peruvian authorities thought, 'We're on to a World Record here. (I BECOME THE PERUVIAN OFFICIAL, TO HIS IMAGINARY ASSISTANT) Hey, if you get any unsolved murders, put 'em on Pedro's tab.

Harold never had that kind of support over here. All they did was drag him down. You can bet he killed more than 215, Harold. He committed suicide for a start-off. That was never counted.

They say he confessed to over 400 murders in his suicide note. Of course, being a doctor, no one could read the fucking handwriting.

It was a stroke of luck that I'd recently chosen to stay in when they had Serial Killer night on one of those true crime satellite channels. There was an hour-long documentary on Shipman. A stand-up comic never knows whether he's slobbing around or doing a detailed research job. Everything goes into the sausage machine and you never know which bits will end up in sausages. There is that moment when an incident, or something you read or watched or just thought about – maybe a recent thing, maybe from years ago – suddenly looms up in your imagination. But now it's as if a comedy spotlight has been shone upon it, illuminating the tiny recesses, laying each detail open to comic exploitation. It was just a chance remark in a shop, or an article you read in a magazine, but suddenly it is transformed. It has gone into a backroom and reappeared in a clown-suit, all squirty-flower and whiteface, ready for show-time.

Of course, some poor clowns have to leave the circus, return to the backroom, wipe their faces and put back on their everyday clothes. Now the misplaced patriotism clown, the Harold Shipman clown, who slumbered in a backroom memory till woken with a jolt by that Canadian comic, must say goodbye to the show. He had a glorious debut, but now he's gone.

That night at the Comedy Café, the jokes were falling off me like windfall fruit, and the crowd were mum-mumble-umming bread-spit and barbecue sauce into their beer. I was laughing because I hadn't heard them before either. But that stuff never went better than it did that night. I suppose the audience were excited because they could tell it was spontaneous; from the context, the nature of the delivery, the jokes were hitting the air, still smeared with afterbirth. The last few times, they've sounded stillborn.

Maybe it's a bit grim – the subject matter, I mean. Maybe the Canadian comic started the ball rolling and gave the night a sort of Shipman Conference feel that justified me chipping in. Maybe, in cold isolation, the 'cheeky chappie laughs at innocent old people dying' angle is too unsavoury to swallow. Maybe it's just not that funny. Anyway, it's gone; a one-night wonder, back in civvies, standing next to a battered suitcase, watching the brightly coloured trucks head for another town.

I hear the rain against my Edinburgh window and smile; one more outing for the Native Americans joke. I came up here hoping for sunshine, but all that's changed. Let it rain for fifteen days, and on the fifteenth I will put something in the warriors' tin. I wonder if they still accept beads.

Tonight's gig was a cracker, even better than the first night. Suddenly, everything is fine again. I'm back. The tour is going to be glorious.

Now it's one in the morning and I'm feeling down. For some reason, I agreed to do a quiz, at midnight, here at the Pleasance Dome. It's called *We Need Answers* and is sort of 'alternative'. When they phoned and said, 'Will you do *We Need Answers*, I honestly thought they said *Weeny Dancers*. My mind was racing, but it turns out to be one of those anti-quizzes with questions like 'How many baked beans would it take to completely cover a man's shirt?' and tasks like putting a duvet cover on a duvet. The presenters are funny but it's not my kind of quiz. I like proper questions. I enjoy getting all competitive and involved. These kinds of quizzes are a bit like England football friendlies. Why am I here?

There was one question, earlier: 'Which spice is said to improve the flavour of men's sperm?' It was probably set up for a Spice Girls joke, but I knew the real answer and I was in there: 'Cinnamon'. I was pleased with myself. It was a proper question and I graced it with a proper answer. Now, that done, I was happy to follow it with a gag.

In fact, if you read any cinnamon packet, it's usually on there as a Serving Suggestion.

I'm up against Anna Crilly and Katy Wix, a newish double act who, I would say, represent the current comedy zeitgeist. They have an intelligent, underplayed performance style; very much not in-your-face; subtle comedy actors with a taste for the surreal. The studenty audience love them. In a way, Anna and Katy ARE them. Or, at least, the them they aspire to be. I am very much not them. I am an old guy talking about spunk. A dirty-mouthed one-liner end-of-the-pier all-about-jokes history lesson in what comedy used to be. I'm out of date.

Stewart Lee is doing a show up in Edinburgh this year. He's a comic who's been around as long as me but who I can't imagine performing even at the beginning of the pier. Stewart has remained true to that word 'alternative'; he's stayed hip, confident in his groove, never chasing the gag but always funny and interesting. He talks clever and cool, wears his brain on his sleeve – and he's forty. It's not about age, it's about attitude, and mine is, or at least is perceived as, still football-fuck-fuck-fuck.

Stewart's Edinburgh show is called *41st Best Stand-Up Ever*. Its title comes from one of those Channel 4 list programmes; in this case, the hundred best comedians of all time. I was at a friend's house the night the programme was shown. I was against having it on, but she works in comedy so wanted to, at least, watch the first half-hour. It was too early to go home so I sat there, muttering that the whole idea of listing comedians, as if one was objectively better or worse than another, was ridiculous. Of course, inside I was gripped with fear that I wouldn't be in it; even seventies, eighties, nineties would be a humiliation. Every comic in Britain was probably watching or recording this stupid programme. If I was in the last thirty, I would feel like I was in a medieval village stocks, pointed at and pelted with brown-slime vegetables by shrill villagers, while dwarves pissed down the back of my jerkin. Time passed. We were into the forties. I walked an internal precipice; on one side I was scoring quite high; on the other, I wasn't in it at all.

By now my friend, who had a location film shoot at seven o'clock the following morning, was starting to yawn and drop hints about bedtime. No fucking way was I leaving that house before I knew my number, or discovered that I didn't have one. I didn't actually say this out loud, but my white-knuckle grip on the arms of my chair was probably a bit of a giveaway.

We'd reached the mid-thirties. She had stopped yawning now. I think the tension in the room had put pay to any sleepiness, but it was still apparent she wanted my number to come up sooner rather than later so I'd fuck off home. Sooner meant lower . . . what kind of a friend was she? Suddenly, David Baddiel was number thirty-four. 'I may have to leave the country,' I said.

'But you said the whole idea of listing comedians, as if one was objectively better or worse . . .'

'I know what I said,' I snapped, 'you don't have to say it back to me.' I think we were both getting worried about what would happen if I wasn't in it. I thought I saw her eyeing a favourite Chinese figurine, wondering if she should transfer it to a nearby cupboard.

The American comedy legend Lenny Bruce was number thirty. When I was a youth, I read a couple of books BY him and one ABOUT him and decided that stand-up comedy might be a great job. It was the beginning of the dream for me. It didn't seem right that I might be higher than the comedian who was my early inspiration. No, fuck him; it was every man for himself.

By now it wasn't a crappy list-programme any more. Each decade was written on a stone tablet sent down from Almighty God. If I wasn't in it, I didn't exist, I had never existed. Was I to leave that house carried shoulder-high by a host of angels, their upper-wing feathers tickling the small of my back, or would I just turn to dust and disappear?

Number twenty-six: Frank Skinner. I exist. Thank God. Oh, what a relief. They showed a clip of me doing an oral-sex joke:

She was shouting 'Deeper! Deeper!'
   I said, 'If I go any deeper I'll be able to taste the chair.'

I looked across at my friend, just to make sure she had laughed. Then the voiceover said, 'A comedian for the *Loaded* generation.' 'Right,' I thought. 'Loaded as in *Loaded* magazine, which was massive in the 1990s; in other words, I'm past it.' Don't ask me who comprised the top twenty-five; I was driving home shouting, '*Loaded* generation, fuck off!' at regular intervals.

Well, the crowd at the Pleasance Dome are not the *Loaded* generation, so that probably explains why they hate me. My only hope is the English students. I might be able to get them on my side because, at twenty past one in the morning, I don't need an overcoat to look like Samuel Beckett.

In fact, Anna and Katy don't seem to be enjoying the quiz any more than I am, but at least they don't look like they might, at any moment, faint from fatigue. How lovely it must be to be young and exploding on to the scene. This quiz is written and presented by a group of fresh-faced new comedians, collaborating, jammin' on a common theme. The new generation of comics are a lot more experimental and inventive than I ever was. They're up here in droves doing plays, sketch shows, musicals and, of course, quiz shows. I just did stand-up. I mean, I did things with David Baddiel later on, but it was all mainly TV stuff. We never tried anything like this. I wouldn't have had the courage to suggest a collaboration with someone in case I got knocked back.

I am always amazed when you get those doubles teams at Wimbledon, with one really good player and one ordinary one. I always figured the ordinary one couldn't have been the suggester or the good one would have laughed in his face: 'Excuse me, Mr McEnroe. You probably don't know me but I was wondering if you fancied being my doubles partner . . . No, no . . . I assure you I am COMPLETELY serious.'

Having said all that, about twelve years ago, when I was just starting to hit, I did get it into my head that I'd like to try a joint project with someone else – maybe a comic play or something of that sort, which we could write together – but who? It should be someone on a similar level to me, but with maybe slightly more experience of comic play-writing.

I must say I got a very nice handwritten letter back from Alan Bennett. He said, yes, he had heard of me and was very flattered by my offer, but felt he was getting too old and awkward to write with other people. What the fuck was I thinking of? And yes, I WAS serious.

Anyway, now it's two in the morning and I'm feeling down; and I'm not talking about my duck-feather duvet. Oh, there I go again. I'm actually trying to give up puns but it's like an illness. I seem to have a brain that's wired for puns; they occur to me all the time in conversation. I've even infected those around me. When I did topical stand-up on my now-dead chat show, I had a team of three or four writers who always wrote with me. I've never used writers for proper stand-up, club-gigs, Edinburgh or tour shows; I feel the material, good or bad, should come from my head, reflect my pre-occupations and what I find funny; it should be me. I'm puritanical about that. If it's stand-up for a TV show, I'm not so puritanical.

I was part of a televised stand-up show in Canada back in the summer, a big comedy gala in Montreal, hosted by William Shatner. I did a ten-minute set which stormed the place, but some of that set was gags my TV guys had written for me in the past. OK, I'd polished and paid for those gags, they were legally mine, but they weren't MINE. Thus the thunderous applause didn't move me much. It's like when someone says, 'That's a nice shirt you're wearing.' I can take some credit for choosing it, but the real praise belongs to the tailor.

Anyway, my writer gang: they kind of did their comedy apprenticeship with me and, during that period, when they were young and impressionable, I think I infected them with my pun virus. They grew to enjoy puns, think puns, just as much as me. The problem is people don't really like puns any more, so I worry I've rendered the poor fuckers virtually unemployable. If they ever sue me for loss of earnings, they should put these gags forward as exhibits A, B and C. An alert prosecutor might also note that, if there was a blood-test, my football and bad-taste viruses might also be in evidence.

I was watching David Beckham's last game for Real Madrid. I think the rumour that he's a bit stupid has definitely influenced the Spanish media. At the end of the match, he was being interviewed on the pitch by a female sports reporter. As it was his last game, the stadium's big screen was saying, '*Adios*, Beckham'. The reporter pointed this out to him. Then she said – and bear in mind he'd lived in Spain for four years – 'Do you know what *adios* means?' Beckham, slightly affronted, said, 'Well, I should do. They make my football boots.'

The Concert for Diana is coming up soon, with lots of people that she used to really like: Elton John, Rod Stewart, Duran Duran. Her tastes always were middle-of-the-road. Of course, if she'd stuck to the middle of the road, there wouldn't be a concert.

The *Daily Mail* says a paedophile alarm has gone off all over Britain. To commemorate this, they're bringing out a paedophile alarm clock. It goes off when the big hand's on the little hand.

Bear in mind, in these three instances I only CHOSE the shirt. Anyway, as I lie in this slightly more familiar bed, it's not my pun disease that's worrying me. It's not even that stupid quiz. It's the fact that, just before I walked out into the light to take part in that stupid quiz, while I was still stood in the gloom of the wings, I picked up a voice-message from a friend of mine that began, 'I was just ringing to say I saw that review in the *Daily Telegraph* . . .' Trapped in the darkness, I launched a blind thumb-attack on the keypad, managing to cut off the message before I heard any more. Now I'm lying in bed, at 2.15 in the morning, imagining what I might have heard if I'd allowed the message to go on.

'. . . that review in the *Daily Telegraph* and they had no right to say those terrible things about you. OK, you're not as funny as you used to be, but you're still pretty good. Only a genius could have written that *adios* joke.'

'. . . that review in the *Daily Telegraph*. You must be a very proud man. I mean, that headline, "*The master returns*" . . . it doesn't get much better than that. Well, except for that bit where he describes you as the "best stand-up on the planet" and says how refreshing it is to see a comic who does proper jokes instead of that quirky character shit that the new lot have the cheek to call comedy.'

'. . . that review in the *Daily Telegraph*. Look, maybe it would be better if you just came home.'

SATURDAY 18 AUGUST 2007

I just had the most horrible dream. Someone . . . I'm not sure I even saw them, I think I just heard their voice . . . was telling me, in my internal darkness, that I'd had 'mixed reviews'. Then there was a sort of film montage, like on *Big Brother* when they say, 'Let's have a look at your best bits', except this was very far from being my best bits. It was me, in various venues, dying on my arse, over and over again. I didn't even seem to be doing jokes, just hesitantly delivering strings of random words in a trembling, cracked-at-the-edges voice. Despite this lack of content, I could still detect the rhythms of feed and punchline; my dream-self trying to give shape to this meaningless sound. After each empty punchline, there was a shot of the audience – in fact, audiences. The personnel changed with each venue, but the expressions remained the same: not angry or puzzled, just bored. I woke in the midst of it, my dream-self passing the baton of fear, panic and embarrassment to the waking me. For maybe three or four seconds, I had the body and mind of a man who was at the Edinburgh Festival, making his much-anticipated comeback after ten years, and dying onstage night after night. In fact, the dream's ever-changing venues took me even further into hell. It wasn't just Edinburgh: the whole tour was a gut-wrenching failure. And I was not just imagining what that would be like: for those three or four post-sleep seconds, I was living it. My gut was wrenched, my throat was dry, my breathing jerky and shallow. Then it was gone.

I'm lying in bed, looking at the sunlit ceiling, reminding myself that the gigs have been going well . . . so far. It was just one of those typical anxiety dreams that performers sometimes get. It means nothing. Though I have to say, I'm glad I wasn't doing actual jokes from my set. I wouldn't want the memory of them stuttered out in that shaky voice; the sound of them dissolving into that void. I think I'm anxious because I'm planning big changes in the show for this weekend. So far, I've done, more or less, the same material every night; an hour that seems pretty solid but that needs to change. I have to leave Edinburgh with ninety minutes of material that works. That's what I need for the tour. And even my Edinburgh hour is about ten minutes of local stuff that won't work anywhere else. I can't tour with the fucking Native Americans. Besides, the weather might pick up. So, yeah, I have fifty minutes that work. That thought: just thinking it makes my gut wrench again, but this time not for dream-reasons; for valid and practical reasons, for public-humiliation, self-loathing and horrible, miserable failure reasons.

I still have a load of stuff I haven't even tried up here. I've been holding back because, in line with my review-avoiding what-I-don't-know-won't-hurt-me policy, I forbid Dan, my publicity guy, to tell me what nights the reviewers are in. Thus, every night feels like an audition; an argument against risk-taking. I hate that. I hate me for it. I've been playing safe, and now the time has come to start playing unsafe, I'm getting anxious.

By the way, when I say 'my publicity guy' you'd be quite right to wonder if he's been off sick for the last three years. Look, I'm in a period of transition, for goodness' sake! Anyway, Dan doesn't just do MY publicity; he does it for all the acts at my management agency, Avalon. Ironically, now I'm finally off my arse and doing something worth publicising, I've hit him with the idea that it would be interesting to see what happens to the tour-sales if I do no publicity whatsoever. Well, except for one newspaper article, written by me. It's in *The Times* today and, as I've written it, it is at last a newspaper article about me that I don't feel the need to avoid.

I'm not totally sure what this 'I never read reviews thing' is about. I've heard actors say it in the past and thought it was fair enough. No one wants to read a big slag-off of themselves, me included, but that doesn't explain the avoidance of good reviews as well. I could easily ask Dan to hide the bad reviews and just show me the good ones. Of course, I realise there's a potential flaw in that system. I can imagine bumping into Dan 'accidentally' every day and, despite my hints, him not mentioning reviews at all. Knowing how I am with these things, I fear the situation would soon develop into a fully fledged niggle.

I always SAY I don't read reviews because the bad ones might sap my morale and the good ones might make me complacent. On the first count, a bad review WILL sap my morale, there's no fucking 'might' about it; my morale was sapped by 'You're going to have a lot of fun on tour', so if I read a bad review, they'd better start checking the rafters. On the second count, the danger of complacency, all I can say is 'hoity-toity'. My only problem with good reviews is I hate how happy they make me. I'm like a dog that's just had his belly rubbed, all excited and pathetically grateful.

Then again, what is a GOOD review? I find that, even in a five-star eulogy, if I REALLY study it, I can generally find something negative. I remember reading a review, years ago, that began, 'Frank Skinner is, to all intents and purposes, a comedy god.' I turned to a friend, who was reading another newspaper at my side, and said, 'What would you say the phrase "to all intents and purposes" actually means?'

He thought about it, then answered, 'I'd say it means sort of "generally speaking".'

'Generally,' I said. 'So something that's generally true rather than specifically, properly true.'

He looked at me suspiciously. 'What's the context?' he asked. I hadn't said I was reading a review, but I could tell he was on to me. He started smiling.

I gave up the smokescreen and continued my questioning less cautiously. 'Well, if someone was described as a comedy god, would you say that was good?'

'Well,' he said, 'it can't really be bad, can it? They're not gonna call . . .'

'Well, hold on a minute,' I interjected. 'Moses probably casually referred to the Golden Calf as a "god"; doesn't mean he thought it was good. I imagine he said it with a slightly sneering tone.' By now my friend's knowing smile was starting to annoy me so I went back to suffering the good review on my own.

To be fair to myself, there is one practical, and not mad, reason for avoiding reviews. Reviewers of stand-up comedy have a habit of quoting the comedian's jokes, verbatim. I have a weird and completely impractical guilt about doing jokes people have already heard. I've done a pretty similar set for the last five nights at the Pleasance. Consequently, when I arrive for the show, I'm having trouble looking the crew in the eye. I feel they're saying, behind my back, 'I can't believe that Skinner guy. He says the same things every night. How lazy can you get? No wonder he's not on telly any more.'

I know ALL stand-ups do, more or less, the same show every night, but that doesn't stop me feeling embarrassed about it. Anyway, it has to be done. You write a routine for a TV show; you do it once; it's gone. You never get the chance to explore its potential; to let its improvised additions blossom and grow; to develop the dexterity, the certainty of delivery, that is honed by repetition; to find its less-obvious magical places. The people who came to those little club gigs saw my initial sketch, its short-cuts and rubbings-out still visible. Here in Edinburgh they're getting the half-completed work; splashes of colour; sections of, as yet, untreated bare canvas. On tour, I hope to be exhibiting something close to the finished work, though the dabbing, the highlighting, will probably carry on right up to the end.

But all this requires repetition of ALL the material, and that's why I need to get brave and put a few more of the rougher sketches up on the easel. Some of the routines I haven't done up here have been held back for a reason: they're a bit ruder, a bit more wince-making, a bit less cosy. I'm wary about doing them because that kind of stuff has to be delivered with complete conviction. If I'm mooting a fund-raising scheme called 'Handjobs from the Homeless', I have to moot it with zeal. If the audience sense any uncertainty, they'll be uncertain too. It needs to be presented with confidence, and it's hard to do that with material you're still finding your way around.

I don't want to sound grand about this, especially not so soon after my borderline-hoity-toity work-of-art analogy. I know at the end of the day it's just knob-jokes, but when you're up here in Edinburgh, when you're on tour, everything gets out of proportion. It's like on *Big Brother* when the housemates are having a massive row about who moved the dishcloth and we sit on the outside, in the real world, thinking they've gone mad. It's reality TV but it's not our reality, it's theirs. And theirs has been twisted and distorted by isolation and a sense of being constantly judged. Well, all this madness – the need for approval, the fear of criticism, the anxiety dreams, the impending obsolescence, the comedy career becalmed – this is my reality. Or at least it is this morning. I'll be all right when I've had a cup of tea. Then I'll feel the old buoyancy start to come back. Two-thirds down the cup and the anxiety dream won't matter. I won't be wondering, like I am now, whether that voice in the dark, that *Groundhog Day* humiliation, that broken man trying unsuccessfully to turn gibberish into gold, actually was an anxiety dream or, in fact, a grim premonition of things to come.

Two sips of tea and I'm already wondering how I still managed, considering the fact I was just spouting meaningless unconnected words, to get 'mixed reviews'. Who the fuck was leavening the critical bread with praise? They probably wrote something like:

At last, Skinner has discarded that tired old trope of carefully constructed fuck-fuck-football one-liners. In this new show, he completely abandons jokes, embraces the surreal and, in a glorious Tourette's-de-force, says some random words. The highlight for me was 'solicitous'.

Anyway, I was talking about those reviews that quote lots of jokes from the show. Well, because I hate doing gags that people already know, because I like to pretend that every routine is like the Shipman routine – made up on the spot – those reviews have a bad effect on me. Even if they've quoted the gags to make the point that I'm funny, I still have a problem the next time I do that line. Because it was in the newspaper, it feels like everyone has read it. Thus I end up doing those quoted gags with an air of apology; a sort of 'sorry, I know you've heard this before' approach that skims the comedy cream right off the top of them. So what I don't know won't hurt me, and what I don't know they know won't affect my delivery. Still, it's too late now. I'm going to be a stammering fool next time I say 'solicitous'.

Having drunk the tea and started on the porridge (made with water instead of milk, and no sugar), I start to think about another dream I had, way back at the beginning of May, between the club-gigs and the arts centre shows. I know it's in my journal, so I just flick back through the pages and check the details. In the dream I was onstage, mid-show, when a guy in a suit suddenly got up from his seat and walked to the front of the stage. I stopped talking and looked down at him. By now the audience were silent, waiting to see what he wanted. Very calmly, he said to me, 'It's not bad, but where's the craft in it?' It was the kind of heckle that would put any comedian on the back foot. And, to add insult to, well, insult, this guy's walk to the stage seemed to suggest that I, at my age, could no longer hear a traditional shout from the crowd; he had to get good and close, as if I needed to use some sort of a heckle-trumpet, held to my ear.

Now I know this wasn't what you'd call an aggressive heckle, but it still required a response and my dream-self looked, judging by his smug expression, like he'd got a real cracker up his sleeve. 'Go back to your seat,' he/I said at last. 'You've gone beyond the limits of audience participation.'

I wrote in my journal that the dream might have been caused by a conversation I'd had at the Sony Awards party, the night before. A woman had said to me, as we spoke of my forthcoming tour, 'You'd better be brilliant. I've been waiting for ages.' There goes that stomach wrench again.

Well, if I'm going to give myself any chance of being brilliant on tour, I need to start a bit of squad-rotation with my material; give the B-team a chance to prove themselves at the top level. I need to start taking risks.

As I stand in the shower, who do I turn to, to inspire me on this courageous course? Which not-scared-to-experiment, risk-taking artist immediately comes to mind? Picasso? Wagner? Bob Dylan? No, it's the former hurdler, and now popular TV personality, Colin Jackson.

Back in November 2005, I had a Chinese-takeaway night-in with the *Strictly Come Dancing* final on BBC1. Jackson and his partner, Erin Boag, were hot favourites to win the contest when it got to the final dance-off against Darren Gough, the cricketer, and his partner, Lilia Kopylova. This dance-off is where we, the audience, see the quintessence of those skills the celebrities have learned during the long weeks of practice and performance. It is their chance to produce a routine that will highlight and illustrate all their strengths and specialities: their party pieces; their sure-fire material. Gough and partner did exactly that: they played safe and stuck to what they were good at, a sort of a Greatest Hits routine, and the crowd loved it. Colin and Erin, however, shunned this opportunity to replay their numerous glory moments from previous weeks. Instead they courageously decided, in front of a frenzied studio crowd and one of the biggest TV audiences of the year, to try something different, to experiment, to risk all on one reckless throw of the dice.

Colin and Erin emerged into the bright light, not clasped together but each paired with a new partner. I stopped, mid-takeaway, to look closer. The new partners were floppy, life-sized dummies, those ones with feet you can strap to your own feet so they appear to dance with you, automatically following your moves; big Muppety puppets in formal evening wear, their wobbly heads swinging around as Colin and Erin put them through their paces. The crowd shrieked with delight, then laughed, then applauded . . . then fell totally silent. It was brave and experimental but it was also shit, a terrible idea that should never have gone further than a tea-break giggle. The four of them – flesh and blood, felt and foam – danced in front of the now almost indignant crowd; even the dummies looked embarrassed. It seemed to last for hours. I couldn't finish my sweet and sour chicken; I was too disturbed.

When the dance finally stopped, Colin and Erin smiled and the crowd politely applauded. Only the dummies, eyes madly staring, heads at a spine-snapped tilt, seemed to reflect what had actually happened.

The judges were outraged: 'You've totally ruined ten weeks of work'; 'What on earth were you thinking of?' And through it all the shell-shocked couple not only had to stand there, side by side, and take the relentless reprimands, the way *Strictly Come Dancing* couples always do, but – perhaps those foot-straps are more fiddly that one might imagine – also had to stand there like the Ancient Mariner and his decaying albatross necklace, with the macabre, death's-head dummies still in their arms. Thus, still smiling as the insults rained down, they literally embraced their own ruin.

Only the crunching sound, as I leaned an elbow against a white plastic bag of prawn crackers, snapped me out of my transfixed fascination. Then I started to applaud with more fervour, respect and elation than any studio audience could ever muster. The gutsiness of it, the sheer bollocks-on-the-chopping-block audacity required to take that risk. At that moment I truly loved Colin and Erin. They seemed to represent every human being in history who had aimed high and fallen flat on their face. We're always hearing about risk-takers whose risks paid off, but they are no braver that those whose risks end in ridicule. Of course, they lost the final, but their courage still inspires me twenty months on. Tonight I'm taking risks.

Oh, but hold on, one of my writer-gang is in tonight. Obviously, because he had no part in the writing of this show, he'll want it to be shit. I can't give him that satisfaction. I'll take risks tomorrow night.

The gig was brilliant, best so far, and I'm back at the flat, soaked. The rain tonight was also the best so far, bouncing off the pavement and whirlpooling in the flooded side-streets. The tartan umbrella just couldn't cope. Adam has taken to walking me home at the end of the night. I'm touched by this. Neither of us has referred to it directly. I don't want to admit that the thought of walking through Edinburgh at midnight even registers on my anxiety scale. I'm not heavy on macho pride; nor am I completely untouched by it. I think Adam senses this. He just walks me home; we say goodnight; he walks away, back the way we came, the detour probably putting a mile or so on his journey. I justify this to myself by saying that, as a recognisable public figure, I run a much greater risk of being murdered due to grudgefulness and why-should-I-know-you-if-you-don't-know-me?-based malice than

FRANK SKINNER

that faceless night-wanderer I was thirty years ago. However, anyone escorted home for reasons that aren't on the scale from goodnight kiss to full sexual intercourse cannot help but feel a little bit pathetic. I could, of course, insist on walking home alone, but I haven't yet.

The Times newspaper still lies on the living-room floor. I braved the rain to get it from a nearby newsagent's this morning. Even though I'd written the piece myself I still managed to find reasons to be pissed off. There was a misprint in the bit where I explain my heart-rate readings. I feel the reader may have been confused and some humour therefore lost. I don't know if it was my misprint or theirs, but it's soured the whole thing for me. The memory of it has throbbed away throughout my day; one article, the full extent of my publicity input for this tour, and now its imperfection nags at me like a toothache. Also, the pictures were terrible. Fifty's a bad age for a face; youth has departed, leaving barely a trace behind, but true old age, when you look wrinkled and interesting like a Bolivian peasant woman on the cover of *National Geographic*, has not yet set in. The boyish grin above the sagging jaw, the thinning grey hair above the excited eyes: it's a face in transition, neither fresh nor foul.

My writer-gang friend turned up and, after the show, we sat sheltering from the rain in the Pleasance's outdoor bar. We talked of football, friends and future plans. He never mentioned the show once. I didn't ask; he didn't bring it up. We spoke for an hour, the post-show joy slowly sucked out of me by his ominous evasion. I would very much like it if no one I know ever comes to see the show again. The laughs, which tonight were massive, are all I need to know about how it went. If I'm going to speak to people who were in the crowd, I might as well start reading reviews. I do jokes, the

65

audience laugh, I leave the stage, they applaud, then I start thinking about the next show. That's how I want it to be.

And now, TV off, teeth scrubbed, the reviewers are still banging at my door, trying to get in. I just got a text from a friend that says *Jesus, even the Guardian likes you now. Keep it up. X.* So I've had a good review in the *Guardian*, that's excellent news. Or is it? I'm thinking that maybe my friend read the piece in *The Times* today and mistook my own writing for a review and *The Times* for the *Guardian*.

You know, maybe I'll put an appendix at the end of this book, full of those reviews I never had the courage, or will have the courage, to read. Then you can explore the light and darkness of their opinions, hear another voice apart from mine, and make some attempt at finding an objective truth amidst my paranoia and their professional judgements – a bit like me trying to find the truth of that Velázquez painting. The other thing about a reviews appendix is that I quite like the idea of an author having a no-go area in his own book, like a locked room in a gothic novel – a chapter too scary, too potentially painful, for him to ever enter.

WEDNESDAY 22 AUGUST 2007

I've just been to a talk at the Edinburgh Book Festival in Charlotte Square, ten minutes' walk from my flat. The Book Festival has a very different feel from the rest of the city. There's none of the venue-up-every-alley sprawl of the Fringe. It's all concentrated in this one square, a sort of bookish types' encampment, its four walls formed by white marquees, all of various sizes, enclosing a grassy quadrangle where people sit on very damp benches, drinking coffee and reading, or at least talking about, books; and where I sit on a bench, writing this.

I love buying books, but I find reading them a long-winded affair. I very much approve of reading them, but I don't actually do it that much. When I DO read it tends to be in bed, but I don't go to bed until I'm tired; why would I? Thus, I hit the pillow, already flagging, finish off my journal for the day and then, if there's any life left in me after that, I'll pick up a book and read about two pages. Despite this snail's-pace consumption of books, I probably buy a new one about once a week. This new book is like a new girlfriend – mysterious, fresh and appealing – so it lures me away from my now-familiar and functional, week-long relationship with the previous book. Thus, I own many books which have a book-mark at or around page fourteen.

Occasionally, I'll cash in on one of those three-for-two book offers and live a sort of Hugh Hefner existence, rotating the three books at whim, my nose in one while my finger is still in another. Inevitably, I like one better than the other two, and the less-popular pair get gradually discarded. And then a new book arrives and the process continues. During this cycle, I do actually get hooked on some books and read them all the way through; but no more than, say, six books a year. And then there's *The Discovery of Heaven* by Harry Mulisch.

I'm not usually keen on novels, but I really like *The Discovery of Heaven*. I bought the book two and a half years ago and I'm now on page 134. I read three pages on the train journey up here. It's been replaced at the centre of my affection by dozens of other books, but I always end up going back to it. About a month ago, I was home alone, at a bit of a loose end, when I suddenly said, out loud and with an air of reckless abandon, 'Fuck it! I'll have a bit of Mulisch.' It was the first time I'd read it for ages and I ended up rattling off about six pages! It's like that friend of the opposite sex that everyone says you should get together with but you never do; you just stay friends, keep it casual and non-committed, maybe don't see them for a month or three, then call them when you're dumped or disillusioned. They're cosy and comfortable, always interesting, always there. That's my Mulisch.

I like going to public talks like the one this morning. It's all good for the sausage-machine. Mind you, I had a scary glimpse of the future at one event I went to, in May last year. It was at the National Film Theatre, on the South Bank of the Thames, and it began with a showing of the classic spaghetti western *The Good, the Bad and the Ugly*. This was followed by an interview with ninety-year-old Eli Wallach, who co-starred in the film as the sneaky Mexican bandit.

Early on, the interviewer asked Eli how he'd got the part. The old actor said, when he'd first heard about the film he didn't understand what it was supposed to be: 'Spaghetti western?' he said, turning to the audience. 'It didn't make any sense . . . like Hawaiian pizza!' It got a big laugh and Eli looked happy. Thus the evening continued, with lots more entertaining anecdotes and other crowd-pleasing moments.

Towards the end, the interviewer called for questions from the audience. One guy asked Eli something about Sergio Leone, the film's director. Mid-answer, a flash of excitement crossed Eli's face. My comedian's instinct told me he'd just thought of something to say that he knew would bring the house down. 'The thing is,' he began, 'I almost didn't do the film.' I knew the punchline was approaching fast. Eli was generating light. He could see the big laugh coming and couldn't get there quick enough. I was on the edge of my seat. What was Eli lining up as a comedy coup-de-grâce? What was the gag that would have us still giggling as we filtered out into the warm night air? At last, Eli closed in on his punchline. 'I thought to myself: spaghetti western?' A sense of sudden dread descended on the crowd. They knew what was coming. Please, no. Eli's eyes widened with anticipatory glee. Film fan looked at film fan: 'How can we stop him?' But they couldn't.

'It didn't make any sense,' spluttered Eli, now almost beside himself. His impending simile hung over us all like the guillotine's blade. Go on, let it drop. If he's going to say 'like Hawaiian pizza', I don't want to live any more.

'Like Hawaiian pizza!' said Eli at last, his eyes wider still, his mouth agape, his hands extended into a Jewish comedian gesture that said, 'Can you believe how funny I am?'

I suddenly had an image of myself in a private care home, on a drip. My eyes blankly staring into the mid-distance, my mouth hanging loose, my trembling head sending little ripples across the tiny birdbath of saliva that has formed between my lower lip and my decaying lower teeth. My shaky hand beckons a nurse towards me. As she leans into a wheeze of fetid breath, I stammer out, in a feeble whisper, 'W-w-when it comes to s-s-serial-killers . . .'

'I know,' she says, calling out, over her shoulder, as she turns on her heels and heads off towards the laundry, 'it's not quality, it's quantity.' Having already forgotten this exchange, I raise my reading glasses, on their wipe-clean lanyard, and turn to page 206 of my shit-smeared Mulisch.

I'd guess most of the people at that event had similarly grim flash-forwards. Eli gazed out at us, frozen in his own confusion. What the fuck had happened? It was one of his best lines. How could it have fallen so flat? About six people had laughed. They were either polite, or the same age as Eli. Their laughter just served to confuse him further: 'THEY liked it, what's wrong with these other bastards?' The interviewer wound up shortly afterwards. Eli had spoilt everyone's night, including his own; perhaps ESPECIALLY his own. At least we knew WHY the wheels had come off the evening; all Eli knew was the sudden sound of a scraping axle.

It has occurred to me more than once that I might do a similar thing during this forthcoming tour. I haven't tried to learn a ninety-minute set for a long time; ten years, in fact. During the warm-up gigs, and even for these Edinburgh shows, I keep my set-list in my back pocket. If push came to shove, if I just blanked, the list would be my humiliating last resort. A few times, during those club-gigs earlier in the year, I did forget. I had no choice but to take a crappy bit of Biro-scribbled paper from my trouser pocket and, in full view of the audience, peer at it in shadowy stage-light, to see what came next. And they were only ten- or twenty-minute gigs, a much lesser feat of memory than a ninety-minute full-length show. I really don't fancy getting my bit of paper out at the National Indoor Arena in November, in front of 5,500 people.

Anyway, today's talk had no senior moments. It was given by a philosopher called Dr John Gray, a genial floppy-haired academic with a South Shields accent and spectacles. I say 'genial' but, amongst other things, he said that progress only ever occurred in technology, never in politics and ethics, and that the Iraq War would escalate and probably continue for about thirty years. Obviously, this was great news for any aspiring Vera Lynn-types that were in the house, but generally speaking it seemed to put something of a downer on the audience. Questioner after questioner probed and pressed Dr Gray for a ray of hope but he wasn't having any of it.

Now I'm sitting here thinking that, if the war's going to last that long, I really ought to write some jokes about it. That kind of comedy shelf-life is quite a lure. It's a terrible thing, but comedians often base their emotional responses to current affairs on how it affects their jokes. I was genuinely distraught when the Queen Mother died. I lost about fifteen minutes of good material. Likewise, I had about ten minutes on Osama bin Laden after the early try-out gigs. It had gone well three times. I actually found myself thinking, 'I hope they don't catch him, or find him dead, till I've finished the tour.' Here's a taster of the routine:

He had that one big hit and then he disappeared; like a sort of terrorism version of Macy Gray.

Of course, he does send the occasional video to Al-Jazeera. There's one video where he says the Americans will never catch him because of his sophisticated security system, another video where he says Al-Qaeda will soon have its own nuclear weapons, and a third where he says Al-Qaeda laboratories are developing germ-warfare capabilities. It seems to me, if he's got a sophisticated security system, nuclear power and high-tech laboratories, maybe it's about time he stopped sending videos to Al-Jazeera and started sending DVDs.

You know, bin Laden and me are almost exactly the same age. I bet we've got all sorts of things in common that you'd never expect. For example, there might be an attack on Barnsley tomorrow. Say a lot of Middle Eastern types parachute in, all dressed in white overalls, and spray acid in the faces of the local residents. There'll be experts on the news saying they know Al-Qaeda have claimed responsibility, but it just doesn't ring true. This sort of attack is not at all bin Laden-esque. It's like nothing he's done before, and why Barnsley? Then it'll turn out it's just him trying out some new material in a smaller venue.

The key, if the routine had any hope of working, was to somehow remove bin Laden from the horrors of 9/11; to make him a human being again, domesticated, potentially ridiculous. I'm not sure the audience ever quite bought into that. The original version of the routine included lines that did seem to unsettle the crowd. I used to follow the Macy Gray analogy with:

Of course, I know that Macy Gray had a second, minor hit that got to number eighteen, but that's like the plane that hit the Pentagon – neither here nor there.

It actually got a decent laugh, but the sound was shot through with some sharp intakes of breath. I had it in my head that the Pentagon plane-crash was a sort of damp squib with no casualties, but maybe I was wrong. I decided to Google it. If the Pentagon incident turned out to be a BIG tragedy instead of a small one, the joke was off. The crash, as a potential joke-subject, had, I felt, certain plusses. It happened quite a distance away from the UK (in Washington), with a reasonable time-buffer: five years had passed, and it had been relegated at the time to the lower-front page by the big story. These three facts, I thought, combined to suck quite a lot of the tragedy out of it for a British crowd. But it all depended on the death-toll. I figured ten deaths or fewer meant I could still do a joke about it. Wikipedia told me that 189 people were killed in the Pentagon crash; 64 on the plane and 125 in the buildings. The joke had to go. Besides, out of nowhere, Macy Gray suddenly appeared on the Jonathan Ross show at the end of March. If there was a comeback in the offing, the joke was done with anyway. In normal circumstances, I would have held on tight and hoped that her comeback passed by unnoticed, which it duly did, but those people were still going to be dead. I cut the gag.

There was a second part of the routine in which I told a true story about a phone call I got from America on 7 July 2005, the day of the London bombings. I was in a traffic jam in central London, listening to news on the radio, feeling sick with the horror of it all: bombs on three underground trains and a bus. My mobile went. It was an old friend of mine, calling from his home in New York. He said, 'I just wanted to make sure you weren't on one of those trains, or that bus.' I was moved, though there was a tiny part of me thinking, 'How DARE you suggest I use public transport? I might not be well-known in America but I can assure you . . .' I carried on with the story:

'We're getting garbled reports over here,' my friend said. 'How many people were killed?'

The radio estimate, at that time, was eighteen. So, obviously, I said, 'Eighteen.'

'Eighteen?' he said. The phone-line was a bit crackly so I couldn't discern his exact tone but, nevertheless, I panicked. This guy was calling from New York, the home of 9/11, and I'm telling him we've got eighteen deaths. I felt like a loser, like I was wasting his time. I actually heard myself saying, 'I mean, there'll be more. I'm sure of that. That's just a conservative estimate and erm . . . There's a lot of injured. Some of them are bound to . . . er . . .'

I know. It's unbelievable and horrible and ludicrous but it's what went on in my head at that moment. It was a terrible day, I was shocked and upset, but even so. Anyway, it happened so I decided to tell the story onstage. It was, it seemed to me, a story about my stupid insecurities rather than those bombings. But the audience couldn't seem to get past the fact that the backdrop to the story was so terribly sad. I gave it a second chance, a few weeks later, but the yellow card soon became a red.

Of course, as always, it's quite possible that the story simply isn't funny, horrific backdrop or not. I just felt I detected unease in the room both times it was aired, something beyond the this-isn't-funny unease that I know so well and would fully expect to come tap-tap-tapping at my door during any new-material gig.

I remember one unsatisfactory outing for the Osama stuff back in May. After that gig, an old comic who I'd worked with a lot in the eighties and nineties showed up backstage. He'd continued doing the clubs after I'd gone off to do theatre tours, telly and all the other stuff, so you can probably imagine the dynamic. There was something very 'it's not as easy as you thought it was going to be' about his smiling demeanour, but it was still good to see him. He had remained on the shop floor. He knew the modern comedy-crowd sensibilities: their likes and dislikes, their safe ground and their thin ice. I was still working it all out, rubbing out the rules I learned twenty years ago and rewriting them as I went along. 'It's hard with terrorism stuff,' he said. 'People are a lot touchier than they were ten years ago, and not just about that . . . paedophile jokes, gay jokes, all best left alone.' This, I thought, would explain the stone-cold response to some stuff I'd tried a couple of months earlier; a routine that, ironically, was supposed to be about how attitudes to terrorism, homosexuality and paedophilia had changed.

Instead, the routine accidentally highlighted several other changes: changes in audience sensitivity that I was chronically unaware of.

It's odd the way a bad guy becomes a good guy when a slightly WORSE bad guy arrives in town. You take the IRA. Ten years ago they were hated and feared. Then Al-Qaeda turned up and people were suddenly saying, 'Well, one thing about the IRA – they'd never have flown two big airliners into a skyscraper. They liked the personal touch. They'd make house-calls if they had to.'

The same thing happened with homosexuals. Homophobia used to be everywhere; gays were abused, marginalised, forced to live secret lives. Then the paedophiles turned up. Suddenly, the gays are off the hook. And you've got the old woman at the bus-stop saying, 'I don't mind these civil partnerships. At least it's two people with pubic hair.'

Maybe I should have spoken to this old comic earlier. Still, I was slowly learning what was acceptable and what wasn't. Those early club-gigs were interesting because the bills were filled with lots of extremely competent young stand-up comedians, all with business cards and websites, doing TV-friendly material in the hope they'd get discovered and get a sketch show on BBC3. Then some old guy turns up, a guy who's been doing nothing but television for ten years and is excited to be off the chain. He's there to get all that stuff he was never allowed to say on TV out of his system. An unkind person might say it was the difference between being on the way up and being on the way down. I was like a drink-addled homeless bloke who'd sneaked into a trendy restaurant just for the sheer pleasure of shouting, 'Suck my cock!'

Don't get me wrong, the kids were good. A lot of them were REALLY good: clever material and polished delivery. It didn't take me long to realise I'd been fucking lucky to start comedy when I did. If I'd been starting out now – fresh from Birmingham, unknown – there's a very good chance I would have sunk without trace.

There are two reasons for this. Firstly, a lot of the new breed actually ARRIVE on the comedy-club scene at a stage of development it took me about twelve months of gigging to get to. This is because they have sharpened their skills, developed their material and stagecraft, while attending various comedy courses all over the country. Some of these courses are part of a recognised Performing Arts Degree; some are less-formal gatherings in church halls and rooms above pubs, run by working comics eager to pass on all they've learned on the job: how to construct material; how to sell a gag; how to deal with hecklers.

It means these new comics aren't going into their first gig like a pasty white-guy in Speedos, walking on to a blistering beach. I wonder how many people who could have gone on to be top comics got fried on their debut and couldn't face going back . . . and all for the want of sun-block.

Maybe I should have done a refresher comedy course, like people do when they haven't driven for years. That last routine, from Provos to Paedos, could've died in a classroom instead of a club; still a humiliating failure but with fewer witnesses. You know, part of me would miss the tragedy of it; the unique but scary world of a post-punchline silence; a glass replaced on a table, the muffled biddley-beep of the fruit machine in the downstairs bar, the creak of boards as I prowl the stage wondering if I'll ever hear laughter again. Maybe that's why I eschew the Jay

Leno method. Some dark part of me likes to be there in the void that Frank built.

Every new joke is a dream of future laughter; not just laughter at this gig but at dozens of gigs to come; laughter in people's homes when they hear it on telly or DVD; laughter in the pub or playground when it's half-remembered and badly told, or heard on a replayed scratchy bootleg from someone's mobile phone; laughter when it's read in a memoir months or even years later; and, yes, laughter when it's read in a fucking review.

Some new jokes make that journey, gather those laughs, become old jokes. Some, though they arrive on stage with the same pomp and preparation, the same dream, as the successful ones, die as soon as they hit the air. But despite those seconds of pain and disappointment, I would not rob them of their moment. They deserve their chance to woo the crowd.

Any audience, certainly any comedy audience, is a mystery: unpredictable and perverse. I've been a comic for over twenty years. I'm still surprised at what they laugh at and what they don't laugh at. But that post-punchline moment, filled with laughter or bleak silence, belongs to the audience. They decide. And when they decide against, to be there at that moment – to suffer their verdict, to witness their exhilarating, merciless honesty – is horrible but exciting. For some, probably masochistic, reason, I'd be loath to give up those moments. Terry Griffiths was spot-on. There IS a certain beauty in defeat. But I don't know how much beauty there is when some comic-turned-teacher, in a draughty church hall, kindly and diplomatically suggests that his pupil has 'stronger lines than that' and maybe it would be better if that particular joke stayed in the notebook, thus denying it the terrible glory of a public execution.

Of course, I'm getting all romantic about stand-up again. I'm sure the idea is that the joke would be identified as endangered at classroom level and then rewritten to improve its chances when it finally goes public. So never mind the new comics that got fried and never went back, what about the new jokes; MY new jokes? How many of them died on debut for lack of sun-block? That thought nags at me. That and, 'Would my stand-up be much, much funnier if I'd got Mrs Dawkins to read me the whole thing out loud?' Imagine the music she would have found in my handjobs-for-the-homeless routine. Anyway, in short, I think the joke-schools are a great idea and their glory is in their graduates.

The other reason I fear I might have got lost in the modern comedy-club mix is the size of that mix. When I started on the London circuit, back in 1988, there were about forty-five comics getting regular, paid work. I spoke to a comedy promoter at a club earlier this year. He told me he had a database with over four-hundred working comics on it.

I think the change has come because this kind of comedy offers much greater rewards than it ever did in my day. When I did my first club-gig, I knew – or I thought I knew – just how far it was possible to go. The example was right there, in front of me, leaning against the bar: the successful club-comic who got regular gigs in the best clubs and went well most of the time. That was as good as it got, and I was more than happy to have that as a dream. There was, to be fair, the possibility of a slot on Channel 4's *Friday Night Live*, but that show disappeared while I was still a raw beginner. Television comedy, in those days, was about Cannon and Ball, Bobby Davro and Russ Abbot; people your Auntie Gwen liked. Now, television comedy is not so different to the comedy that goes on in those little clubs where I did my recent try-outs; so one of these good young comedians has the potential to go up, up and up. The dream isn't to be a good club comic any more, it's to have an American film star say you're funny.

I suppose I might have played some small part in this transformation of alternative comedians from late-night cult-heroes to mainstream millionaires, but I'm not sure that I take much pride in it. I remember sitting alone in the dressing room at the old Comedy Store in Leicester Square at two in the morning. It was rare to be alone in there, but I had just come off stage, having gone on last, and the other comics had gone home or were in the bar. In the distance, I could hear the compère rounding off the night, improvising his way to some big laughs, getting a little extra love from a great crowd, loath to let them go. I thought of that thing Bela Lugosi says in the old black-and-white *Dracula* movie: 'Listen to them. Children of the night. What music they make.' It was like being part of a special, almost-secret world. I wasn't dreaming of bright lights; I was happy underground.

I suppose my return to stand-up, to those clubs, to those dressing rooms, was an attempt to find that feeling again, but it was never going to happen. Whether you're loved or hated for it, you're that famous guy; not one of the gang; in this world but not of it. My integration was minimal and I didn't exactly help myself. The very first try-out gig, back in January, was at a great little club in Kingston-on-Thames called Outside the Box. When I arrived, the other comics on the bill – fresh-faced, charity-shop chic – were huddled in a corner. They looked at me with a stare that my new-kid-on-the-block insecurity interpreted as: 'Who does he think he is, turning up here like some kind of Big-Time Charlie?' I decided I had to be humble and sweet and then they'd like me. One of them, though I didn't know this at the time, was a funny new comic called Rich Wilson. He had obviously decided to break the ice. He moved away from the huddle and walked towards me, hand outstretched, as his comedy companions looked suspiciously on. We shook hands.

'Hello,' he said, 'I'm Rich.'

'Yeah, so am I,' I replied.

Unsurprisingly, this seemed to alienate the other comics, but I just couldn't resist it. I went on stage, about forty minutes later, and told the story verbatim. It got a big laugh and has been in or around my set-list ever since. If this keeps up, I thought, the set is going to write itself.

I have to say, though, that I never encountered any real hostility from the new comics. I was largely ignored and left alone. Those that did speak were sometimes complimentary. I remember, I'd just come off stage at the Ginglik, a subterranean club in West London that used to be a gentleman's toilet; in fact, the actual gentleman's toilet where Wilfrid Bramble, the star of the classic BBC sitcom *Steptoe and Son*, got arrested and charged with trying to procure a sexual partner. I liked that the place had been the setting for such a particular moment in British comic history. I was very happy to be walking in Wilfrid's lightly imprinted footsteps.

When I returned to the dressing room, pleased with the audience response, a female comic, who was also on the bill, approached me. 'I didn't want to say anything before you went on,' she said, 'but, well, you're a hero of mine. One of the reasons I went into comedy.' I wasn't sure how to reply, other than to say thank you. I put my arms around her in a slightly awkward way. It was a beautiful thing she'd said but I felt embarrassed, even a little anxious. If these warm-up gigs, if Edinburgh, if the tour, if the whole return-to-stand-up thing failed, this was the sort of person

I'd be letting down: someone who remembered me as sharp and funny. If I came back as a *Stars in Their Eyes* mediocre impression of my old self, I'd not only fail now but also fail retrospectively; her memory of me rendered forever questionable and unsound. It's like when old boxers fight for too long. They can look so shit in their twilight years that you can't believe, despite the video evidence, they could ever have been good.

We chatted for a few minutes, mainly about her comedy career and how it was progressing. Then she broke off to say, 'I'm so glad you're nice because I'd heard that you weren't.' Ah, those crew members, in their smelly black t-shirts and head-sets had spread their message well; resentment-evangelists, bringing the bad news to the people. I decided against querying the source of this gossip, just in case their grudge was wholly justified. I made to leave and, midst our goodbyes, she said, 'You know, whenever I die' – a phrase one only ever hears in comedy dressing rooms and Buddhist meetings – 'I think of you dying at the Royal Variety Performance, and that always cheers me up.' I felt so proud.

Despite my comedy-elder-statesman status, I was only once, during the course of those try-out gigs, ever asked for advice. This paucity may have been caused by awe or contempt but, either way, I was grateful for it. On the rare occasions I do give comedy advice, I always end up contradicting myself and saying something I don't actually believe. That one time I did get asked was when I'd just done a particularly fluid fifteen-minute gig on a Thursday night in Crouch End. It's a downstairs space, with a low ceiling and the front row so close you have to watch you don't trip over their feet. I was loose and keen to explore them. One was an Asian guy called Abul who, in the course of our intermittent banter, suggested we might, at some point, have a night out together. I said, 'Yes, as long as we don't go to a china shop.' The audience took a while but I was happy to wait. Yes, it was a pun, but I enjoyed it; and the chances of me ever using it again were slim so I decided to seize the day.

I closed the first half that night. As I leaned, job done, against a wall during the interval, sipping flat cola and feeling good, a young comedian – nervous, intense, sweaty even – approached me.

'You know that thing you do,' he said, 'that thing when someone says something and, even though you didn't know what they were going to say, you say something back to them, and it's funny?' I was just about keeping up.

'Well, yeah, that happens sometimes,' I said, tentatively. I thought he was about to test me with a random remark to which I was supposed to make a hilarious reply. I was worried I'd fail and disgrace myself, like when that student punched Houdini in the stomach with no warning, to test his famous stomach muscles, and Houdini's appendix burst like a wasp on a windscreen.

'No, but, like, tonight,' he continued, undiverted, 'when people in the audience said stuff and you said something straight back and everyone laughed.' I just looked at him and waited. 'How do you do that?' he asked.

'It doesn't always work,' I admitted.

'No, but how do you DO it?' he said. I was too nonplussed to find flattery in this.

'I erm . . . I . . . I honestly don't know,' I said. I could see he felt this reply just wasn't good enough.

'Oh, come on, tell me,' he said, slightly pleading, slightly pissed off.

I muttered something about needing to speak to someone else and moved off. His look, as we parted, said I had denied him, that all I'd had to do was explain this simple technique and he'd have been laughing – or, rather, the audience would have been laughing – and this fucking comedy thing that he wanted so bad, that was so difficult and elusive and was driving him crazy with frustration, would suddenly have flowered and he'd be confident, funny and sharp. At last, being a comedian would have started making him happy and stopped making him sad. The truth is I'd make a lousy tutor at comedy school. I'm doing jigsaws in the dark, same as everyone else.

I'm meeting Adam for lunch today. We need a bit of an air-clearer. Yesterday we lunched at Rick's restaurant, just up the road from my flat. We were there to work out some of the nuts and bolts of my forthcoming tour. Adam had lots of notes and a big road atlas of Britain. He was particularly keen to work out the hotels. Did I want to stay in the town where I'd just gigged or head towards the next town and stay there? Did I want to stay at home, in London or my Birmingham flat, when convenient, or always in hotels? I smiled at these enquiries, not because they were foolish but because I knew I was about to answer in a way that was contrary to the whole ethos of my previous tours. In those days I always, unless it was just practicably impossible, stayed in the town where I'd just gigged. Otherwise, how was I supposed to have sex with a woman from that town? I didn't want her in the tour-bus, being driven miles away from home and then, the next morning, dropping hints about a lift back, or help with her train fare, as we squelched our way through a bon voyage knee-trembler against the half-empty mini-bar. And the idea of taking one of these temporary sweet-hearts back to my own home, London or Birmingham, was, of course, out of the question. What detrimental effects it can have on an erection when you return to your bedroom, struggling into the rubber gloves you've just been to the kitchen to get, and find your *shag du jour* rifling through the en-suite bathroom bin for an eccentric souvenir.

'Yes, I'm happy to stay in any town, in my own flat, whatever . . . anything that's convenient for you and generally good for the tour. I won't be fucking anyone so it doesn't matter.' The last sentence slightly sticks in my throat, but I manage to get it out without too much dry gulping. I mean it. I won't be fucking around this tour. The reason arrives tomorrow, on the 3.20 from St Pancras.

A tour-book about a churchgoing, drug-free teetotaller who's not shagging strangers; I won't think ill of you if you leave now.

So, anyway, the tour-lunch was going well until, in the midst of working out these logistics – how to avoid knackering late-night journeys; how to guarantee me a lie-in; how to stop Adam from deliberately driving head-on into oncoming traffic when he's had two hours of 'Shortnin' Bread' from the back seat – I asked a simple question that anyone in my situation might have asked: 'Where the fuck is Dorking?' Adam looked blank and reached for the enormous road atlas. 'But surely,' I said, 'if you've spent weeks planning the tour, you should KNOW where it is without having to look in the atlas?'

'I DO know where it is,' he explained. 'I'm just double-checking the mileage.'

This is where the picky me always kicks in: Mr Picky, the crew members' dark nemesis.

'OK, so if you're DOUBLE-CHECKING the mileage, that means you must already have a pretty firm opinion of what it is; otherwise, you would have nothing to check. To "check", after all, is to seek to confirm something that you're already pretty confident about. So, without looking at the atlas, what is the mileage?'

Adam was trying hard to be patient. He took a deliberate deep breath, in and out, before speaking. 'What mileage are we talking about?' he said with yogi-like calmness.

'You tell me,' I said. 'You're the one who brought up mileage. All I said was "Where the fuck is Dorking?" Apparently, even though you've spent three weeks preparing the tour schedule – a tour which includes a gig in Dorking – you don't know.'

I must say, celebrity brings many things – shitloads of money, quality time with Velázquez, dirty sex in clean hotel rooms – but it also brings a certain amount of cuntiness. I've tried to drive it out, over the years, but it still lurks just beneath the surface, waiting to release its slimy, sarcastic, little-man-in-a-big-coat venom.

A very dear friend of mine bought me a large, framed, orange sign with black lettering on. It says, 'WORK HARD and be nice to people'. I don't know if it's meant to echo a philosophy I already adhere to, or point me in the direction of a life changing rethink, but I DO know that I recently caught myself wondering why the 'and be nice to people' bit is in a lower case. I think I was looking for a loophole.

Nevertheless, it hangs above my bed and I try my best to live by it. But if there's one thing I hate, one thing that REALLY annoys me, it's when people just won't own up, won't raise a hand to acknowledge guilt, like a footballer accepting he's committed a foul; won't say, 'OK, it's a fair cop. I don't know where Dorking is.'

'Frank,' he said – I'm not sure he's actually ever called me that before – 'I know where Dorking is.' A sentence few can have said with such pride. I still wasn't convinced. I considered grabbing the giant atlas and giving him a formal test. 'All righty! Is it north of London or south of London? Is it nearer Southend or Southampton?' In the end I opted for just raising my eyebrows in an 'I think we both know you don't' kind of way. At this, he barked 'FRANK!' in a slightly scary manner.

'Oh, that's it,' I thought, 'he's a nutter. We're going to be driving along some dark road in the early hours of the morning, I'll make some innocent remark – maybe twist the dashboard dial and mutter, "Radio One isn't what it used to be" – and he'll suddenly swerve on to a patch of waste-ground, switch off all the lights and beat me to blood-mush with his big atlas.'

We moved on, monosyllabled our way through coffee, and went our separate ways. Then, some eight hours later, as I sat in my dressing room after that night's gig – so down about handjobs-from-the-homeless not getting laughs that the idea of my splatter-headed body being bin-linered up and left in a ditch didn't seem so bad; certainly a much better plan than spending three months on a miserable, unfunny tour – Adam suggested part two of the logistics meeting for lunch today. I feel I'll have to tell him I didn't like being barked at, which might stir the whole thing up again, but I'll also do some peace-making. This is going to be a long tour.

This time, we've opted for an Italian restaurant. It soon becomes clear that the waitress, slim but hairy, has an approach to customers best summed up as service-with-a-sneer. She throws a couple of menus on the table, like a bitter bankrupt handing over deeds to a greedy landowner, and storms off. Even her tight, denim bottom seems unnecessarily brusque. Luckily, her manner doesn't seem to be rubbing off on Adam. He is bright and breezy and has all the confidence of a man who's looked up Dorking. 'Before we start,' I say, 'I think we should discuss what happened yesterday.'

'Oh, OK,' he says cheerily, as if I'd just said I think we should share an antipasti. 'Look,' I continue, 'I know I was a bit picky about the . . . er . . .' I, stumbling to a halt, am trying if at all possible to avoid the word 'Dorking'. 'But, anyway,' I continue, 'I felt that when you said "Frank!" quite sharply' – now I could hear myself sounding ridiculous – 'well, it was a bit aggressive, and I thought there was no need for that.' The waitress appears, as if drawn in by the word 'aggressive'. She stands over us in silence but her dark eyes seem to be saying, 'So what the fuck do you two losers want?'

'Shall we order?' I say, suddenly quite bright and breezy myself; camp, even. We do order. He goes for salad, which, for some reason, seems to calm me. I would've been edgy if he'd gone for raw meat and Red Bull. I bravely ask the waitress, who by now is looking at me in a manner which suggests her grandfather was killed by comedians during the war, if she would be kind enough to fetch us a large bottle of fizzy water. Her expression on departure suggests she is just as likely to come back with a large axe.

'Well, I didn't mean to sound aggressive,' Adam says, with an air of kindness. I hear Mr Picky saying, 'Well what kind of mood WERE you trying to communicate then, when you chose "loud", "staccato" and "snarling" from your voice-tone ingredients list?' This time, I decide to keep Mr Picky out of it. I do a little speech about how it's going to be a long tour and how I hope we'll have a laugh, and Adam agrees, and I say if he's got any gripes or worries I'd like him to be straight with me, and he echoes this sentiment, and pretty soon everyone's smiling except the waitress.

I think our Dorking moment has passed. We chat some more about hotels and stuff, but eventually, as I approach my last meatball, the talk becomes more human, more from the heart. Adam tells me how, for most of his life, he's been crippled with rheumatoid arthritis, and how, only quite recently, hours and hours on an operating table have released him from that nightmare; from the pain and the pain-killers. It explains the shuffling gait and identifies that snowstorm he looked like he was shuffling into. That slightly annoying deliberate jauntiness is now redefined as a self-crafted shield, a courageous determination to remain unbowed.

It's one of those moments when the superficial divide between two individuals – and it can be ANY two individuals – suddenly dissolves, and you look into someone and seem to see all your own gut-wrenching fears and confidence-shattering insecurities, your own personal punch-the-air elations and dewy-eyed dreams, swirling within them, and feel theirs in you. And you know the essence of those things, the core, uncustomised truth of those things, flows through everyone and that we're deep-down the same; and that's why we should do unto others as we wish them to do unto us; and that's why we say the Our Father and not the My Father. And I'm confronted by the embarrassing, hard-to-say truth that if we could all feel like this and remember the feeling, not only would there be no wars and no starvation but there wouldn't even be a big kid pushing over a little kid in a primary school playground. And for the seven seconds it lasts, I know that Heaven might have harps and clouds and wings, and then again it might not, but it WILL have this; it might even BE this.

And then Adam uses the word 'interweb' and Heaven slips away. The waitress returns with the bill and my barriers are back in place. She catches me eyeing her long denim legs and scowls, causing her mono-brow to buckle in the middle. It seems unwise to say I was just checking her for disabilities that might explain her apparent rage against the world. I resolve instead, revealing faint traces of

Heaven still in my system, to tip heavily; so heavily that her face, at last, is illuminated by smile. Her mono-brow remains mono, but her moustache opens like Tower Bridge to let that smile pass through.

Those moments like the one with Adam, those suddenly-I-see-it moments when there's a hole in the fog, are rare but can come upon me at any time. On one occasion I was talking to someone, a virtual stranger, a man in his late fifties, when suddenly, for no perceivable reason, I was overcome with great love for him; perhaps love that should have a capital 'L'. I wanted to embrace him, to physically express our oneness, but it was inappropriate; I'd only met him about seven minutes before. To make things worse, I was in the middle of recording a television chat show and he was Alice Cooper.

I'm not really an Alice Cooper fan so it wasn't that excitement one feels when meeting a hero; it was simple, indiscriminate, soul-to-soul Love, the glimpse of Heaven. It made no difference that it was a celebrity. It could have been a seamstress or a Grenadier Guard. It came upon me as it always comes upon me: from nowhere; apparently triggered by nothing. There was a silent pause when I gazed at Alice and Alice gazed at me. I was thinking, 'Truly, the river of God's love flows through us all.' (I now reduce the moment by retrospectively translating it into words.) Alice, I'm guessing, was thinking, 'This ass-wipe has forgotten his next question.' The moment was beautiful but I couldn't run a chat show in that heightened state, couldn't conduct an interview that was just a blissful smile. I had to look at a member of the crew to snap myself out of it.

It's 6.30 and I'm back at the Book Festival to hear a talk by Karen Armstrong. It's tight but I can just about squeeze this in before my gig. I hate not having my pre-match chill-out, I'll literally have to dash to the venue, but I really want to hear this woman speak. She's an ex-nun, ex-Catholic writer on religion, who seems to be still fascinated by Christianity but also by Judaism, Islam, Buddhism and many other Eastern religions. She's just written a 'biography' of the Bible, and that's what she's plugging today. This talk is being held in a much bigger tent than the one this morning. It probably holds about eight hundred and it's totally crammed.

The Catholic Church has an interesting attitude to the Bible. It venerates it as the Word of God but it doesn't feel that it's the whole story. In brief, it works like this: Jesus lives as an obscure carpenter for thirty years then, one day, he disappears into the desert and his family and friends hear nothing from him for six or seven weeks. When he returns, he's not interested in carpentry any more; he's transformed into some kind of über-preacher. The pun-sick me wants to say he'd moved to a higher plane. (It's a carpenter joke.) He then spends three years über-preaching, gets crucified, dies . . . and what happens next is, shall we say, open to conjecture. Anyway, the Catholic Church argues that, in three years of über-preaching and thirty years of prep, there must have been a lot more words and deeds than you could squeeze into the four Gospels. The people who hung out with Jesus – especially the Apostles, who were like the inner circle, his posse – heard him say, and saw him do, loads more stuff than ever got written down, and, unsurprisingly, they told people about it. So there's an oral tradition kicking around the Church with a lot of Jesus biography and associated stuff that never made the Bible.

Also, the early Christians, the sort of Fathers of the Church, being so close to the source, had a deeper insight into the truth of

Jesus than people who came later, so their thoughts and writings also got included in the mix. To top it off, because the Catholic Church believes itself to be the boss church, directly descended from the Apostles, it also believes it has a unique capacity to suddenly get truth revealed to it – it could happen today – so truth is like a living thing, growing and developing over the years. All these – the written truth, the spoken truth, the absorbed truth and the magic truth – go together to form a whole Catholic truth that can be drawn upon as a source of teaching and wisdom.

It's like that Holy Day of Obligation last week, the Assumption. If you go looking in the Bible for the bit where it says, 'Mary got taken up, body and soul, into Heaven', you're going to be looking for a very long time. It's not there. It comes from Catholic tradition. In fact, it didn't truly become official Catholic teaching till 1950, one of the truth's later flowerings. So, although the Bible often enters a Catholic Mass held aloft and chinker-chinked with incense, you could argue that it doesn't have the clout, the ultimate authority, that the Protestant Churches give it. It's just one source of the truth.

Some have suggested it's a kind of a climate thing. Protestantism was forged in Northern Europe – Germany, Holland, Scotland – cold, dark places where people stopped in at night, with the wind wooh-woohing through the window-gaps, reading the Bible by flickering candlelight and pulling apart every word because there was nothing else to do. This created an approach to religion that was thundery and puritanical; a cold, dark existence eventually evokes a cold, dark God. 'We don't like incense and pretty paintings round these parts; we like a big, black, scary book.'

Meanwhile, the Southern Catholics, their souls full of poetry rather than prose, were hanging loose alfresco on a balmy evening in Rome or Seville, saying, 'Do we really need Bible classes on a beautiful night like this? We could be with our family and friends, feeling the love, as we sip house red at a pavement café. Let's just try and be good and the priest will keep us informed if there's anything we REALLY need to know.' I generalise, but you get my drift.

Being a dark-nights Northerner, I have been known to have the occasional bash at the Good Book myself, but, if I'm being totally honest, it's always been more of a chore than a life-changer. I've heard all the best stories before, and the other stuff's too Jewish.

Anyway, Karen Armstrong doesn't seem to support any particular team so I'm keen to get her angle on the whole Bible thing. She's slimmish, in her early sixties and has dyed blonde hair, short and parted into curtains like a grown-out Purdey-cut. She has a middle-class accent and a general air of Miss Jones from *Rising Damp* about her. For some reason, I can't describe her without referencing seventies British TV.

She says the whole idea of the literal interpretation of the Bible is a nineteenth-century Protestant invention. The Bible is, in fact, she says, a long mystical poem that offers insights into an unknowable God. It is continually growing, expanding in meaning with each reader.

It is, she says, a way of teaching us compassion. She tells a story about a rabbi who was challenged to stand on one leg and recite the Bible in full, from memory. He offered to do it there and then. He stood on one leg and said, 'Love God and love each other.' He put down his leg and explained, 'Everything else is commentary.'

She is very insistent that the reader of the Bible must respond personally. Maybe I should apply my three-stage art-appreciation technique to Bible reading. I look at my watch. She's over-running a bit. I really don't want to be late for my gig. Then she says, 'Lectio Divina' and it snaps me back into the lecture. It's a phrase I first came across back in May, in a book about monastic life I read the first fourteen pages of. It's a sort of Bible-based form of meditation with a distinct mystical element to it. I haven't tried it but, for some reason, the phrase keeps coming into my head. She moves on but I will investigate further. I might be able to make my own hole in the fog. Shit, I really need to go or I'll never get to the gig for eight.

I'm back at Fred Street and feeling pensive, sprawled out on the sofa with my feet sticking over the edge, television off so my thoughts can marinade. In the main it was a storming gig, but I think I lost another routine tonight, and not even one of the dirty ones. The trouble with losing a clean one is that the act needs light to accompany its dark; otherwise the power of the filth is lessened. You can't just eat bacon; you want to have a bit of bread with it. Not that this particular routine was exclusively light, few of them are, but it had a certain warm cuddliness about it that I shall miss.

Like most of my act, it was based on something that actually happened to me. I was asked to be the mascot for West Bromwich Albion, in their home game with Norwich City. When I say mascot, I don't mean that I dressed in a replica kit and walked on to the pitch holding the hand of one of the Albion players. No, I was on the pitch long before the players came out and I was dressed as a giant thrush – I mean the bird, not the infection. I didn't come dashing out of the tunnel, dressed as a vaginal discharge, and then get chased around the pitch by another man, dressed as a tube of Canesten. You'll notice I've slipped into the routine without giving you prior warning, probably because the first joke is a pun, and again, I'm ashamed of my lack of resolution. Anyway, I continue:

So I walked around the track at the side of the pitch, dressed as a giant bird, with just a narrow slot to see through. No one knew it was me in there. I was totally anonymous. The younger Albion fans love to have their photo taken with the club mascot, so I posed for dozens of photos, with my wing around various excitable kids. For each picture I adopted my usual photo-with-my-arm-around-someone grin. Then, about twenty photos in, it occurred to me that the grin was completely unnecessary. I could grimace, stick my tongue out or just look bored . . . who would know the difference? The privacy and thus freedom this gave me was exhilarating. I suddenly realised why Muslim women are reluctant to give up the veil.

This realisation, combined with the warm smiles on those children's faces, led me to a further conclusion. The suspicion and fear many non-Muslim people experience when coming into contact with the Muslim community would be greatly reduced if, instead of wearing the slightly sinister, traditional all-black robes, Muslim women were, say, Disney characters.

The woman's privacy would still be protected, but the tension which is so evident in modern Britain would be greatly reduced. OK, you might want a quick sift through Winnie the Pooh's honey pot before you'd let him on an aeroplane but, generally, the current situation would be diffused and the mood lightened.

And it's not just religious tensions. Take the nation's anxiety about paedophilia. It's produced a situation where the subject has become taboo, been driven underground. Universal anger and hatred is rained down upon these monsters, whereas some attempt to understand and listen to them might lead to an eventual cure and, ultimately, a safer society for children to live in. Here's my idea: instead of the paedophile dashing, as the baying crowd scream and swear, from courtroom to police van, with the traditional blanket over his head, why not cheer things up a bit, get rid of the blanket and have him come out dressed as, for example, Road Runner – apprehended at last.

Perhaps that brutish oaf in the leather bomber jacket who runs, slamming a clenched fist against the side of the police van, would be pulled up short, forced to consider the long-term ineffectiveness of this vigilante approach, when a plaintive 'beep-beep' emanated from within.

It felt tonight, and not for the first time, that when all these words left me, the transmitter, they were elaborately bejewelled with nuances, ironies and social satire; but, somehow, by the time they reached the audience, the receiver, they had become nothing more than racism and pro-paedophile propaganda. Suddenly the comedy was dead, hanged on a tree with no trial or testimony, no lets-just-hear-him-out, no appeal. Then again, the old proviso: maybe it just wasn't funny. But a comedian has to challenge taboos, has to say the unsaid.

Anyway, it's gone. Another routine bites the dust. Over the course of these last four nights, well into my last period of pre-tour experimentation, the final selection of what material comes with me and what stays at home has begun in earnest. I've been using my act like Sven-Göran Eriksson used to use England friendly games: first half, play your strongest team and make sure all is well with them; second half, bring on your squad players and see how many of them are good enough to make the grade, make the final squad, get on the aeroplane. So my first half-hour is the safe bets and my second half-hour is the risks. Inevitably it's been hit-and-miss but, frustratingly, it's been largely non-decisive: some ticks, some crosses, but mainly recurring question marks. Half a dozen of the newer routines are playing OK, looking fairly at home in an England shirt, showing potential to be match winners; but the tour starts in seventeen days, with each show ninety minutes long, and I've only got an hour and ten minutes that's match-fit. It's getting a bit late for 'OK', 'fairly' and 'potential'. I thought I'd have jokes to spare by now. If these question marks turn into crosses I'll be in a position where I have to write a last-gasp, all-new twenty minutes of material for the tour, with no time, and no gigs, to try it out.

Still, the fact remains, my football mascot routine – though it stormed the little rooms above the pubs, stormed the art centres, stormed Montreal – has suddenly Devon Loched on me, and tonight was its sad farewell. I took my chance like Colin and Erin. I jived with the giant thrush, waltzed with Winnie the Pooh and rumbaed with the Road Runner. When the verdict came, I smiled through the silence but the contest was lost, the courage unnoticed; and the crowd left the Cabaret Bar, saying, 'It wasn't a bad show, except for the racism and pro-paedophile propaganda.'

It was a long routine as well. Thirty-two ticks.

SUNDAY 26 AUGUST 2007

I woke up stupidly early and I'm lying in my now-very-familiar Edinburgh bed, thinking about last night's gig. In the midst of a wayward improvisation, I found myself talking about the fact that the Prime Minister, Gordon Brown, has only got one eye. I pointed out that one-eyed people can't judge distance. There is a simple Johnny Ball-type way of demonstrating this. You point your index finger upwards, at just-above-waist level and then get another person to stand an arm's length away, and bring their index finger directly down till it meets, tip-to-tip, with yours. They do it easily. Then you get them to try the same thing with one eye shut and they virtually always miss, either under- or over-reaching. Hey presto: you can't judge distance if you've only got one eye. I was moving towards a gag that involved Britain under nuclear attack, and a desperate Gordon Brown trying to press the nuclear button but missing it over and over again.

However, before I could do that pay-off, I had to convince the audience that my can't-judge-distance thing was actually true. If I was just making the whole thing up, the joke was pathetic, so I asked a guy, a very friendly sort of fellow, in a sweatshirt and jeans, to join me onstage. I held my index finger aloft, told him what he had to do, and we began the first part of the fingertip-to-fingertip experiment. But the guy just couldn't do it. Three goes, three misses. 'I don't get it,' I said, 'this is the straightforward bit.' My keen-to-be-helpful assistant had a sudden thought. 'I'm blind in one eye,' he said. 'Might that make a difference?'

I've got two gigs today, my usual eight o'clock show but also a charity gig at 1.30. One thing I forgot about Edinburgh is that it's a real pleasure to have the occasional night off; just to have twenty-four hours when the little fire isn't burning inside. Lots of comics half my age are having one night off a week while they're up here; I've just done thirteen nights on the trot and it's a double-header today. They're driving the old war-horse into the ground.

Still, tomorrow night is my last show. Then I have twelve days before the tour and . . . unnnng! My gently meandering mind is suddenly wrestled to its knees. My thoughts take me in a rough headlock and, though I struggle against the turning, force me to face my dark dread: not a disastrous tour but a disappointing one; an OK tour; seven out of ten; 'I quite enjoyed it but he's not as good as he used to be'; average. All this week, in the middle of a meal, in the middle of the night, that fear keeps rising up and suddenly I'm Scrooge confronted by Christmas Yet to Come.

As I've said, I thought that by this stage I'd have mound upon mound of totally nailed routines and would be delicately stroking my chin before selecting the choicest jokes, like a Parisian dandy picking his way through a tray of petits fours. As it turns out, a more suitable analogy would be a man with a fifty-foot ladder trying to get over an eighty-foot wall. Thus my glorious twelve-day break has become my terrible twelve-day intensive, sink-or-swim, sixty-seven-date tour-rescue programme. I say sixty-seven but I spoke to my manager yesterday and he's suggesting we add a third Birmingham NIA and a second Hammersmith Apollo; that would be an extra nine thousand tickets to sell, an extra nine thousand witnesses to my mediocrity. I gaze, unblinking, at that version of the future then, at last, neck-muscle my way out of the headlock, look at the still-dented pillow next to me and think about Cath.

She arrived two days ago. I was standing at the railway station and she suddenly emerged from a doorway, surrounded by friends, looking like she'd just got up. Talking too loudly, swearing too loudly, blue-grey manga-comic eyes flashing, long dark hair all over the place . . . a foul-mouthed, chaotic cross between Pigpen and Jane Russell in *The Outlaw*. She saw me waiting for her, smiled, kissed me casually, like a friend might kiss me, and said, 'I'm bursting for the toilet, I'm fucking starving, I've got a fucking headache and I'm meeting Mum ten minutes ago.'

Someone who'd just been introduced to her might have asked, 'Why didn't you use the toilet on the train, eat on the train, take an aspirin and call your mum to tell her you'd be late?' I didn't ask those things. I knew the answers. I knew she didn't use the toilet on the train because her claustrophobia makes her too scared to lock the door; didn't eat because she might get food-poisoning and her vomit-phobia might give her a panic-attack; didn't take an aspirin because she likes to keep her body pure and, anyway, they aren't strong enough to cope with her worse-than-anyone-else's headaches, headaches that can only be lessened – not actually cured, of course – by Solpadeine, a much stronger pain-killer that she, pure body or not, takes on a regular basis. I also knew she didn't call her mum because she forgot to charge her phone. 'I forgot to charge my cunting phone,' she said, as she frantically went through her bag, pockets and purse, trying to find her train ticket.

I considered asking what had caused the headache – not because I wanted to know; I doubted there even was a headache – but because I knew her answer would be borderline astonishing. During the time I've known Cath, she's had a series of headaches caused by Epstein-Barr, an illness which, whenever I quizzed her on the subject, she always defined as 'that thing that nearly killed Barbara Windsor'. Then she discovered migraines, and had one that lasted for three days, leaving – according to her elaborate and utterly sincere explanation – so much electricity in her body that her mobile phone crashed, my plasma screen died and her work computer exploded. Best of all, there was the accidentally self-inflicted headache caused by wearing a stripy dress. Strangely, she has never had a headache caused by coffee, even though she often has four mugs of it for breakfast.

Despite all these fears and foibles, I knew she had spent the whole journey, not cowering in a corner like a frightened child but, rather, describing the details of her latest ailment, telling highly animated, outrageous stories about her chaotic life and repeating with utter faith the latest crackpot theory she's read on the Internet – 'Dates are the most fattening food you can possibly eat, but at least they don't give you cancer, like avocados' – and generally showing off to her little group and anyone else on the carriage who wasn't wearing industrial headphones.

This 'little group' includes her younger and much more sensible sister, Rachel, who Cath has somehow managed to convert into an elder sister; regularly phoning and texting her for advice on the most trivial and non-urgent things. Rachel has long brown shiny hair, like a shampoo advert, and is always immaculately dressed and make-upped. Cath doesn't brush her hair because she read, on the Internet, that brushing is bad for it; she is happy to use make-up but is usually running late and doesn't have time to put it on; and when she does wear an item of clothing that looks great, she is always keen to tell you that it cost £4 from TK Maxx.

I tagged along as the gang headed for town, with Cath asking me where we should eat – a tough question because any chosen restaurant would have to cope with the fact that Cath is allergic to wheat, probably allergic to potatoes and possibly allergic to tomatoes. Oh, and she doesn't like dressing on salad, sauce on fish or cream on anything.

I've known Cath, on and off – with quite a lot of off – for about seven years. We started out in a sort of casual relationship, then split for about a year, then got together on a more formal basis. Our relationship then swerved erratically from breathtaking starry-nighted wonder to snarling bad-blooded bitterness and back again, and back again, and back again. Each day like the throw of a dice: odd-number, a head-in-hands nightmare; even-number, a wrapped-in-each-other joy. Our last split – I've lost count of how many we've had – was almost a year ago. Over the last few weeks we've gradually crawled back towards each other; wounds healing but not quite healed.

Last month we had a weekend in Brighton, a chance for us to reacquaint and for me to chill out before Edinburgh and beyond. One of our arguments there took my heart-rate to 136 bpm. Admittedly, not as bad as the Aldershot gig but, still, a rate you'd normally expect to encounter on a biggish fairground ride. That same weekend, we read the whole of Voltaire's *Candide* to each other, and Cath had a down-on-her-knees laughing fit when she caught me on the balcony smoking my clay pipe. We weren't back together. I think Cath wanted it but I was scared; scared to step back into the cold, cold night where that drab carousel grinds onward, the same arguments coming round, again and again; scared of that post-fight emptiness when you can hear the clock ticking and see the marks your fingernails have left on the palms of your hands.

A few days after Brighton I was in Canada, doing the Montreal Comedy Festival. While I was there, I had some really good gigs, some OK gigs and one horror. As well as three nights of my own one-hour show and the William Shatner TV Gala, I was also doing a thing called *Britcom*, a show on four consecutive nights, exclusively made up of British comedians. The Canadian organisers had decided that, because I was the big TV comic, I should close the show. This didn't allow for the stand-up comedy ring-rust I was still trying to oil away. Nor did it allow for material I was still trying to refine. The other comics on the bill had been gigging regularly for years. I could hear the wham-bam certainty of their punchlines as I stood in the shadows, watching each of their storming eight-minute sets. I had twelve minutes, the privilege of the headliner. I would have been happier with five.

The first night was OK. I closed the show, did my twelve minutes, mixed some old material in with the new and scored a workmanlike seven-out-of-ten. Even so, I was still the weakest act on the bill. The second night, I decided to be brave and try a completely different set. It was something to do with that old embarrassment about repeating the same routines. I didn't want the other comics to think I was scratching around for material. Six minutes in, my mouth was dry, a woman in the audience had called me an asshole and I could hear my feet moving around the stage.

The trouble began when I told the audience about a speed-dating club I'd been to in Montreal the previous evening. I explained I had never tried speed-dating in the UK, but because I'm anonymous in Canada, I thought I'd give it a go. I continued:

So I sat opposite this Canadian woman, very attractive, and we each had two minutes to sell ourselves. I went first. I saw this as an opportunity to speak as a man, not as a celebrity; to be liked for myself, not just for my fame. But after about fifty seconds she was already beginning to look bored. I panicked and, well, I'll tell you what I did. You'll probably hate me for it, but just remember, it was motivated by insecurity rather than arrogance. I needed something to impress this woman, something to draw her in. So I said, 'As you may have noticed,

I'm not actually from Canada. I travel quite a lot, what with me being a millionaire and everything.'

The crowd, as I expected, groaned, and, as I said, a woman called out, 'Asshole!'

'I know,' I said; not my best-ever response to a heckler. I continued with the story:

Anyway, this speed-date woman stops me, mid-sentence, and says, 'Oh, right. And because you're a millionaire, I'm gonna get down on my knees and suck your tiny dick!' I said, 'Well, that's a great opening but it's not your two minutes yet.'

There was some clapping but it came before the punchline. It was the 'Asshole' woman and about six of her girlfriends, applauding the phrase 'tiny dick'. Some guys laughed at the punchline but some women, in the crowd, booed. Suddenly I was Mr Sexism. The speed-dating story wasn't even true.

Anyway, I had planned at this point in the set to move on to some ten-year-old material about having a teenage girlfriend. Clearly, that routine had been rendered completely inappropriate. The women in the audience already hated me and, anyway, I wasn't even sure it was funny any more. However, for some inexplicable reason, I did it anyway.

Fame has many perks. I've actually got a seventeen-year-old girlfriend at the moment. (Boos now from most of the women in the room. One fat guy in a leather bomber jacket applauded. Internally, I was with the women, but my mouth was favouring Fatso.) We actually get on pretty well, though we did have a row the other week when she broke one of my old sports trophies. (What the fuck was I talking about? Did I look like a man who had sports trophies? In the original routine she broke 'my favourite mug', but I had a sudden fear that Canadians didn't use the word 'mug'. A woman in the crowd whooped in support of my imaginary seventeen-year-old girlfriend and her now gender-war-based symbolic destruction of my probably phallic, imaginary sports trophy.) It's always hard to take if a girlfriend breaks something of sentimental value – especially if she does it skipping.

Of course, there were more boos. Why was I doing this stuff? It was even offending ME. However, in all of my routines about sex, even those from twenty years ago, any laddism is always defused by self-deprecation. Maybe that would turn things around.

I was standing naked at the side of the bed one night and she said, 'You know, you're like a tiger.' I felt really good; inclined to snarl, even. Then I realised she was referring to the stretch marks on my arse.

A woman actually shouted, 'Go girl!' At that, I decided to swan-dive into the flames.

The other day, she said to me, 'You're not going to put me in your act, are you?' I said, 'You're kidding. If I said how old you were, I'd get booed off.' She said, 'You could always add a couple of years to make it more palatable.' So I did, but it hasn't really helped, has it?

A woman shouted, 'Paedophile!' I'd never thought of that joke in those terms but it was an interesting historical point. When I wrote the routine, in 1997, the whole paedophile thing seemed vague and unreal. Now it's in the papers every day and the grim truth of it is all too obvious. At the same time, that transformation from seedy sub-culture mystery to bring-out-the-monster melodrama has made the subject impossible to discuss rationally. But it should be discussed; all taboos need un-tabooing; every elephant-in-the-room needs a good hard slap across the arse. You might think stand-up comedy is the wrong place for that discussion, but we're not talking about the crime itself – the crime isn't open to debate; it's cut-and-dry indefensible – we're talking about society's sometimes bizarre and contradictory response to the crime. That, surely, is a suitable subject for comic analysis. Of course, this is my in-an-ideal-world theory. Whenever I've put it into practice, the resulting gags have bombed. Note the short life of the civil partnerships joke, the Road Runner joke, and another joke I tried and dropped, one of my Devon Loched routines from the art centre gigs.

This particular piece of material referred to the Bill Wyman–Mandy Smith affair. Back in 1993 it was revealed that the then thirteen-year-old Smith was having a physical relationship with the forty-seven-year-old former Rolling Stone Wyman. At this point I would usually ask a younger member of the audience if they knew about the scandal. Invariably, they didn't. In which case I would ask them to guess what happened to Wyman when the story broke. They always guessed prison, a ruined career, a lonely exile abroad. When I explained that the police basically just gave him a bit of a ticking off, they were shocked. And then came the social comment:

You see, it's not just comedy where 'timing is everything'; paedophilia is the same. You know those movies where the hero is in a room and there's a big, solid metal gate slowly sliding downward; and if he doesn't get out of the room, he's definitely done for; and so he runs and he slides along the floor, and he just gets under the gate before it slams down shut? Well, THAT was Bill Wyman. And then along comes Gary Glitter. Splat! Face-first into the gate.

The Canadian audience had brought up the subject. I could have tried the Bill Wyman bit. But no, I decided against it. That crowd would never have got the irony, would never see it was a joke about changing fashions in social outrage, about moral bandwagons. All they would hear was a joke about paedophilia. Maybe it IS just too grim a subject, even as background to a joke that is actually about something else. Besides, the joke about the fifteen-year-old girlfriend was, I suppose, a bit harder to defend. It hardly qualified as social comment.

In the cold light of day, it wasn't the crowd's fault, that terrible gig in Montreal; it was mine. I chose the wrong material. I did old stuff I didn't believe in any more. It was a former me talking, not the comic I am now. The difference might not be readily discernible to the outsider, but I could feel it in my gut. It was like going out in 2007 wearing a suit I bought in the 1990s. It was out of date and, what's more, it didn't fit me. A British crowd who knew me, who knew my comedy back-story, would have seen the thing in context, would know where I was coming from before I began. But it wasn't a British crowd, and that wasn't their fault. It was my fault for not factoring that into the equation. I fucked up. Anyway, I ended the gig by saying:

As you've probably guessed, I'm not a famous British comedian at all – I'm actually a reality TV contestant. There are cameras hidden all around this room. I've never actually done this before and . . . erm . . . you can bet I'm never gonna do it again. But anyway, thanks for listening. Goodnight.

I left the stage to some confusion and quite a lot of you-almost-had-us-fooled warm applause.

I mention this Montreal gig for three reasons. Firstly, because I feel some Ancient-Mariner-type need to talk about bad gigs; I suppose, in a way, it's cathartic for me. Secondly, let's face it, bad gigs are far more interesting to read about than good gigs. It's true of many things. If a friend is in love and his relationship is going great, it's a fucking boring story. If, on the other hand, his girlfriend's been shagging someone else and when he confronted her about it she took an overdose of sleeping tablets, that's a ripping yarn you just can't get enough of. The same applies to tales about holidays, parties, physical health and any number of other matters. Happy endings are just about tolerable, as long as they come with unhappy beginnings and middles. The third reason for telling the Montreal story is slightly more complicated. I wonder now if that nightmare gig stripped me bare, made me feel like a stranger in a strange land, left me open and exposed. I wonder if it made me realise that I didn't want to face life alone and unsupported. I wonder if it made me realise how much I loved Cath, and how much I needed her. If it did, that's one fuck of a silver lining.

So, it was Montreal, the day of the big TV gala, four days after that nightmare gig. William Shatner was familiarising himself with the autocue in a downtown theatre and I was sitting in my hotel room, looking at the giant hilltop cross that overlooks the city. It's illuminated at night, and I'd taken to sitting at my window last thing, just staring at it; not thinking big religious thoughts, just liking that it was there. But now it was daylight, and the cross looked grey and metallic in the distance. It could have been a radio mast or a crane. I was thinking about Cath; I'd been thinking about her since Brighton. I remembered the Samurai code: that every decision should be made within the space of seven breaths. I got to five and called her. In some ways, it wasn't a romantic conversation. I said, 'I've been thinking. Let's face it, whatever happens we're going to end up together so we might as well just accept it. Where am I going to find another woman who'll read *Candide* to me?'

There was silence and then an understandable 'What's suddenly brought this on?'

And that seems to be the current state of play. I'm still keen. In fact, I feel the closest I've ever felt to that elusive 'knowing' that people in relationships sometimes talk about. I've had the conversation a million times, trying to find out their secret, to understand what they've got and I've never had. They'll say something like, 'One day you meet someone and you know they are the person you want to spend the rest of your life with.'

'What do you mean, you KNOW? How do you know?' I always ask.

'You just know,' they say, in a tone that makes it clear that any lack of communication is down to my inability to grasp their truth, rather than their inability to express it.

'The fact is I don't KNOW anything,' I retort. 'Doubt is my constant sidekick. I doubt my work, my faith, my relationships. If you're a human being, doubt comes with the job, doesn't it? When Jesus is dying on the cross, he suddenly looks up and shouts, "My God, my God, why hast thou forsaken me?" Even Jesus! And then he dies. He couldn't die until he'd become wholly human; and he couldn't be wholly human until he'd experienced doubt.'

Then I get that look that says, 'Poor old Frank, the weirdo loner with his strange references that nobody's interested in, a little bit separate, a little bit dysfunctional. How could he ever understand what it's like when you "just know"? No wonder he's not on telly any more.'

I, for my part, arrogantly think my doubt, my not knowing, is a sign of intelligence. But then, of course, I can't be completely certain about that. I've always responded to people who 'just know' like the atheists respond to people like me. I think they're kidding themselves; they believe because they WANT to believe. Oh, it's so lovely and comfy to 'just know'; until one day you suddenly start getting those flash-frames of uncertainty out of nowhere. 'Julie is dull; we have nothing in common; I'm lonely; I bet I could fuck Susan in the office.' And the flash-frames become whole evenings, whole weeks, and Julie has no idea, or if she has she's too scared to mention it because mentioning it might make it really happen; and suddenly it HAS really happened, and there's tears and a hastily packed suitcase; and you're on an old mate's sofa-bed thinking you've done the wrong thing and thinking you've done the right thing.

My friends are right about the weirdo-loner thing, though. I was like it as a kid, playing on my own for hours, cowboy hat and Colt '45. One of my favourite paintings is *Excursion into Philosophy* by Edward Hopper. An anxious man sits on a bed, an open book at his side. I'd guess he's been reading all night. Behind him, on the bed, lies a sexy woman, fast asleep; her dress has risen up to reveal her curvy arse. He doesn't notice. He just stares at a patch of sunlight on the floor and thinks.

One of my favourite poems is 'Danse Russe' by William Carlos Williams; where, while his family sleeps, the protagonist dances naked in front of the mirror 'in my north room', waves his shirt above his head and sings, 'I am lonely, lonely/ I was born to be lonely/ I am best so'. It seems beautiful to me. And he ends, 'Who shall say I am not/ the happy genius of my household?'

Why would these two appeal to me? Why do I get tense at the end of a Western movie, when the woman asks the man to stay, and he looks at her and then he looks at the distant prairie? Why do I SO want him to get on his fucking horse?

I was walking near the Thames once, alone. It was a warm summer evening around six o'clock. I stopped to cross the road. A convertible, with the top down, pulled up at the traffic lights. In the front seat, two grinning men, shirtsleeves and shades; in the back seat, two beautiful young women, summer dresses and hair swirling in the breeze. That, I'm told, is what MY life should be like, could be like; that's how celebrities are supposed to live. I crossed in front of the convertible and soon arrived at the cinema. I sat alone in the dark and watched *Grey Gardens*, a thirty-year-old documentary about an ageing mother and daughter who live a reclusive life in a dilapidated old mansion full of cats and spend their days singing songs from old Hollywood musicals. Of course, I loved it.

Where are the showbiz parties? I stopped going to them ages ago. Where are the weekends spent sipping cocktails, poolside, at a fellow celebrity's country home, or maybe on their yacht in the South of France? Where are the ski-trips, the white-water rafting? I don't drink, I don't swim, I don't ski; I hardly know any celebrities. I have friends who I love but I don't call them most of the time – who knows why? It's not me who should be worrying about three months with Adam; it's Adam who should be worrying about three months with me.

But Cath's aware of all that and she's OK with it. She's a bit of a weirdo loner herself, despite the loudness and the jokes. I've been known to do loudness and jokes myself. It doesn't prove a thing. She once bought me a book and she had written on the inside cover, 'You don't have to be by yourself to be yourself'. That, I think, is the whole point. And I have never met anyone I can be more 'myself' with than her.

Anyway, Cath hasn't actually said yes to us getting back together. She's being cagey.

Of course, many might feel this is extremely bad timing on my part. To go into a relationship just before a tour – it's crazy! The thing to do would be to put everything with Cath on ice, go away for three months and sow the last few bottom-of-the-barrel wild oats I've got left. Then, when the tour is over, have a good rinse, turn up at Cath's door and tell her I'll love her forever; probably. But the truth is, I don't want anyone else, even for a night. Shit, it's strange to write that. Maybe it's age. I read that George Melly, the jazzman and writer, when he lost his sex drive, said it was like getting off a runaway horse. I haven't dismounted; I've just managed to get hold of the reins. I'd become disenchanted by fucking around – the addiction, the weakness of it. And also the long, dull chats into the early hours, the slow, tentative crawl to reach the fruit at the end of the bough . . . I don't know that I could be bothered any more. So, maybe it's that: age and apathy. Or maybe I'm downgrading it. Maybe it's love.

I think it might be the prospect of the tour that's holding Cath back. Things happen on tour: resolutions fade; a lamplit cleavage outside a shadowy stage door; a come-hither smile in the hotel.

There's a saying: 'What happens on tour stays on tour'. Likewise, there's a thing up here called Edinburgh Rules: 'Whatever happens stays secret, and is not rewound, not even referred to, when everyone gets back home.' Maybe those loopholes will draw me in. Maybe I'll weaken. Then again, if love, age and apathy prove insufficient reason, maybe my weirdo-lonerness will pull me through. The idea of a full gig followed by an empty hotel room, me sitting alone on a king-size bed, a single lamp illuminating my Mulisch . . . it makes me feel warm inside. This new resolve is strange to me, but I gave up alcohol, drugs, cigarettes, milk and sugar in porridge; I might as well give up casual sex as well. I like the chill of giving up; the cold denial of hot, basic instinct; the shock of the no. I'm very good at Lent, a sort of converse-Oscar Wilde. He could resist anything except temptation; I can give up anything except giving up.

The problem is, even if I don't weaken, Cath will be convinced that I have. Cath is a beautiful woman – a fifties pin-up figure and those manga-comic eyes; she still gives me the tingles – but she is convinced that men, if it's on a plate and easy, cannot refuse sex, regardless of what's back home. It's not an outrageous theory, I'll admit, but I still resent the implication that I'm too weak, too cock-led, to say no. I have occasionally said no in the past and actually found it quite liberating. If the woman's attractive it's an out-and-out buzz. This is dangerous ground, I know, but I spent a lot of non-celebrity years being knocked back left, right and centre by attractive women, often only slightly attractive; and, while I'm not saying anything so crass as 'it's payback time', there is a certain novelty in the tables turned.

I read a story about Liam Gallagher, the Oasis frontman, which may or may not be true, but which made me wonder if he'd had similar thoughts. Certainly, his approach was a bit more rock star, cruel even, but I could see some dark logic in it. The story goes that Oasis were dining in a café when Liam asked the waitress for her phone number. She smiled and walked away. Shortly afterwards she returned and handed the singer a piece of paper with all her details, giving him a knowing look as she did so. Liam took the paper, ripped it into several pieces and threw it on the floor.

Now, I know Liam did a bad thing; he should have put the pieces in an ashtray. I also know that it's hard to imagine a big, good-looking lad like him ever getting many knock-backs in his pre-celebrity days, but, ignoring that, my tables-turned theory does seem to make sense of his behaviour. Of course, it's still bad behaviour. Then again, the Columbine shootings were BAD behaviour, but when I heard that the two kids started the spree by killing pupils who were good at sport, well, I was shocked and horrified but I DID feel I knew where they were coming from.

Anyway, I don't think Cath believes I won't be shagging on tour, even with age, apathy, weirdo-lonerness, novelty and love as my five-fold motivation. In fairness to her, we haven't actually discussed the first four. The thing is, Cath gets a little bit . . . Well, look, let me offer you the following story by way of illustration.

During one of our numerous breaks, I was dining out with a very good friend of mine called Marie. Marie is an attractive, bright and funny woman who I have known for a long time. There's never been anything physical between us. Anyway, somehow or other the subject of dancing cropped up during dinner. Marie said she'd love to be able to tango and I agreed. She suggested we might take lessons together and I said I'd love to. It's the kind of resolution friends make all the time but never actually pursue. A month or so later, Cath and I got back together. We were watching TV one night when some tango dancers appeared, and I said, 'Oh, I saw Marie a few weeks ago and she was saying she'd love to learn to tango. We actually talked about going to lessons together.'

'And DID you go?' Cath said nonchalantly.

'No,' I said.

'Well, why don't you?' she asked. I was surprised by her liberalism. Maybe this was the new Cath, laid-back and trusting.

'Well, we were apart then. Now we're back together it doesn't really seem appropriate,' I explained.

'Why not?' Cath asked, as if I was being ridiculous.

'I don't know, really,' I said. 'It just seems a bit odd.'

'Well,' said Cath, very matter-of-fact, 'just for the record, if you do ever want to learn tango with Marie, it's fine by me.'

I was very heartened by this exchange. I remember sinking back into the sofa with a sense of great calm. Cath had finally sorted out her jealousy thing and I could see only blue skies ahead. A few weeks later we were away for a week in Brighton – as you will have guessed, a favourite haunt of ours. We would go abroad more but Cath doesn't like flying. Anyway, it was the last day of the holiday and we were on the balcony, stretched out on sun-loungers, seagull shadows punctuating the glare, when I got a text from Marie. There was a one-off tango class the following Saturday morning, in Islington, North London, and she wondered if I wanted to go. *Let me know soon*, the message said, *because they expect it to sell out so I'll need to buy tickets*. I told Cath what the text was about and she asked if I would be going. 'Are you sure you're OK with it?' I said.

'Yeah, totally,' she replied, not even bothering to look up from her magazine.

'The thing is,' I explained, 'I don't want Marie to get the tickets and then . . .'

'Look, I don't have a problem with you going,' she insisted. 'Text her.' I composed the return message, but just before I pressed 'send' I felt the need to get one more endorsement, just to be quite certain that this decision was fine with Cath. 'Look,' I said, 'I'm about to press the button. Once I've said yes . . .'

'Oh, for fuck's sake!' Cath snapped. 'I don't have a problem with you going to the cunting tango lesson with Marie. Now send the fucking text and stop fucking going on about it.' Endorsement received, I did as she suggested.

How many people have pressed 'send' and then been filled with terrible regret? Even with a posted letter, you've got a chance. You could return to the box before the next collection, pour paraffin into the slot and set fire to the whole lot. It would be reckless and illegal but you could do it if the need was desperate enough; but once you've pressed 'send' . . . Not that I had that sense of terrible dread as I sat on the sun-bathed balcony. No, what I had was more of a nagging doubt. Like that tightening in the neck and shoulders you get when you're on your way to the airport, convinced you've forgotten something; or that shallowness of breathing you experience when you're sitting on the bus, trying to remember if that lump you felt on your left testicle in the shower that morning had definitely always been there. As far as I knew, nothing was wrong; but how far did I know, and what horrors lay in that region just beyond the extent of my knowing?

I think this mild anxiety was brought on by the fact that Cath hadn't spoken for about forty-five minutes; in fact, not since I'd sent the text. Still, it was very warm and maybe there was something interesting in the magazine. Very interesting. Very interesting and VERY long. 'Cath,' I said, my voice a little higher than usual, 'are you all right?'

'Yeah, I'm fine,' she said. I rolled over to give my back a few more rays and, while my motionless exterior stewed in sunshine, sweat and Ambre Solaire, my interior converted into the head-quarters of a major intelligence agency. Cath's 'Yeah, I'm fine' was rushed to the voice-tone laboratory for extensive tests. Men in white lab-coats and horn-rimmed spectacles held headphones to their ears and looked at each other pensively. There was, they agreed, a definite extension of the 'i' sound on 'fine'. One boffin even claimed to hear a slight dip in the middle of it. The others listened again and nodded. Their faces grew anxious. A man – no women worked in this department – began feeding the data into the WTFDSMBT computer, its title an uneasy acronym of 'What The Fuck Did She Mean By That?' but the results were inconclusive. They needed more data.

I rolled on to my side to face Cath. She lay on her front, on the sun-lounger, her eyes fixed on the magazine that was open on the floor, just below her head. The boffins examined the scene on an internal monitor. 'You just seem a bit quiet,' I said. She continued looking at the magazine.

'Oh, I'm just tired,' she said. A flurry of activity in the laboratory. Was it the 'tired' that meant 'fatigued', or the 'tired' that meant 'fucking furious'?

'It's nothing to do with the tango lesson, is it?' I enquired, with as much casualness as I could muster.

'I've told you,' she said, still looking at the magazine, 'I don't give a shit about the tango lesson.' The boffins were completely stumped. One lay his head on a desk; another sighed and moved towards the smoking area.

Beep! Beep! No, it wasn't a paedophile being transferred into a waiting van on the promenade below, it was a text message. Cath, at last, looked up from the magazine. One of the boffins noted that her facial expression would not have been very different if a used condom had fallen out of my work-clothes. The text, of course, was from Marie. 'It's just Marie saying she'll get the tickets,' I said. Had casualness ever been more carefully conveyed? Cath returned to her magazine, without comment. There would be no more contact with Marie today; nothing to add to the story. The crisis had passed, for the moment. I could relax. I started to drift away into sun-stupor.

Meanwhile, back in the intelligence centre, lights flashed and alarms sounded. One sharp-eyed boffin had noticed something. He'd whizzed back through the tape and zoomed in close. There could be no doubt. Ever since the arrival of the initial text message, a period of some fifty-five minutes, Cath's magazine had been open at the same page. She wasn't reading; she was raging. The boffin was on the hotline to me. Ring-ring. Ring-ring. Where the fuck is he? But I was slipping and sliding into sleepland. Aaaaaaaaaaahhhhhhhhhhmmmmmmmmm . . .

'Well, actually, I AM fucked off about the fucking tango lesson!' Cath suddenly snapped. My mouth and eyes popped open like I was the victim of unanticipated sodomy.

'What? B-But I asked you THREE times!'

'Yes, but I don't want to be the sort of girlfriend who stops you doing a tango lesson with another woman.'

'Great! Well, don't be that sort of girlfriend then.'

'I'm not! But I'm still fucked off about the fucking tango lesson.'

We drove home that night in silence. I started to wonder if I'd been unreasonable. Would I like it if she was having tango lessons with another guy? Or any kind of lessons, for that matter? I didn't want to say any of this out loud because I wasn't TOTALLY sure I was in the wrong and I knew Cath would take any conjecture as a confession. If I spoke now, and then, after further consideration, decided I was after all in the right, she would beat me over the head with my own rash words: 'Look, you fucking admitted you were in the wrong; now you're trying to wriggle out of it.' So I stayed silent.

Cath and I have never lived together, but we were due to hang out the following day. By mid-afternoon, the shrugs and grimaces were so unbearable I texted Marie to say I was, after all, working next weekend and simply couldn't do the class. I was really sorry and, of course, I'd pay for the ticket, and I hoped that she'd have a nice time. I didn't actually tell Cath I'd done this. I thought it would be a nice trick to have up my sleeve, something to produce with a flourish during her next rant on the subject: 'Well, let me tell YOU something, Cath. You've ruined my day out. You've ruined Marie's day out. And you've forced me to go against all my instincts and tell a lie. I hope you're pleased with yourself.' Just the thought of it brought a smug expression to my face – the same smug expression, no doubt, that I'd be wearing when I actually delivered the speech. It was as if I was putting my face through a smug-expression dress rehearsal, so everything would be perfect when my big moment finally came.

I did not have long to wait. Cath ranted; I smugged. She pulled up short. 'You did what?' she asked. I suddenly lost my nerve. Where I had expected shame and remorse, there seemed, instead, to be indignation. I nervously fingered a shirt button as I repeated, in a muttering, apologetic style, that which, only seconds before, I had declared with great gusto: 'I-I texted Marie and I . . . erm . . . told her that, you know . . .'

'Well,' Cath said, suddenly energised, 'you can fucking well text her now and tell her you ARE fucking going.'

'What are you talking about?' I said. 'I thought you didn't want . . .'

'Listen,' Cath said firmly, 'either you go to that fucking tango lesson or I walk out of this relationship.'

In my internal intelligence agency, people ran in all directions. Smoke belched from doorways, flames licked control panels and sirens blared. It was like the end of a Bond movie, when you get the shot from 007's slightly scorched speedboat as the whole high-tech island-complex blows to smithereens.

I needed help. I needed a voice from the outside world, someone who could confirm that this was madness. I picked up Cath's mobile. 'Right,' I said, 'I want you to phone your sister and tell her what you just told me.' Cath, suddenly deflated at the prospect of repeating her words to Rachel, sheepishly took the phone. She pressed a couple of buttons and I could hear Rachel's voice, small and scratchy through the tiny speaker.

'Hi,' said Cath. 'You all right?' I made an impatient gesture. 'Frank wanted me to tell you what I just said to him.' The small and scratchy phone-voice sounded intrigued. 'Well, Frank's texted Marie and cancelled the tango lesson.' The phone-voice seemed strangely saddened. 'So I said if he didn't feel free to go to the tango lesson, maybe we shouldn't be in a relation . . .'

'No, no,' I protested, 'that's not what you said. Tell her exactly what you said.' So Cath reluctantly repeated her threat, verbatim. I couldn't be sure, but if the phone voice DIDN'T say, 'Oh, for fuck's sake', it said something very similar.

Anyway, although Rachel's admonishment, and their resulting chat, seemed to calm Cath down, she still insisted that I should go to the tango class, and assured me that she would cope. She really DIDN'T want to stop me doing things with friends, she said, and she would continue to battle with her jealousy until it was beaten. I kissed her warm lips and everything seemed good. A flashing red warning light pierced the thick grey smoke of the ruined intelligence agency, but there were no boffins left to respond.

I didn't want to walk into a crowded tango class on my own, so I arranged to meet Marie in a pub round the corner. She wore a red dress and red heels, and had tied back her long black hair. She had decided to look like a tango dancer, even if she couldn't actually tango. I had made no such efforts. The sight of me leaving the flat in a cummerbund and bolero jacket might well have pushed Cath over the edge. The class was full and, though I liked the music, I danced like I always dance: stiff and ugly. We rotated partners every few minutes but, whichever woman I danced with, it was always like the Tin Man dancing with Dorothy. To make matters worse, I had two hot patches in the middle of my back: Cath's searing gaze travelling across London, bent on spoiling my fun.

Most of the women seemed to be no-nonsense housewife-types who determinedly held me at arm's length, like they were repelling the advances of an over-excited plumber on a rainy Tuesday afternoon, between *Loose Women* and the school run. As it was, I definitely wasn't making any advances, either to them or in the art of tango. The class ended, I said goodbye to Marie and went to pick up Cath, who was shopping in Covent Garden.

She was a little stand-offish. I figured that if I didn't respond, the mood would pass and we'd soon be back to normal. We drove to my flat. I was forecasting to myself a tense rest-of-the-afternoon, clearing to produce a crisp but surprisingly mild evening.

'How was the tango?' Cath asked at last. I was happy to tell her the whole truth of it.

'It was probably the least sexy thing I've ever done in my life.'

This was pushing it a bit because I used to be in a cribbage league. However, I was very keen to prove that her fears had been unfounded. 'It was a lot of fat, ugly housewives, with BO and bingo-wings, dancing like they had rickets. I wish you could have been there. You would have laughed out loud at the very thought of it being some sort of school of seduction.'

'Did Marie have a good time?' she asked.

'I don't know,' I said. 'We barely spoke.' I was starting to feel glad that I'd had such a crap time. We parked outside my flat and headed for the front door. I reached for my keys but they weren't there. I went through my pockets. Cath looked at me, and eventually I looked at her. 'I must have left them at the tango place,' I said. Cath said nothing. When we arrived in Islington, I asked her if she was coming in with me. She preferred to stay in the car. 'Oh, come on,' I said. I knew, when she saw the drab, empty hall, she'd realise nothing sexy could possibly have happened there. At last, she grudgingly agreed to accompany me.

We reached the building, I opened the door to the hall . . . and suddenly we were in Lust-ville. The loud, violently sensual tango music, gut-stirring and jagged at the edges, ripped through the heat-haze atmosphere of the room. Wild-eyed angular men, their muscles wrestling to get out of tight black vests, made shapes with beautiful long-necked women. Haughty but hot, male and female, stick-thin and throbbing, threaded together like locusts fucking on a shiny-stone cave-floor. They were magnificent in their union. You couldn't tell where the man stopped and the woman started. There was no sign of Colin Jackson.

Cath's mouth hung open. I'd been in the Beginners' Class; this was the Advanced. Shell-shocked, I edged forward to talk to the man. He said he hadn't seen my keys. I ferreted around the room, dodging the four-legged sex-fiends. Cath stood, photoshopping them with her eyes, replacing his head with my head, her head with the head of Marie. The keys weren't even there.

We walked silently back into the sunshine. 'You DO realise that was the Advanced class, don't you?' I said at last 'The one I was in was nothing . . .'

'So where are the fucking keys?' Cath asked.

'I must have left them in the pub,' I blurted out, unthinkingly.

'Pub? You never said anything about going to a pub.' She managed to say the old-fashioned, incredibly English word 'pub' like it was French for 'cum-guzzling fuckfest'.

The keys were indeed at the pub, but my relief at their recovery was somewhat marred by the barman saying, 'Oh, yeah. You were the couple in the corner.' I didn't look at Cath. I didn't have to.

Anyway, we recovered. We always recover. You may have picked up clues during the course of this journal which have led you to suspect that I, also, am capable of being a little difficult. In truth, we're both a bit odd but two odds make an even. And she is the most loving, kind, gentle, funny, outrageous, sensual, complicated, frustrating but ultimately beautiful person I've ever met. I really hope the tour, for reasons of absence, jealousy or my own self-pity, doesn't fuck things up for us. I'll get to see her whenever I can, but those sporadic meetings are always tricky; the post-separation strangeness; the pressure imposed on brief periods of 'quality time'.

If the shows are going badly, I'll be a nightmare: morose, edgy and preoccupied. It happened a few weeks ago. We were lying on the sofa in my flat while Cath told me about a music gig she'd been to during our eleven-month interregnum. I could hear the words, see the gestures, but it was just sound and movement. I was thinking about this story I'd been telling onstage over the previous weeks about a kid at my school who claimed that if you slept upside-down, like a bat, you got more intelligent because all the blood went to your brain. A couple of kids in our class seriously considered trying it before the mock exams. One spoke about tying his feet to the top of the wardrobe; the other to his younger brother's upper bunk. I was much less keen to give it a go:

My first thought was 'What if I have a wet dream?' I'll wake up the next morning and say (SWITCHING TO A VERY BUNGED-UP VOICE), 'Oh, I had a filthy dream last night. And terrible catarrh this morning!'

Then I'd blow my nose on a bit of toilet paper, leave it by the side of the bed and everything's back in its rightful place.

They were laughing at it till about three gigs ago. Maybe I'd accidentally changed my delivery in some way; perhaps a new facial expression or added emphasis was making it too gross.

'And there was this pulse-like bass-sound and the singer was sort of screaming,' Cath was saying, as I fell back into real time. 'Are you listening?' she said.

'Yeah. Pulse-like bass-sound,' I said.

'Yeah, but were you listening before that?'

'Your hair looks great,' I said.

'It fucking doesn't,' she said.

I'm still looking at the dent in the pillow on my now-familiar bed. She hasn't even said we're officially back together. Anyway, I need to get moving. Eleven o'clock Mass at St Patrick's.

The Mass is pretty good but not greatly inspiring. I champion the Old Church with its mysterious rituals and supernatural traditions, but sometimes, probably more often than not, the Mass is a bit pedestrian. I mean, just consider what they're selling: spiritual enlightenment, forgiveness, eternal life and, for an encore, bread and wine mystically transubstantiated into flesh and blood. That's quite a set-list; it should guarantee a great gig every time but I can't say it does. For example, I've probably heard twenty or so really moving sermons in my lifetime, and I've been to Mass hundreds and hundreds of times. They are usually too long, under-rehearsed or under-written. The priest often tries to make several points instead of concentrating on making one really well; and the sermon rarely has reference to any topical themes that might make it seem more relevant and immediate to the listeners. I feel bad saying all this because I'm sure priests are mega-busy and can't give as much time as they'd like to sermon-writing, but I speak, for a change, as an audience member and I've got my rights. If I do a crap stand-up gig, I don't expect the crowd to think, 'Well, I know he was rubbish but, to be fair, he's probably got a lot on.' I have a duty to do the job as well as I possibly can, regardless of other commitments. A sermon doesn't need to be intellectual, probably shouldn't be, just pithy and pertinent. I don't see why, given the subject-matter, the whole experience has to be like the third reading of a white paper on traffic-filtering, going through the House of Lords.

I once went to a Spanish Mass and, at the end, the congregation applauded. I didn't understand a word the priest had said, but it sounded like he'd gone down a storm. I'd like to see this convention become universal. Believe me, you can tell a lot by a crowd's closing response. I think it would have quite a motivational effect on any priest if he knew he'd be leaving the altar to ecstatic, warm, non-committal or perhaps even non-existent applause; a direct and measurable verdict on his performance. Of course, I'll probably discover that there is no convention in Spain for closing applause at Masses. It'll probably turn out that the priest had just made a closing comment that went down particularly well, like 'Next week there'll be no sermon'.

As I say, I hate to blame the priests because they've got tough jobs and, in post-Dawkins Britain, ever-dwindling kudos. Also, the average Roman Catholic congregation could, with some justification, be described as a tough crowd. Oh, they wouldn't boo or heckle, but the lethargy is deafening – people arriving twenty minutes late, screaming kids, talking, yawning, mobile phones going off – and they often don't join in with the hymns or responses. It's like the corporate seats at Wembley. The Old Church needs a shot in the arm, but I can't imagine what that will be. Though, obviously, the Second Coming might well turn it round. Still, to paraphrase JFK, 'Don't ask what the Mass can do for you; ask what you can do for the Mass', and I'm in St Patrick's concentrating on the words, singing all the hymns and trying to get into the zone.

In fairness, this Mass isn't so bad, and at one point the sermon actually makes me laugh out loud. The celebrant tells us about the farewell speech of a former priest who was leaving this parish some years ago. The old man, we're told, closed his address with, 'And let me just say that if I offended anyone during my stay here, I invariably meant it.'

I didn't enjoy this afternoon's charity gig. It was in Pleasance One, twice the capacity of the Cabaret Bar, but it felt stilted and restrained – the ruder stuff in particular. This may have been because the audience, I'd say, were a little older than the ones I've been getting in the evening gigs; there was a lot more white hair than usual. For this crowd, granny porn was not so much a joke as an everyday reality. It may also have felt flat because it was an earlier show. I'm not sure sunlight twinkling through a curtain-gap is a suitable accompaniment to jokes about prostitutes, cancer and girlfriends with well-endowed exes: 'Eventually, she sort of shrunk to fit.'

And yes, it may also have been because I just wasn't very good. But, anyway, it raised ten-and-a-half grand for people with HIV, so I died that they might live.

Now I'm outside the venue, hiding from the departing crowd, with a thank-you card in one hand and a bottle of champagne in the other. I accepted the latter with an 'I'm a recovering alcoholic but thank you anyway' smile, and headed for the exit.

A guy approaches me and, before I can apologise for the show, he introduces himself as Rolf, one of the stars of *Auto Auto*, a German production staged in the venue I just vacated which features a car being destroyed and its parts turned into musical instruments. Rolf, a native of Hamburg, explains that he's just seen my show and was amazed at how much of it he understood and actually enjoyed. 'I like that it's you just talking about your life,' he says, 'with not many difficult references.' It's essentially a comedy-as-a-second-language compliment but I'll take what I can get. Though we only speak for ten minutes, I really quite like Rolf. I'm not one of those people who can only think of Germans in terms of World War II. But, anyway, he's got a show to prepare, and I've got one to cry about, so we shake hands and pass like U-boats in the night.

I meet up with Cath and she picks up on my despondency, not so much because our intimacy borders on the telepathic, but more because she asks me how I am and I say, 'Despondent.'

'But it's going really well,' she says, as we walk along North Bridge in the sunshine. 'I read a review that described you as "one of the greatest storytellers of our generation".'

She suddenly stops walking, realising what she's just said. She looks back at me – I'd stopped walking on the word 'review' – and says, 'Oh, fuck, I'm sorry.' I close my eyes and speak very calmly and carefully: 'I've told you a thousand . . .'

'I know. I'm sorry.' She waits for me to catch up with her, and we continue together, across the bridge. 'What are you going to do with that bottle of champagne?' she asks. I dismiss, as a possible reply, 'Drink it, all alone, on waste ground', and opt instead for, 'I'll think of something. I'm not carting it back to London.' We walk on.

'One of the greatest storytellers of our generation'. Oh, the pain. The pain of nearly but not quite . . . of maybe but not sure . . . of anyone but not Cath. In normal circumstances, hearing that review-fragment would send me spiralling into high elation. No doubt there would be something else in the rest of the review that, if I saw it, would send me spiralling back down again, but this sweet selection was uncontaminated by context: a lovely, juicy compliment, simple and unspoiled. But it came from Cath; went through the Cath scrambler that jumbles up words and syntax till no linguist, regardless of rank, could predict the outcome. Cath has a habit – most of the time, an incredibly endearing habit – of misremembering and misquoting things. For example, during one of the many late-night conversations we've had about our relationship, we moved on to the subject of basic gender differences. 'Maybe we should read that book, *Men are Venus*,' she suggested. I laughed so much she laughed at me laughing, but didn't know what I was laughing at. Coincidentally, on another foray into this subject-matter, we talked about how different we were in many ways, but how that difference still seemed to work. 'Yes,' said Cath, 'it's like Jack will eat no Spratt.' In fact only yesterday she told me she'd been introduced to someone at a gig but the resulting conversation was very hard work. 'It was like pulling blood,' she said. How could I NOT love her?

But now, as we turn into Princes Street, the charm of this habit is not quite so apparent. 'What did it REALLY say?' I ask myself. Even with a deliberate effort to be optimistic, I can only aim as high as 'one of the greatest storytellers of the *Loaded* generation'. At the opposite end of the scale, the bleak and despairing end, I'm wondering if, where she read 'storytellers', it actually said 'cunts'. Still it will give me something else to torture myself with during the twelve days of hell that link a lukewarm Edinburgh to a disastrous tour.

Now it's ten past midnight and I've put aside worries about reviews and the forthcoming tour to worry, instead, about the show I just did. The first half, the reliable half, went well. The second half, the experimental half, was an enigma – most notably the sex-from-behind-in-a-shirt and the oral-sex routines. What is it with these two? Every line seems to get a good laugh; several get a great laugh:

I read in *Marie Claire* that some men suffer from a thing called clitorophobia. They're actually scared of the clitoris. I don't have that problem. In fact, nowadays, it's one of the few things in a hood that I'm NOT scared of.

You see how I've evolved since that joke I did on the one hundred greatest comics programme? My oral-sex jokes used to just be about oral sex; now they're about psycho-sexual illness and the traumas of urban decay.

Nonetheless, while each separate joke got a laugh, neither of the routines seemed to function as a whole. It was like watching a football side full of talented individuals, but not playing as a team. None of the gags deserve to be dropped, but they won't win matches if they continue like this. I've been a stand-up since the eighties, but I can't remember this phenomenon occurring before. My normal method of improvement is pruning and/or rewriting, but with these routines, neither seems appropriate.

'Can you move your right foot about three inches to the left, please?'

I'm in the hot tub with Cath, Cath's mum Sandy, Cath's sister Rachel and Rachel's friend Danielle. The ladies all came in bikinis and I came in my trunks. (Forgive me, the chlorine's making me skittish.) I used to dream that showbiz would be like this, me and four women in a hot tub, though I never thought it would include my girlfriend, her sister and her mum. Even though they're drinking what I've unfortunately come to think of as 'the HIV champagne' and I'm smoking my pipe, the overall effect is not so much 'Playboy Mansion' as 'family bath-night'.

The ladies leave Edinburgh tomorrow; me, the day after. I've kind of enjoyed it but I wish I was further up that eighty-foot wall. Suddenly, the city, spread out beneath us, reminds me of something.

A couple of years ago, in July 2005, I was invited to the premiere of *Festival*, a sort of comedy-drama about the Edinburgh Festival. It wasn't a star-studded event; I was only there as Cath's plus-one. It was mainly trendy media types and journalists. I couldn't have called myself a stand-up at that time. I was a chat-show host; a

TV presenter, even. But, as the film progressed, the slumbering stand-up within me started to stir. Not through nostalgia or a desire to emulate the heroic exploits of the comics in the movie. No, this stirring was motivated purely by rage. The fictional comedians in the film, all up in Edinburgh doing their fictional shows, were portrayed as self-centred, insecure, misogynistic drunks. Having read this far, you're probably thinking, 'Yes, what's your point?' But I was angry. If these criticisms were spoken by nurses, working with the poor of rural Africa, I could have taken it, but coming from the mouths of fucking actors, it sounded a wee bit hypocritical. I resented the satisfied sniggering of the audience, the oh-yes-that's-what-comedians-are-like smugness of it. I felt like a black man at a BNP meeting. The film even had a paedophile Catholic priest to add topping to my already substantial alienation-cake. My outrage reached its high point during a speech which centred upon the question 'Why do we need comedians?' 'Hey, why do we need music?' I thought. 'Why do we need football? Let's just go to cool bars and do cocaine.'

In the midst of all this rancour, I suddenly stepped back from myself. Why was I getting so hostile? I didn't know the writer of the movie, didn't know the audience, so how could I justify wanting them to suffer severe facial disfigurement in a series of seemingly unconnected house-fires? Then it struck me. I would not be getting this angry if I wasn't a comedian. If the film had been about chat-show hosts or TV presenters I'd have been sniggering along with everyone else. It was a beautiful moment. Deep down, I was still a comedian. I'd almost forgotten.

So the club-gigs, the arts centre shows, the Edinburgh run, have all had their lows as well as highs – but I'm doing it. The reviews might, for all I know, be saying I'm a shit stand-up, but they can't really deny that I AM a stand-up. I'm on that stage, one man and a microphone, doing jokes; that's all the essential ingredients. It can be disheartening, humiliating even, but it's also a fuck of a great job.

I've gone all sentimental now. Maybe it's the pipe-tobacco. The chink of champagne glasses snaps me out of it. I look at my legs, dappling through the blue-glow water. Life is sweet. I look at that dark, brooding castle against that ink-blue sky. I have a lot of work to do. Then, for some reason, it suddenly dawns on me: those twelve days I have to turn the disjointed results of sixteen Edinburgh gigs into an 'all killers, no fillers' ninety-minute tour-show aren't actually twelve days at all. I've got an hour-long show in Birmingham on 5 September and another the next day. They're at the Hare and Hounds, the pub where I made my Birmingham reputation back in the late eighties. The shows were my idea. A fiver a ticket, a bit of a laugh, a way of trimming down the mountain of knockout material I'd be triumphantly bringing back from Edinburgh. So it's eight days. Eight days of writing and rearranging; two days of Birmingham gigs; two days of building a tour-show from what's left after that. This pipe is horrible. A ninety-minute tour-show; I've got a lot of holes to fill. But then, I bet I'm not the first man, sat in a hot tub with four women, who's thought that.

PART TWO

LOOKING BACKWARDS

AND FORWARDS

WEDNESDAY 29 AUGUST 2007

I've been back in London for three days now. The work started immediately after my last Edinburgh gig. I went straight back to my flat and, with the sound of late-night Bank Holiday revelry rising up from the street, I sat in a pool of table-lamplight and spent two hours going through each of my routines: charting their progress, or lack of it, during these last sixteen shows; swirling the grit and gravel in search of glistening gold. The remaining question marks have made my mathematical calculations difficult. I still have, I would say, about an hour and ten minutes of material I feel confident with. The rest is guesswork. These upcoming gigs in King's Heath are my last chance to test stuff before the tour proper, so my plan is, over the two nights, to throw everything at them. Maybe some borderline stuff I rejected earlier on in the process, when my performance skills were still in storage, could find new life now I've regained some of my strut and swagger.

I've also thought about adding a couple of songs to the act. On the last series of my chat show, I wrote a topical song each week and performed it as Bob Dylan, *circa* 1966, with massive black curly wig and shades. David Blunkett's affair, bird flu, the Paris riots, Madonna's leotard, Gary Glitter's imprisonment . . . they all got the Dylan treatment, with me playing guitar and kind of playing harmonica. I loved it. It was my favourite part of the show. In my current stand-up set, I touch upon the old British tradition of singing comedy songs about warfare, particularly World War II:

mildly abusive attacks on the enemy leader – 'Adolf' by the Billy Cotton Band or '(It's just too bad for) Nasty Uncle Adolf' by Ambrose and his Orchestra – and more general comic ditties about the experience of war, like George Formby's songs 'I'm Guarding the Home of the Home Guard' and 'I Did What I Could With My Gas Mask'. In my act I bemoan that this tradition has died out. It seems, I say, like a very British way of coping with the horrors of war. I then go on to wonder how modern audiences would react if, in the current climate, I brought out a Formby-type song about the War Against Terror. I even sing a brief snatch, in my best George Formby voice, of how that song might go:

> My mate Ali was a dentist
> Now he's a Muslim fundamentalist.
> Bang! Bang! Baghdad.
> He's gone bomb-mad.
> Bang! Bang! Baghdad-Boy.

It's a simple idea, incorporating a comic dance, and it almost always goes well, often getting a round of applause. Now, I don't get much applause mid-set. I find applause from a comedy crowd often means 'we agree' rather than 'we think that's funny'. Thus, jokes about George Bush being stupid get applause; jokes about granny porn get laughs. If I'd wanted applause, I'd have gone into politics. There is something about a comic song – in fact, any song – that makes people feel they should applaud at the end of it; even a brief, unaccompanied snatch of a song like the one above. I don't want that – some sort of hollow politeness – but, if they LAUGH at the song as well, if that song is a series of deserve-to-be-there put-to-music gags, that's a different story. So, I'm writing a couple of more fully formed George Formby-type songs, this time to be accompanied by my banjo-ukulele.

Just a quick note: a banjo-ukulele is like any other ukulele except it has a circular, drum-like body, like a banjo, rather than the tiny, wooden, guitar-like body that characterises the standard uke. This makes it louder. George Formby used a banjo-uke so he could be heard in big theatres. Every day's a schoolday.

I want these new songs to reflect the realities of the War Against Terror, while retaining a Formby-esque jaunty innocence. George often sings about his sweetheart, so that was my first port of call. You'll have to trust me on the tune, but the words begin:

She's my little suicide-bomber girl.
Don't know where our relationship is going.
She's my little suicide-bomber girl.
It's so sexy when her wires are showing.
She likes me cos I never ask about the tanks of Calor gas
    piled in the back of her black Subaru.
She likes me cos I never tut or tell her off or argue, but she
    likes me most of all because I'm not a Jew.

With the plinka-plink-plink of the uke and lots of grins and knowing looks from me, it might just work. I'm still working on the second song, but it will continue the lighter-side-of-terrorism theme. The big question is, will I have the guts to try them out at King's Heath? I'm a crap ukulele player and, also, the words to these songs aren't really sticking in my memory at the moment. Besides, I'm a stand-up. I like the no-props, no-songs, no-gimmicks purity of that. With the odd exception, I usually find turns that do comedy songs a bit embarrassing. Still, the songs might provide a bit of light relief amidst the smut. The audience appreciate an occasional sunbeam, especially when they're in the murkier parts of the forest.

I also like the idea of my act continuing to evolve. I heard a programme on Radio Four during which they interviewed a scientist who studied sea anemones. He said it was sometimes hard to be sure whether the anemones were alive or dead. 'The most crucial factor is growth,' he said. 'If there's no growth, there's no life.' I would say that's probably also true of people's minds, and their stand-up acts. Six weeks ago, instead of using my usual upward or downward stroke, I tried shaving my throat sideways. Ever since I was a teenager, I've never managed to get my throat really smooth post-shave; it's always retained a slightly stubbly feel. This newly introduced sideways stroke, the result of a mid-shave whim, left me suddenly smooth and stubble-free. Now, if I, a fifty-year-old man, can still improve, at this late stage, my shaving technique, surely I can do likewise with my act.

However, I've spent much more time holding a razor than I have a ukulele. My true Formby initiation was only twelve months ago. As part of the banjo documentary, I spent a warm Friday night in Barnsley, in the tiny function room of a local amateur football club. It was the monthly meeting of the George Formby Appreciation Society, Barnsley Branch, and I was greeted in the car park by their president, Dennis Taylor. Obviously, he greeted me in the car park because the documentary's director had told him to, but even the television bullshit couldn't hide the fact that Dennis was a big, friendly man in spectacles, who loved George Formby. As we chatted, in that slightly awkward, self-conscious way that people often chat on television, a steady stream of inexpensive cars pulled up and various men and women, mainly men, emerged carrying tiny ukulele cases and made for the function-room door.

When Dennis finally led me in, there were about seventy people sitting at tables and, onstage, a little old lady played ukulele and sang a song I didn't know, but which had George Formby written through its core like 'Blackpool' written through a little stick of rock. Almost everyone at the tables had a uke-case at their feet. The monthly meeting of the George Formby Appreciation Society, Barnsley Branch, was not just a spectator-sport, it was all about getting up and having a go; and this being a see-the-celebrity-humiliated sort of a documentary, I realised I'd walked into a trap. I was taken into a back room and introduced to Andy Eastwood, an extremely dapper man in his late twenties with an electric-blue suit and a whiff of after-shave, who I guessed would be equally at home on a cruise ship or exchanging business cards at a Variety Club of Great Britain dinner. Andy epitomised mainstream entertainment. He'd just got back from a summer season in Bournemouth with Ken Dodd and had made CDs called *Ukulele Serenade* and *Ukulele Mania*. I imagined him singing Formby songs as if the last half of the twentieth century had never happened; jogging the memories of two-dozen pensioners in a three-hundred-capacity theatre, somewhere in nowhere. I was wrong.

Pope John Paul II once said that the really bad thing about pornography is not that you see too much but that you see too little. I've said the same thing myself. The difference is I was raging about the Japanese porn industry's obsession with pixilation; John Paul was saying that pornography reduces the people in it to their physical being and deliberately removes the person within: the spirit, the soul. They become bodies, mere bearers of physical functions. A Catholic priest once said to me that we all adopt a similarly reductive attitude to strangers, deciding who and what they are with a single glance, a mindset that could be described as social pornography; we see too little. I once wrote a sitcom called *Shane*, in which I played the eponymous hero. In one episode, Shane meets a homeless bloke called Harry and takes him home for dinner, a few drinks and a chance to spend some time in a family environment. As Harry leaves, he says this:

> Look, before I go, I want to say thank you. Especially to you, Shane. Not many people would welcome a tramp into their home, because not many people look through the grime and see the human being that's underneath. Those broken figures you see on the streets might look like the spectres you rattle past on the ghost train, but the difference is they're flesh and blood. They don't have homes, but they have hearts.

Yes, I know it's a bit *Diff'rent Strokes*, but the sentiment is sound. At first glance, I had reduced Andy Eastwood to a stereo-typical mainstream performer, all cufflinks and corporate gigs, but I soon discovered he was a bright and interesting bloke. In fact, he'd studied music at Oxford University and was the first-ever student there to major in ukulele; he studied piano and violin as well. I wonder if Ken Dodd likes Velázquez.

Andy took me into a corner and showed me a few ukulele chords. They are the same shape as guitar chords but with four strings instead of six. He handed me a banjo-uke and said, 'You can borrow this one if you like. It belonged to George.' I'm not kidding, I felt a definite shiver as I took hold of it. Sometimes great men linger in their belongings. I said I'd like to play 'Leaning on a Lamp Post', a Formby classic. Andy smiled and pointed to some pencilled handwriting on the uke's drum-like body. Incredibly, George only ever played in one key, so when he sang songs in other keys he switched to a uke that was tuned accordingly. George had used this particular uke on his last-ever TV show and he'd written on it so he'd know it was the right tuning for a particular song. I peered at the scratchy, pencilled writing. It said simply, 'lamp post'.

In about forty minutes, Andy taught me enough to be able to get up on stage and play the song. I wasn't note-perfect but I really loved playing the uke and singing like George, and the members of the George Formby Appreciation Society, Barnsley Branch, seemed to like it too. I once heard a classical pianist say that, sometimes, when playing Beethoven, he actually felt like the spirit of Beethoven was operating within him, inhabiting his body, playing with his fingers. Suffice to say, it doesn't sound quite so dramatic when it's George Formby, does it? There was something that night, though; something about playing George's uke.

I had a great time in Barnsley. I met a very polite nine-year-old kid called Christopher, who was dressed as George and carried the uke he'd been given when he won *Junior Stars in Their Eyes*, and, as I left the building, I saw a bloke dressed in 1930s motorcycling gear and riding a 1930s motorbike, replicas of George's clothes and bike in the 1935 film *No Limit*.

Anyway, I drove away from that football club in Barnsley and I haven't played a banjo-uke since . . . until now. So, I'm writing two songs, learning two songs and learning the instrument itself, all in eight days. I'm back to thinking about this British comic-tradition thing. Obviously, most people who like George Formby nowadays would be appalled by my act but, in his day, George was considered risqué; 'With My Little Stick of Blackpool Rock' was banned by the BBC in 1937. I'm wondering now if I can take the Formby form but update the content; my own comedy mindset, wrapped in a plinkerty-plink and a winkerty-wink. I just take out the gas masks and the Home Guard, take out the Hitler, recycle a bit of already extant stand-up, add a jolly tune and:

> What happened to that nasty man
> So pally with the Taliban?
> O-O-O-O-Osama bin Laden
> He had one big hit then he went away
> Like a terrorism Macy Gray.
> O-O-O-O-Osama bin Laden.
> Every now and then he sends out a video tape
> To say he's doing great and he's full of hate.
> If he's doing so well then please tell me
> Why a video tape, not a DVD?
> O-O-O-O-Osama bin Laden.

Meanwhile, as the songs continue to develop, the search for straight stand-up material from the previous eight months' work that might be good enough for a reprise is proving to be a painful but interesting process. It involves going through all my post-gig check-lists and digging a bit deeper into some of those ticks that Devon Loched; even the odd question mark that might have been too hastily dismissed. I won't actually be rescinding any straight red cards – that gag where I pull my coat right up over my head and stick my tongue out as far as it will go, as a visual postscript to the clitorophobia joke, will not be invited back – but there might be a few yellows I didn't persevere with at the time that now deserve re-inspection. And, of course, now the Osama material has found a new home, rehoused in a cheerful tune, I might construct an encore that is, essentially, *Handjobs-from-the-Homeless: the Musical.*

I'm reading through a bagful of scribbled bits of paper. I always work on a computer except when I write stand-up. For some reason, I can only write that by hand. I can type set-lists of already written material, but the original joke always gets to paper *sans* PC (you can say that again). Anyway, just picking through these scribbled notes is, for me, a slightly harrowing walk down Failed-Gag-Memory Lane:

Things are pretty bad at West Brom at the moment. I've started staying till the very end of the match to avoid the traffic.

You see those guys who paint themselves silver and pretend to be statues? People come up and put money in their tin. They get paid just for keeping still! I tell you, if that quantum physics work ever dries up for Professor Stephen Hawking, he could make a fortune in Covent Garden.

I hate it when a mobile-phone conversation just cuts out in the middle and then the person on the other end of the line calls you back and says, 'I don't know what happened then!'

I always say, 'Well, how could you? In order to know "what happened then" you'd have to be in some sort of mobile phone nerve-centre, with a big computer-map of Great Britain showing network coverage, colour-coded reception areas and prevailing weather conditions. Even then, there'd have to be a certain amount of guesswork involved. The truth is you'll never "know what happened then", neither of us will; just accept that.'

I even wrote a line to follow jokes that died – self-contained and insertable at a moment's notice. The only problem was that died as well.

Don't worry about that last joke. It's gone for ever. Writing jokes is like having children for me. It's terrible if they die but all you can do is just let go. I don't blame you people. I'm like the bereaved parent and you're like the surgeon who's come into the waiting room and said, 'Sorry, we did everything we could. It just wasn't strong enough.'

It's the polar-opposite of Jay Leno's 'if I don't react to it, they might not notice' approach. Anyway, I don't think any of those gags will be getting a second interview. This pre-tour period is obviously all about the nuts and bolts of making the show as good as I can get it, about attention to detail. At the same time, I've found myself wondering why I'm doing this at all, why I'm doing stand-up again after all these years. What's the real no-showbiz-bullshit from-the-heart reason? In the old days it was sex, money, personal pride and sheer enjoyment, with the latter two very much dominating the pie-chart. Nowadays, as I've already established, sex has been channelled into one particular person. As for money, I had a meeting with my bank manager in December 2005 and I opened by saying, 'Look, I'm nearly fifty. I'm coming towards the end of a seven-year contract with ITV. They're not begging me to stay, nor are there a host of other broadcasters kicking my door down. You know how much money I've got. You know how much money I spend. How's it looking?' He smiled. The pause that followed seemed momentous. 'In my professional opinion,' he said, with some gravitas, 'if you never work again, and don't suddenly switch to a more extravagant lifestyle, you will probably remain financially secure for the rest of your life.'

Admittedly, he could have been a bit pithier in his delivery, but it was still quite a moment. I have always considered myself to be a non-materialistic person; I drive a modest BMW Compact and I'm not big on designer labels or jewellery. But the bank manager's smile was not in the same league as the one creasing up MY face. It was the best news I'd ever had. 'Fuckin come on!' I said as I punched the air. The bank manager and his assistant both smiled, as bank employees tend to do when in the company of an affluent client. 'Well,' I said, having somewhat calmed, 'that really is splendid news.' Then, in a second wave of excitement, I burst out laughing and spontaneously applauded.

Those born into money will never know the very special pleasure derived from having none and then having plenty. Likewise, the lottery winner, while obviously thrilled by a sudden windfall, cannot enjoy the added pleasure of having worked for it: the nights sleeping in cars; the unpaid gigs; the humiliations of failure; the early hours writing stand-up while still holding down a full-time job . . . it had all paid off. OK, I might get cancer tomorrow, but, even then, rich cancer is better than poor cancer. Finally – and this is a fact – in my bank manager's oak-panelled office, I sang, with gusto, the old thirties ballad 'Ah! Sweet Mystery of Life'. You may remember it from Mel Brooks' *Young Frankenstein* movie:

Ah! Sweet mystery of life, at last I've found thee.
Ah! I know at last the secret of it all.
All the longing, striving, seeking, waiting, yearning,
The burning hopes, the joys and idle tears that fall.

I was not embarrassed. In fact, I felt the bank manager and his assistant would happily have joined me in a three-part harmony, had they the technical know-how. Anyway, this news had a surprising effect on me. Throughout my comedy career, I'd always sincerely believed that I was very much NOT in it for the money. Of course, financial gain was a lovely side-effect but, as the pie-chart showed, my priorities were always more noble; more spiritual, even. Now, however, I wondered if, by continuing my career, I would lump myself with those idiots we used to take the piss out of when I was a young man living on ten quid a week: those knob-heads who won the football pools and then said, in the local paper, 'It won't change me. I'll carry on being a lathe-operator.' Someone would read that out loud, in the factory or the pub, and we would fall about laughing. Rarely has the word 'twat' been delivered with such vim. I know being a comedian is not quite the same as being a lathe operator, but nowadays, when the alarm clock goes off because I have to get up early to film something, or write some-thing, or have a meeting or whatever, the ringing sound of that clock always seems to have an echoing chorus of 'twat' at its core. Happily, it doesn't seem to echo quite so loudly when I'm getting up early to write stand-up.

What I never really understood was when rich people – and I'm talking MUCH richer than me – did jobs that were clearly just for the money, with no creative input or potential for job-satisfaction involved, like Nicole Kidman doing a perfume advert. How much fucking money do you need? I used to howl when I saw massive American film stars doing adverts that, contractually, could only be shown in Europe, like that meant no one would ever find out. I was in Germany and I saw Dustin Hoffman doing a car ad. Dustin Hoffman! Fuck off!

I remember, during the ninth and last series of my chat show, leaving the Avalon offices one Sunday night at nine o'clock. I said goodnight to the security guard, a devout Muslim who often sat in reception reading the Koran – I once walked in on him actually at prayer, on his knees in the corner. The security guard returned my goodnight and added, 'You work a great many hours, don't you?' I agreed but explained that I wanted to do the best show I could do; no pain, no gain, and so on. The guard looked at me with a degree of concern in his eyes and said, 'There is a saying in Arabic: "When a man has a mountain of gold, he wants to build another one."' As I drove home that night, the phrase played on my mind. 'Is that what I'm doing?' No English security guard would say a thing like that. The best you could possibly hope for would be, 'Another day, another dollar', but most likely it would just be a grunt, still smelling of lunchtime's beer. Anyway, I didn't want another mountain of gold; I didn't want to waste my days and nights working for that. I'd rather spend my time and effort doing something beautiful and fulfilling. I'd rather be learning the lute than earning the loot.

But then, tragically, I too fell into the greed-sweet trap. I had an offer from Tesco, the supermarket chain, to voice-over an advert for their new slim Christmas tree. In a way, it was the distant memory of my factory workmates' derision that made me do it. You're a twat if you've got money and still work, but surely, I reasoned, you're an even bigger twat if you say no to fifteen grand, just to sit in a sound-studio for thirty minutes, reading a one-page script. So I did it. Twelve days later I was sitting home alone, watching Sky TV and reading the newspaper, when I suddenly became aware of my own voice. I looked up from the paper, just in time to hear myself say, 'Tesco – every little helps'. Now, don't get me wrong, Tesco is a perfectly fine supermarket chain that sells nice things at reasonable prices, but I must have washed my hands ten times before I went to bed that night, like the crazed Lady Macbeth trying to scrub away imaginary blood. At least she had only been party to murder; I had done an advert for a slim Christmas tree.

In my defence: lesson learned, I did, a couple of months later, turn down good money to be the voice of an interactive comedy pub-game called Jokey-Cokey. And, a few months after that, David Baddiel and I turned down even better money, when the food-company McCain's wanted our permission to change the lyrics of the football song 'Three Lions', which we'd written with Lightning Seeds' frontman Ian Broudie, so it could be used in an advert for their oven chips. They wanted to take part of the original song, a couplet which combines nostalgia for England's 1966 World Cup triumph, with great hope for the future . . .

> I know that was then
> But it could be again.

. . . and rewrite it in a more, well, oven chips kind of a way:

> Less than five per cent fat
> Who can argue with that?

I'd have still been washing my hands now. Anyway, what I'm saying is, it isn't the money. And that's incredibly liberating. I heard a great story about Max Miller, the famously risqué comic of the thirties, forties and fifties, whose catchphrases included, 'I don't care what I say, do I?' He did a Royal Variety Show and did about three times longer onstage than he was supposed to do. Eventually, the powerful impresario Val Parnell appeared in the wings, angrily gesturing at Max to come off. In a PR masterstroke, the comic turned to the crowd and said, 'They're telling me to come off, but they give the American acts plenty of time – what about backing an English lad for a change?' Of course, the audience cheered wildly and Max carried on. When he finally left the stage, an outraged Parnell confronted him and said, 'Miller, you'll never work in my theatres again.'

'Sorry, Val,' said Max, 'you're £80,000 too late.'

Needless to say, £80,000 was an 'Ah! Sweet Mystery of Life' fortune at the time.

So what about personal pride? Well, in the past I've had the BBC and ITV fighting to sign me; three-year contracts that included more or less anything I wanted as long as I delivered three series a year; comedy awards nominations running into double figures. When that dries up, it does throw you a bit. It's nice to feel wanted and not so nice to feel less-wanted. It happens in this line of work. I believe the Americans call it 'franchise fatigue'. 'You're lovely but we've sort of seen you now. Oh, and can you leave your car park pass on reception?' Let's face it, it's the kind of turnaround that's happened to much better people than me: Sunday it was 'Hosanna'; by Friday it was 'Crucify him'.

Oh, I still get offers: one-off appearances on panel shows and chat shows; documentaries; mainstream game shows, reality TV

. . . but rarely anything I actually want to do. And that is the crux. Broadcasters aren't banging on my door with some fabulous idea for a new comedy show, but then again they never were. I went to THEM with ideas. That's what's stopped. Somewhere down the line, I seemed to mislay my mojo, my inner drive.

I'll give you an example. When I did the chat show, twelve episodes a series, we'd record the programme the night before it was due to go out. I would finish the studio record – usually about two hours long – then go up to a viewing room with the producer and watch the whole thing through, making notes and decisions on what bits were in and what bits weren't good enough. The process often went on till about two in the morning. Five hours later, I'd meet that same producer in an edit suite. We'd watch what remained of the show after last night's cuts and then set about cutting it further till it was the fifty minutes that constitutes an ITV hour. (You lose ten minutes for adverts.) It was an exhausting process; poring over and debating each line to make sure the best bits got in and the show was as good as it could possibly be. The rest of the week, I was writing jokes, planning interviews and recording inserts, so it was full-on. But I wanted to give it my best shot and that included being part of the editing process. However, come series eight, I said to the producer, in our first pre-series meeting, 'Look, I've been thinking. We pretty much agree on most of the decisions in the edit. Why don't you do it without me this series? Then I'll have an extra day to write and I won't be so knackered from the late night and early morning.' I wasn't skiving – like I say, I was taking the opportunity to do an extra day in the office – but, looking back, it suggests slightly less pride in the finished product. If anyone had said to me during, say, series five that I needn't be in the edits, I'd have dismissed the suggestion as laughable. Anyway, I didn't do the edit for series eight, or series nine. There never was a series ten. I'm not saying the shows were worse because I wasn't in the edit. I wouldn't know. I never watched a single episode of either of those two series. That, let's face it, is not a very good sign either.

During that same period, I was doing an improvised show for ITV with David Baddiel, called *Baddiel and Skinner Unplanned*. That was recorded and edited in the same way as the chat show. In the previous series, Dave and I took it in turns to edit with the producer. Then one day I said, 'Dave, you enjoy editing, don't you? Why don't you do it EVERY week?' In this instance, however, I still had to watch the show – Dave would test me on it the next day – but I don't recall ever quibbling about what did or didn't get in. I no longer had the right to do that and, also, it suddenly didn't seem that important.

However, if there's one thing that makes me laugh about celebrities, it's the way they try to sell career problems as things they decided for themselves. We all know when they say, 'I went to Hollywood and had some really good meetings, but they wanted me to move out there and I didn't want to uproot my family', they actually mean, 'I went to Hollywood and managed to persuade two minor producers to see me but neither have called back.'

So let's be clear. I used to be on television all the time. I'm hardly on at all now. This is partly by choice, as far as things like panel shows and reality TV are concerned, and partly because of my own lethargy. It is also down, in no small degree, to the undeniable fact that broadcasters are not as keen to have a Frank Skinner series on as they were three or four years ago.

And now we're in this deep, let's get even deeper. That sitcom called *Shane* that I mentioned: the first series went out about five years ago and did OK in the ratings. Obviously, I don't know what the reviews were like, but ITV commissioned a second series which I wrote and duly recorded. Several years later, it is still in the bottom of a cupboard, somewhere in Network Centre. Now, how bad does a sitcom have to be to be rejected by ITV? They, as a channel, are good at many things, but it is, I would say, universally accepted that sitcoms have not been their forte for twenty-five years or more. To be a sitcom that is considered not funny enough to get on ITV is like being a celebrity who is considered not famous enough to get on Sky One's *Cirque de Celebrité*. And we're not talking rejected script here. It wasn't a case where the powers-that-be at ITV read a few pages and said, 'Sorry, we don't like this and we're not going to make it.' They DID make it. They paid for the sets, the actors, crew and studio time and, still, after that massive investment, they watched it and thought, 'We would rather lose all that money than subject our audience to this crock of shit.'

Still, I've had plenty of time to get over it. As the former *Stars in Their Eyes* presenter-turned-actor Matthew Kelly, who played Harry the homeless bloke in the doomed series, said to me, as we stood chatting outside the gentleman's toilet of the Covent Garden restaurant Joe Allen, 'Well, we all got paid.' And that we did.

Looking back, it was an odd concoction. Like an old-fashioned sitcom, it was recorded in front of a studio audience and was about an ordinary family. In some ways, it was VERY old-fashioned, more like vaudeville or a war-time radio show. Like when Shane's daughter, Velma, tells him about her new punk-rocker boyfriend:

VELMA: Oh, he's lovely, though. He's got a bright-red Mohican.
SHANE: I'm not a big fan of caged birds.

Or when Shane tells his best friend, the Leyton Orient fan Bazza, about the problems of watching a daughter grow up:

SHANE: It only seems like yesterday I was sitting on the edge of her bed, explaining why she couldn't have a pony.
BAZZA: It's a terrible thing, constipation.

Or again, when Shane gets home with his wife, Myrtle, and their son Lenny, only to find the house has been burgled:

LENNY: (WHISPERING) Dad. He might still be in the house.
SHANE PICKS UP A CHUNKY GOLF CLUB FROM THE FLOOR.
SHANE: I'll go and have a look upstairs.
MYRTLE: They always wear dark clothes.
SHANE: Who?
MYRTLE: Burglars.
SHANE: Well, just for now, I'm adopting the policy that any complete stranger I find in the house, no matter how garishly dressed, qualifies as a suspect.
MYRTLE: Well, be careful. I'll try and tidy up a bit. Do you want a tea?
SHANE: (LOOKING AT THE GOLF CLUB) Oh, no, I'm just taking this as a weapon.

I know: too many puns. I like the garishly dressed stranger bit though. And there was some nice observational comedy in it too:

SHANE: So the copper said to me, 'There's been a spate of burglaries in this area over the last few months.' I said to him, 'Why do the police always say a SPATE of burglaries or a SPATE of muggings? All "spate" means is "a great number of". There's no reason for it to be particularly associated with crime.' I said, 'Never mind campaigning for more Special Constables; what you lot need is more collective nouns.'

I sound like I'm trying to sell it now, don't I? It's slightly pathetic really, but after all that work – I never missed an edit on this one – it should qualify for at least a brief moment in the spotlight. I am prepared to admit that, all things considered, it didn't really work. Its subject-matter was a bit dark – like when Harry the homeless bloke talks about his younger colleagues:

HARRY: Agh, they've got no idea. I see them sitting on the pavement, with their hands outstretched, wearing baseball caps and Nike trainers. They're supposed to be begging, not collecting an MTV award. If people are going to give you money, they like to see you've at least made the effort to become filthy, bearded and bedraggled. That's what turns fifty pence into a pound.

And sometimes it was just too dirty. I even wrote a speech where one of the characters argues seemingly with Shane, but at the same time with me, the writer, about the filth they are forced to speak. The speech is also, I suppose, a defence of ITV as a channel which has an understandable commitment to appeal to Middle England. It comes at the end of a pub scene with Bazza and the pub's land-lady, Sheila. Shane has just told Bazza that Velma is living with her low-life boyfriend in a squat in Piccadilly, a house owned by a man who keeps a stainless steel dildo in his bedside cabinet, seemingly for his own use. (Yes, I know! Primetime ITV.)

BAZZA: Well, Shane, I know what it's like to be lonely. You have to grab love when you can.

SHANE: Yeah, but stainless steel.

BAZZA: Oh, I think the 'stainless' element is part of its appeal. It's a word that suggests no sin has actually been committed. Besides, when you support Leyton Orient, you'll take any opportunity to shove a bit of silverware in your cabinet.

SHEILA: You shouldn't judge Velma too harshly. I lived with a boyfriend when I was seventeen.

SHANE: Yeah, but I bet you never squatted in Piccadilly.

SHEILA: Well, once, but I went behind a car. The trouble was he wasn't parked; he was kerb-crawling. I ended up walking incredibly slowly, still crouched, at the side of him; like I was doing a very tentative Cossack dance. Honestly, the tears were running down my face.

BAZZA: Was it laughter or sadness?

SHEILA: No, I think it was just the acidity of the steam.

SHANE: You know, Sheila, I don't know why you bother with these stupid brewery promotion nights. What's brilliant about you is the honest earthiness of your character. You're a bit more real than all this nonsense.

SHEILA: Yes, Shane, but I run a public house, frequented, funnily enough, by the public – simple ordinary people who don't want promotional nights based around stainless-steel sex-aids and anecdotes in which the proprietress urinates at the side of a slowly advancing car driven by a man searching for prostitutes. Oh, of course, they'll snigger at a Wicked Willy greetings card or someone breaking wind on *You've Been Framed*, but they don't want to walk the dark road that we walk. To be honest, I'm not really sure that I do. There are times when the aftermath of our conversation hangs on me like a heavy ermine cloak. (SHE EXITS)

Like I say, it didn't really work and was never the sitcom I dreamed it could be. Maybe Jon Plowman was right about comedy being about character, not jokes – certainly as far as sitcom is concerned. And I'm probably not that good at character, or plot, or lots of those other ingredients that make a sitcom human and involving; something people develop a real love for, rather than just a cobbled-together vehicle for gags. But there were times when the poetry, the darkness, the filth and the vaudeville jokes mixed to form something, if not good, at least unusual: a sort of Beckettian *Carry On* film. Like the scene when Sheila and Bazza stand almost indistinguishable in the eerie gloom of an unlit and otherwise deserted pub:

BAZZA: You know, there's something about a power-cut; the omnipresent darkness, diluted only by the flicker of candle-light. It seems to stop the world. We feel hidden, invisible, able to say things we wouldn't normally say.

SILENCE

SHEILA: I'm desperately lonely, Bazza.

BAZZA: So am I. Maybe we could make each other . . .

SHEILA: It's not THAT dark.

Anyway, it's dead and gone. A sitcom – I'll say it again – not even funny enough for ITV. Despite that, career-wise I'm still doing OK. I'm not waving to the cheering crowd as I ride my donkey over palm leaves, but nor am I, as I write, nailed to a cross, in between Michael Barrymore and Les Dennis. And even if that were the case, any or all three of us would still have the possibility of resurrection. You'll know when there's a crisis. I'll start telling anyone who'll listen that I'm 'passionate about radio'.

When my ITV contract ended, and no one offered me another one, I decided to look on the bright side. I'd been doing three TV series a year for six years. It would do me good, I thought, to spend a year doing something different, something a bit less high-profile and pressured – a chance to step out of the limelight and quietly badger away at a new challenge. I wrote a book, *Frank Skinner by Frank Skinner* (can you believe I didn't put a pun in the title?), that turned out to be the third-best-selling autobiography of 2002. In first and second place was *A Child Called 'It'* and *A Man Named Dave*, both by Dave Pelzer, the pioneer of what came to be known as Misery Literature or Mis Lit. The first book charts Pelzer's horrible childhood, with tales of starvation and being forced to drink ammonia and eat his brother's shit; the second book starts with a childhood memory of being hit in the throat with a broom and ends with Pelzer sort of making peace with his mother. Both books beat me, fair and square, but, given the choice, I'd have settled for my happy childhood and third place.

After the success of the autobiography, my publisher offered me a two-book deal and suggested that, next time, I might try a novel. I hardly ever read novels so it was a strange prospect for me, but I thought my lack of knowledge, certainly of MODERN novels, could be an advantage. Maybe, I thought to myself, it would ensure some sort of originality. I couldn't be influenced by something I had no experience of. I signed the contract at the end of 2002. Three years later, I still hadn't delivered – indeed, still hadn't started the novel. But by then I was anticipating the non-renewal of the ITV contract and so was starting to wonder what I might do in 2006. After a recording of *Baddiel and Skinner Unplanned* in July 2005, I spoke to Tim Firth, the successful playwright and screenwriter, and told him I was thinking of writing a novel. He said, 'You should definitely write one because no one has ever written a really funny novel and it's what everyone wants to read.' I made up my mind, there and then: 2006 was to be the year of the novel. 'It will be lovely,' I thought to myself, 'tucked away in a cosy little office, tapping away at my computer, with music playing in the background and a nice cup of tea on the desk. A thousand words a day for a hundred days and then an afternoon writing my Booker Prize acceptance speech. Blissful.'

I fuckin' hated it. I don't know why. The autobiography had taken me six months to write and the first three months were hard. I don't normally tend to sit around, dredging up the past, and it had quite a strange effect on me, a sort of emotional detox. And remember, we're only talking about light-hearted family stories like the one when my dad burned all his sheds or when a chimpanzee pissed on me at Dudley Zoo. When Pelzer wrote his he must have been in bits. However, come the second three months I really started to get into writing the book, actually enjoyed it, and I came out of the whole process feeling sort of cleansed and well ordered. In fact, I'd go so far as to say everyone should write their autobiography, even if there's zero chance of it ever being published. It's definitely good for the head.

I suppose I basically see myself as a stand-up comedian who does other things as well. I know that sounds odd coming from a man who didn't really do stand-up for ten years, but it has remained, somehow, at the core of my being. That's why I think the autobiography worked. It was true and so is most of my act. I will embroider the stand-up a bit – I didn't actually ASK the didgeridoo man to play 'All by Myself' and I've never seen an anal wart in my life – but essentially it's the sausage-meat of my experience turned into stand-up-shaped sausages. Or autobiography-shaped sausages if required.

Novel-shaped sausages are a bit more complicated. Where the fuck does the meat come from? I know some novels are thinly disguised autobiographies and I can definitely see the lure of that. For example, if I decided to turn this journal into a novel about a comedian, I would have all that experience of making the second series of *Shane* to draw on, but I could then top it off with the show not only being broadcast but also winning a host of awards. That kind of novel is a sort of opportunity to edit life. But I didn't write that kind of novel. I'd barely read any fiction since I finished my English MA in 1982 – except comic books. I'd read a lot of them.

Thus, I decided to write a novel that could have been, maybe should have been, a comic book. It was called *Thunderman and Geoff Phillips*. The title was supposed to refer to those classic comic-book duos like Batman and Robin or Captain America and Bucky, but with a twist. I wanted it to be clear that one of the duo wasn't a superhero at all, and chose Geoff because it's a typically English spelling of that name, thus stating from the off that this was a British, rather than an American, superhero story. I'll keep this brief, but the basic plot concerned an English kid who was so impressed by American comic books, he'd headed to America to actually become a superhero of the self-made-with-no-super-powers Batman variety. Thunderman, as he came to be known, had an illustrious crime-fighting career, but now, aged fifty, had slowed down somewhat and was enjoying the fruits of his labours: a best-selling autobiography, a resulting bio-pic and various lucrative sponsorship deals. He was in the United Kingdom doing a promotional tour. Like I say, there were no parallels with my own life. In the UK he meets Geoff Phillips, a lifelong fan who is angered by what he sees as his hero's selling out. Geoff suggests they could become a crime-fighting duo and sets about persuading TM, as they call him, to take on one last battle. You know, now that I read that, it actually sounds quite good. Maybe I should have another crack.

Anyway, a novel is usually about 80,000 to 100,000 words and I got up to 60,000, but I just couldn't go on; it was too hard. I never got to the stage, like I did with the autobiography, where I was coasting and enjoying it. *Au contraire*: it was like a snail moving across broken glass. I always hate to be a quitter, but the factory chorus was deafening and I was the twat operating the lathe.

I know you're desperate to read a bit of it, so I'll give you a very small taster. This really is becoming the Frank Skinner's Failures Hall of Fame. At least I killed this one myself.

The book opens at a press conference, in London's Majestica Hotel, to promote the paperback edition of Thunderman's autobiography, *It's a Thunderfull World*. (I'd managed to resist a punning title for my own autobiography but it seemed acceptable here.) Karen, the sweet, slightly overweight, slightly promiscuous hotel events manager, a woman 'whose heart was as big as her ankles', is suddenly confronted by the superhero:

Thunderman towered above her in a black catsuit, black body-armour and black-leather fifteen-hole assault boots. You had to say he was themed. He was dressed for elegant enforcement – a sort of Armani riot cop. In the old days, he'd been masked, but now he stood broad-shouldered and bare-headed, hair cropped, teeth capped and dark, dark eyes that you hoped, for his sake, were not the windows of his soul. On his chest was the grey-cloud logo that had, in blood-stained alleyways and hypodermic-strewn apartments, in hugger-mugger boardrooms and too-scared-to-scream bordellos, caused the most amoral wrongdoers to pause, to reconsider, and often to run; that same logo that now graced the packaging of Morton's Beef Jerky.

I know it's a bit melodramatic but so are comic books so it seemed sort of appropriate. And if you're not impressed, don't worry; neither was Karen. Once again there are no parallels with my own life:

She knew famous men became cruel and corrupt, like Roman emperors. Star-struck girls hung from them, almost unnoticed, as these latter-day Caligulas indulged their evil celebrity-opportunities. They were sucked as they snorted, rimmed as they raged, begged for kind caresses as they popcorned their way through snuff movies and horse-porn, where crack-slave women looked accusingly to camera as once-noble beasts emptied splattering semen into their sad mouths. That was fame. She knew because her cousin had been out with a guy from *Emmerdale*.

Everyone at the press conference had to wear a name badge. Geoff Phillips, a stranger to such events, was seriously impressed:

He was beginning to enjoy the easy accessibility of these pin-on potted biographies. Would the world not be a better place if everyone wore a badge with their name and profession on it? There'd be no more office juniors sobbing into their alcopops because the manager had called them Jane instead of Julie; no more internationally acclaimed soul divas outraged at being told, as they arrived at the stage door, that the other cleaners were already in the auditorium. Life would be simpler and less painful and, having passed a carefree hour in an all-night amusement arcade, the corpulent businessman would not, in all innocence, offer a lift home to that feverish youth who wore the 'Nathan. Rent Boy' badge.

But Geoff was less impressed when he watched his hero playing to the crowd and pissing all over his own legend.

'There's an old Hollywood saying,' Thunderman continued, '"Always get a piece of the action". But I have my own version: "Always get a piece of the action-FIGURES."' As he said this he produced, from behind his body-armour, action figures of himself and Ed Berry, the serial-killer he had wrestled with on a rickety fifth-floor Brooklyn balcony, while a crowd oohed and aahed in the street below. During the film version of this tussle, Mel Miller, playing Thunderman, called down to the awestruck spectators, 'Sorry to do this on the balcony but the air-con has broken.' In the real-life, non-Hollywood version, Thunderman was too busy completely gauging out Berry's left eye to indulge in such badinage.

So that was my novelist career. Now, I haven't gone through the sitcom and the novel with a fine-tooth comb, but obviously what I've included here are some of my favourite bits. If either work had been consistently good, they'd be on the screen or in the bookshops by now. I have shared a number of failed stand-up gags with you, but they were a means to an end; the sitcom and the novel were just an end. And, you know, even with those failed stand-up gags, there is probably some part of me, deep down, that thinks they should have made it.

If the return to stand-up was all about recovering my mojo, it worked. I really care about this tour, really cared about every one of those little pub gigs. When it works, I'm happy; when it doesn't, I'm distraught. I would say the rekindling of that kind of passion justifies the whole enterprise. Whether or not it was the whole motivation for returning to stand-up, I'm not sure.

I don't know if I can BE sure. I looked back through my daily journals to try and find some clues, but the earlier ones can be quite cryptic at times. The knowledge that these Edinburgh and tour-related journals will be read by others has changed the tone considerably. I'm deliberately making things clearer; more accessible to the outsider. Previous to this period, the journals were a bit more free-form, a bit more oblique. The most puzzling discovery was an entry on Saturday 26 August 2006. It reads like a lovely day. Cath was away at that year's Edinburgh Festival but we had a sweet phone conversation in the morning. I spent the daytime at home playing banjo and watching the C&G cricket final on TV. That night I had dinner with an old friend and we chatted till late, laughing hard. After all that pleasantness, the last sentence in that day's journal seems to come out of nowhere: 'I think I need to do stand-up to save my life.' It was only a year ago but I have no idea why I wrote it. What exactly did I mean?

There was another moment, just a little thing, but it seems to be the seed from which this whole return to stand-up thing grew. My journal entry for Saturday 26 February 2005 reads, again right at the bottom of the page:

> Article about Chris Rock in the paper today (he hosts the Oscars tomorrow). It quoted a joke of his: 'Black guys have got a reputation for being criminals and they blame it all on the media: "the media's created a negative image"; "the media makes us look bad": I gotta tell you, when I'm using the cash-machine at midnight, and I'm looking over my shoulder, I ain't looking for the media.' Beautiful. Made me really wanna be a stand-up again.

I was inspired by that gag: its sharpness; its dangerousness; its intelligence. The next day I wrote a joke of my own. Maybe it was meant to be the beginning of my NEW stand-up career; the NEW sharp, dangerous, intelligent me:

> I would rather have a serious car-crash than a serious cock-rash.

Way to go. There was one other thing that stood out when I read back through those journals, one other clue to why a fifty-year-old, financially secure man would get back up there and put his previous reputation on the line. I got up early to watch England's cricket team play a one-day game in India. The commentator, former Australian test cricketer Dean Jones, was talking about a player who had made a couple of bad fielding errors. He said a professional had to learn to put that behind him. No matter what's happened, 'You've got to want the ball to come to you,' he said.

His words really hit home with me. Television is such a public event that sudden absence from it does not go unnoticed. 'When are you back on telly?' – that's what I get asked all the time. At first I'd just respond with a slightly pathetic 'soon' but, before long, I'd opted for, 'Oh, the bubble's burst; you know how it is. One minute you're the big man; the next minute you're on the scrapheap.' I found it quite liberating to say that, but the person who'd asked me would often look slightly distressed, like they'd said, 'How are you?' and I'd said, 'I've got pancreatic cancer.' The temptation is to hide; to use writing a novel or some other shut-yourself-in-a-room activity as an excuse to slip away. Well, I tried it and I didn't like it. I'm back in my cricket gear and out on the field. The tour starts soon and the ball is very definitely heading my way.

WEDNESDAY 5 SEPTEMBER 2007

I feel terrible and the first King's Heath gig is tonight. I've had this shit cold since last Friday and it seems to be getting worse. I've barely eaten for five days. I'm living on Lemsip, Night Nurse and flat Coca-Cola. I've already phoned my manager this morning to say I might have to cut tonight short and possibly even cancel tomorrow. The idea of cancelling any gig fills me with horror but, the trouble is, once you get wrecked on a tour of this length and intensity it's very hard to get unwrecked. There's no space for recuperation, and ailments that would've lasted a few days last a few weeks.

There's an oft-told story about Grimaldi, the famous clown of the late-eighteenth/early-nineteenth century. He went to see a doctor and said, 'Doctor I feel terrible . . . ill, exhausted and depressed . . . can you help me?'

The doctor, not recognising the great clown, said, 'You need a tonic, something uplifting that will take you out of yourself. Why don't you go and see Grimaldi?'

Comedians are supposed to be the medicine, not the disease. My main worry is my throat, of course. Adrenalin – or Doctor Theatre, as actors call it – will get you through a show, even if you feel awful, but if you lose your voice, you're fucked.

The added problem with this tour is that I'm planning to do forty-five minutes, then an interval, then another forty-five minutes. I don't know how MY Doctor Theatre copes with intervals. I worry I might flop down into the dressing-room armchair, the adrenalin will disperse and I won't be able to get up again. I've played charity football games with ageing ex-players who are brilliant in the first half – you wonder why they ever retired – but after a fifteen-minute rest at half-time, they come out of the dressing room walking like a mummy from an old horror film: muscles seized up, old skills entombed.

I've never done stand-up with an interval before. On previous tours, a support act would do twenty minutes, then we'd have an interval, then I'd come on and do an hour and a half straight through. It always seemed a lop-sided structure to me. No sooner had the audience sat down, it was time to go back to the bar again. Forty-five and forty-five seems much more sensible, and cheaper – no support act to pay. But, aside from the health aspects, I still don't know what effect an interval will have on my act. Will it shackle me? Put an unnatural brake on my momentum? How should I distribute the material between the two halves? I was going to explore and experiment with these things over the next two nights, but I feel too ill. I'm going to do these Birmingham shows as an hour, straight through, hope I end up with ninety minutes of stuff that works, and worry about intervals afterwards. The tour starts, at Leeds City Varieties, in four days' time. Adam e-mailed me the full three-month itinerary yesterday. It didn't make me feel any better.

I'll tell you what did help, though. Cath and I watched a DVD last night, an old black-and-white movie called *Sullivan's Travels*. Cath's mum had bought it for me, saying she thought I'd find it interesting. It's about a film director, John Sullivan, who specialises in comedies. His movies are very popular but he feels comedy is a trivial and essentially worthless pastime. He longs to make a serious film with a strong social message so, in order to research this epic, he poses as a hobo. After a series of mishaps he ends up in a grim penitentiary, where the men are worked hard, underfed and regularly beaten. By the time we near the end of the film, Sullivan has become part of a chain-gang who are taken into a local church hall to see a movie. He sits amidst the downtrodden prisoners and a congregation of dirt-poor black people. A shaky old film-projector flickers on to a sheet hanging from the wall, and a Walt Disney cartoon, featuring Pluto the dog, starts to roll. Pretty soon the battered convicts and poverty-stricken blacks are roaring with laughter at the cartoon. Sullivan looks around him in amazement and afterwards says something along the lines of, 'Laughter ain't so bad. It's all some people have.' Yes, I know it's corny but I need a bit of show-must-go-on to get me up on that stage tonight.

The Hare and Hounds in the King's Heath area of Birmingham is where I used to host a weekly comedy club in the late eighties and early nineties. The club, in a 150-seater room above the pub, existed before I took over the compèring job. I'd done a couple of slots there, just an unknown local comic getting a break, and they went so well, the people who ran the club asked me to take over as host. What followed was some of the happiest times of my life. Every Thursday night I would perform twenty-five minutes of written-that-week new material, in five- or ten-minute bursts, interspersed between three London-circuit acts like Eddie Izzard or Steve Coogan. It soon became MY club and we spent wondrous nights there, the audience and me. I was fresh and new and on fucking fire. They knew it and I knew it. So-called alternative comedy clubs were, at that time, still rarely seen outside of London, but the King's Heath club was as good as anything the capital could offer. Anyway, then my marriage collapsed, I won the Perrier Award and moved to London and the big time; but no tour and no television show has ever compared to those Thursday nights in King's Heath.

I don't suppose many of the old crowd will be in tonight but it's an added pressure, something else to live up to, another chance to disappoint.

I've got together my sets for the next two nights. If, health permitting, I get through the two one-hour shows, I'll trim off the weakest half-hour and do what remains in Leeds. At this point, I feel I should make a confession. I don't know if it's the illness but I've actually been thinking of incorporating a question-and-answer session into my tour-show. It's what comics do when they don't have enough material. It usually lasts about fifteen minutes, so that's thirty-six gags' worth of stage-time. It's very much a last resort but, if these Birmingham gigs go badly, it might be time for damage limitation. I think an audience are more forgiving of an unfunny fifteen minutes if they themselves are actually an integral part of it. There's also the theory that, if someone goes to a comedy show and sees a shit Q-and-A section, they may well, in the light of that Q-and-A's courageous no-safety-net spontaneity, make allowances for its failure and reason that the shitness represents no more than an off-night. It's probably BRILLIANT most nights, the charitable audience member thinks, whereas of course a shit stand-up routine is just a shit stand-up routine, night after night after night. *Baddiel and Skinner Unplanned* was Q-and-A, pure and simple; we made a feature of that fact. It constituted a sort of bottled-water approach to comedy, but if I go to a stand-up show I want to see stand-up. Oh, let's wait and see. Maybe it would work brilliantly and become my favourite part of the show. Maybe.

Of course, now that the tour is imminent, I have the option to write some topical material, jokes about stuff that's currently in the news. There wasn't much point in writing topicals back in the spring; they would have been well past their sell-by date when the tour started in September. But, now the hour is nigh, the news is hot, and I've been going through the papers looking for inspiration.

Incidentally, during my news-trawl, I noticed the tabloids had completely exaggerated that thing in my *Times* article about checking my heart-rate before and after a gig. Now, I read, I am so worried about collapsing onstage that I will be wearing 'a special harness' that will enable me to keep a constant check on my heart during my 'gruelling UK tour'. Maybe I could have the bpm reading shown on a big screen throughout the performance. As we've seen, the rate gets higher during bad shows so this could inject some ooos and aaahs into an otherwise flat audience; similar to the way a bad referee can liven up a dull game or a quiet football crowd.

One potentially helpful thing I read in the papers was that Jade Goody, the *Big Brother* star who fell out of public favour at the beginning of this year by bullying and, some feel, racially abusing her Indian *BB* housemate Shilpa Shetty, is doing a tell-all interview about her resulting we-don't-like-you-any-more ordeal. I describe this as 'potentially helpful' because back in February I wrote a routine about Jade; it was such a big story I felt I had to. It went well at the time but, as one would expect, when the immediacy of the scandal faded, so did the routine. That was a pity because I had a relatively unique angle on the whole incident. Back in December of last year, I recorded a panel show, *A Question of Comedy*, on which Jade and I were both panellists. (I know I said I often turn down panel shows, but this one was for Comic Relief so I wasn't quite so sniffy.) The show was recorded on 20 December but wasn't due to go out until Comic Relief Night, 16 March. In the meantime, Jade laid into Shilpa and, pretty soon, effigies of Ms Goody were crackling away on the streets of Mumbai. I bumped into a senior Comic Relief organiser at the time of the scandal. He said they were planning to edit down Jade's appearance on *A Question of Comedy* till she became little more than 'a smiling presence', but I wasn't sure that would work. It would be extremely odd, I thought, to have the much-talked-about Jade on a comedy show, with no reference at all to the controversy. Sure enough, in late February, I got a call to say the show had been pulled. Two days later I was doing the routine:

I wouldn't mind, but I was brilliant on it. After the show, the producer said to me, 'Frank, you were so funny tonight that, when this goes out, I think it might turn things round for Africa.'

I don't think anyone would have recognised Jade anyway. She was wearing a full Ku Klux Klan outfit. They could have got Jim Davidson to dub his voice over hers and no one would have known the difference. He'd have gladly helped out. He and Jade are big mates. They get on like a cross on fire.

It said in the paper that Jade's friends are on suicide-watch. They had a quote from one friend saying, 'We're worried that Jade might do something stupid.' I'd say you could put money on that.

That last gag might sound a bit callous, but obviously it would have been a tragedy if Jade had killed herself. The whole routine would have been completely unusable.

In truth, I actually felt sorry for Jade. People loved her for being a gobby, slightly thick, working-class girl and now they hated her for being a gobby, slightly thick, working-class girl. Her journey from the donkey to the cross was particularly swift. Still, as a *Sun* journalist once said to me after he'd written an unpleasant kiss-and-tell hatchet-job featuring my ex-wife, 'Come on, mate, it's nothing personal.' Journalists, paparazzi, critics, comedians . . . we all roam the celebrity battlefield looking for the injured and dying, seeing what parasitical pickings there might be, something we can use to reinforce the jealousies and resentments of the folks back home. I did start the routine with a 'does anyone here feel sorry for Jade?' bit, but it only produced boos; thus giving me full licence to make fun of her fall from grace. Just like all the other vultures, I use, when pushed, the 'oh, well, if you choose to be a public figure you have to accept criticism' justification that one often hears trotted out to justify cruelty and spite. I'm sure the Pharisees and Sadducees said something very similar. If I'd been in Jerusalem 2,000 years ago, I don't think I would have been party to the Crucifixion, but I might well have gone on to write a comic song about it.

I sound like I'm beating myself up about the Jade routine, but in truth I'm sitting here hoping her latest tell-all interview will suddenly make my Jade-jokes topical and, therefore, funny again. I'll find out tonight.

Exhibit A in the racism charge against Jade was the fact she referred to Ms Shetty as Shilpa Poppadom. I was wondering if I could get a laugh, especially as I'm in Birmingham, by saying;

You know, I never thought I'd get nostalgic about racism, but Shilpa Poppadom! It's not in the same league as 'Like the Roman, I seem to see the River Tiber foaming with much blood.'

The Conservative MP Enoch Powell made that allusion to the poet Virgil when he made his infamous 'rivers of blood' speech in Birmingham in 1968. I think an ironic literary criticism of the decline of racist language is an interesting idea, but, needless to say, people will just think I'm being racist or won't have heard of Enoch Powell, so I'll play safe and stick to knob-jokes. There are some subjects you just have to leave to Chris Rock. During the try-out gigs, I did a routine that was sort of about race, probably inspired by that Rock joke in the newspaper, but on the two occasions I tried it I got tense, the audience got tense, it just wasn't worth the bother.

It began with a straightforward true story, something that happened to me in a Tommy Hilfiger shop where the assistants were all incredibly cool black guys. I was looking at some winter coats, those padded ones like football managers sometimes wear. I pulled a coat off the hanger and tried it on, disconnecting a security wire on the way. An alarm went off and one of the black guys started to walk towards me, but in an incredibly slow, cool way, like Vivian Richards walking out to bat.

It was the most laid-back response to an alarm I've ever seen. By the time he reached me, I'd already had quite a bit of wear out of the coat; it was starting to get those little balls of nylon on the elbows.

White people can't really do that slow, cool walk. I think the closest I got was when I had a CD Walkman and I used to sort of creep along to stop it from jumping.

This is why some people think most criminals are black. The truth is most criminals that get CAUGHT are black. You get a bunch of guys raiding a warehouse, and suddenly there's a police siren. All the white criminals are going, 'Hey, let's get out of here.' And whoosh, they're gone. The black criminals are going, 'Yeah, we're right behind you (REALLY SLOW WALK), this is a desperate situation!'

That walk is part of black culture, a sign of identity, but like a lot of traditions it's fading away. Hanging out with a lot of twitchy, dashing-around white kids is slowly chipping away at the black kids' walk. I heard two black women talking at a bus stop. One said, 'Hey, Chinchilla, how's your boy, Carlton, doing nowadays?' The other black woman looked distressed. 'Oh, Mesopotamia,' she said, 'he's been hanging around with a bunch of white kids and my mother saw him on Streatham High Road and he was . . . (SHE BEGINS TO CRY) well, the word Mum used was "scurrying".'

OK, it's not the funniest stuff I ever wrote, but what was interesting was the sudden tension in the room; the crowd thinking, 'Is this going to get racist?' and me thinking, 'I'd better stick to exactly what I wrote here because one slightly ambiguous improvisation and the whole thing comes down like a house of cards.' The cool black walk stuff is definitely dead and buried; any material that even slightly involves race is just too fucking difficult. Car crash – cock rash; that's my department.

I'm still toying with the idea of a catchphrase. Twenty years in comedy and I've never had one. People seem to love them. It's the closest a comic can get to that thing that musicians have: the old hits that people always want to hear. It doesn't work with jokes – people complain if you do stuff they've heard before – but it DOES work with catchphrases. You see Robbie Williams, you want to hear 'Angels'; you see Paul Whitehouse, you want to hear, 'Suits you, sir.' I have two catchphrases in the frame at the moment. They both, like 'Suits you, sir', have a fashion motif, but also include a visual element which I hope will give them a distinctive stick-in-the-memory quality.

The first one comes right at the top of the show. I walk on with both my arms wrapped around my neck, my fingers interlocked at the back. I walk up to the microphone, still in its stand, wait for ten or fifteen seconds, till the audience are wondering what's going on, and then say, 'It's as good as a scarf!'

The other can come at any point in the act. With the four fingers of my right hand outstretched, I suddenly start sliding the thumbnail of that same hand down the right-hand side of my stomach. 'Sorry,' I say, 'I usually wear a waistcoat.'

I've tried them both a few times and, generally speaking, the waistcoat goes better than the scarf, but how are you supposed to make a value-judgement on a catchphrase? Most people will only see me ONCE on the tour, so how will they even recognise that either of these IS a catchphrase? They could just as easily be casual one-off remarks. I suppose, ideally, I need to do them every week on a TV show but, as I've explained, that isn't really an option. Besides, lots of old music-hall performers had famous catchphrases, like Jack Warner's 'Mind my bike' or Sandy Powell's 'Can you hear me, Mother?' and they didn't have TV to popularise them. I suppose I just have to stick with it. What I need is a publicity splurge, a headline like '*Man on motorbike killed doing scarf-catchphrase*' – something that fixes it in people's minds. Whatever happens, as long as I don't collapse, vomit or lose my voice, tonight should be educational. Even when I was a Thursday-night local legend, the Birmingham crowd were always happy to NOT laugh if they thought the joke wasn't good enough. I'd be surprised if that honesty-of-response has changed, ten-year absence or not. I did a West End play once called *Cooking with Elvis* where I had to drop my trousers and pants and simulate sexual intercourse; happily, with my back to the audience. About two weeks into the run, I was mid-simulated-stroke one night when a loud Brummie-accented voice shouted, 'Frank Skinner's arse!' I wondered if he might have been a toastmaster by trade. I'm expecting a similarly straight-forward approach tonight. If they see the emperor's bare arse, they'll be quick to point it out. I think it's time for another Lemsip.

The gig is due to start at eight but as the room is already crammed at seven, I suggest we get the ball rolling so I can do the show and then get to bed as early as possible. Entrance to the gig was a fiver on the door, with no advance sales, so when we got here there was a massive queue disappearing up the street. There were local journalists and a film crew outside. It feels like an event. It's a shame about the people who didn't get in, but at the moment, sitting in the dressing room drinking honey and lemon, desperately trying to remember revamped routines and ukulele chords, the only person I'm really feeling sorry for is me. It's 7.03. I can hear The Fall's 'Containers Drivers' blasting out in the distance. I walk out of the shabby dressing room that hasn't really changed since I did the club eighteen years ago, down the corridor and into the darkened room. The music is really loud in here. It's a short walk to the stage; down the aisle; three handshakes and about a dozen pats on the back and then I'm up the stairs and onto the stage. The light is in my eyes and my right hand instinctively reaches out for the microphone. The roar of the crowd drowns even the music – a roar that would fill a much bigger room but, somehow, it's been squeezed into this one. I put the mic stand out of the way. Shit, I forgot to do my scarf catchphrase. The noise continues. I don't speak yet. I just stand and look out at them, microphone in hand. The noise is still increasing. I'm waiting because I feel a bit teary and I know they will hear it in my voice. They cheer long enough for me to get a hold of myself. And then I begin.

I can hear myself doing the stuff, ad-libbing and milking the laughs, but it sounds different. It isn't the voice I heard in Edinburgh saying these same gags; it's another voice. It's me from eighteen years ago: the accent as heavy as it was; the attitude restored. The routines that didn't make sense in Edinburgh, suddenly, emphatically, make sense now. If you're going to talk about blow-jobs and fucking someone from behind, it has to be like this: goggle-eyed and unapologetic; a leering, loud-mouthed Harlequin, pointing a bony finger at a grinning victim in the second row. The sophisticating, mellowing, rough-edge-removing, comfortable rich-man London years roll back and I'm me again – or is it 'him' again? I don't know. But some of this stuff, I suddenly realise, wasn't written for London-me; it was written for Birmingham-me. And now I hear Birmingham-me doing it, it all makes sense. I start laughing at the gags like I've never heard them before. In Canada, I did old material in my new voice, and it didn't work; tonight I'm doing new material in my old one, and it's storming.

I'm back at the flat feeling really ill, worse than I did this morning. The gig lasted an hour and a half, and I only did about two-thirds of my stuff. It didn't all work. Some of the Jade stuff was good; handjobs-from-the-homeless . . . never again. And I mean it this time. I decided, about halfway through the set, not to do the songs; then I changed my mind again and did them both as an encore. 'Suicide-Bomber Girl' was OK, but the Osama song brought the house down. He'd better keep safe for the next three months. I was up there, singing, getting big laughs, with a ukulele – just like George. But no check-lists tonight; no more analysis. It's 21.19. My head is splitting. Two Solpadeine and bed.

THURSDAY 6 SEPTEMBER 2007

Slightly restless night but I woke up feeling a bit better. I bought this flat in Birmingham about ten years ago for fifty-two grand. It's on the tenth floor; I like to be high up and away from everyone. It's sunny today. I'm drinking tea and eating custard creams on the balcony as, at the Edgbaston Croquet Club below, old people dressed all in white are swinging mallets and chatting in huddles. A football match is about to begin on the pitch to the right of the

Croquet Club. Men in their thirties, in blue or red, stand around, lazily aiming shots at goal or doing sketchy versions of warm-up exercises they've seen footballers do on the telly. In short, it's all gone a bit Beryl Cook.

I don't normally eat biscuits but this is one of the plusses of illness. If you've hardly eaten for a week and then you actually fancy something, it's allowed, no matter what it is. On the way back from the gig last night, I got Adam to stop at a garage and I loaded up with biscuits, crisps and meat pies so I can junk-food myself back to health again. Stuff that makes me feel sick when I'm well seems to make me feel well when I'm sick. The plusses of illness are something you think more and more about as you get older. When you're twenty you lie in bed and think, 'I feel terrible; I'm going to die; I'll never see any of my friends again.' When you're fifty you lie in bed and think, 'I feel terrible; I'm going to lose at least half a stone; I'll be able to get into those jeans again.' And, no, it isn't only women who think that – it's only women who ADMIT they think that.

The other plus is an excuse to stop in. That's another age-thing. When you're twenty and a night out is cancelled, you're devastated: 'It's too late to rearrange anything now. What am I going to do all night?' At fifty, a night out is cancelled and it's like you've suddenly been handed a wondrous gift: 'Ah, I can stay in, eat food I've chosen and use my own toilet.' Nowadays, I basically want to stay in every night, nice and cosy, tracksuit-bottoms and television. However, hanging over my head is the fear that this staying-in constitutes a terrible waste of life and, when I'm old and unable to leave the house, I'll look back and think, 'Oh, why didn't I go out when I had the chance?' So I DO go out, most nights, motivated by a regret that I MIGHT have IF I live long enough to be old and house-bound. The imaginary old me is bullying the real, here-and-now me into going places I don't want to go and speaking to people I don't want to speak to, and for what? The old me probably won't be able to remember whether I went out or not anyway. Still, illness, as I say, is a great excuse to stay in; the best excuse. Rubbish food, rubbish telly, rubbish clothes: beautiful.

I suppose someone about to start a big tour is bound to get sentimental about staying in; the comfort of the womb and all that. There was an article about last night's gig in today's *Birmingham Evening Mail.* I got Adam to check it first to make sure it wasn't actually a review. When I read the first sentence, 'From superstar to lowly pub performer', I wondered if, in some sort of sci-fi time-warp situation, I'd accidentally picked up a newspaper from two years' time; but it was a nice piece. It was basically interviews done before the show with people in the queue, all saying lovely stuff – even the ones who couldn't get in. There's a photo of me onstage, playing my banjo-uke. I look more at home with it than I expected.

I've been thinking about my comedy-voice thing from last night. It has to be ME up there. I don't want to be playing a part, portraying someone I was twenty years ago – or even ten years ago, when I did my last tour. I've changed . . . or have I? A good friend of mine, a poet, was booked to do a reading at the Swedenborg Institute, near the British Library, in London. It was a Wednesday night, he was staying at my flat, so of course I was going to go and see him read. A couple of nights before the poetry reading, David Baddiel phoned to say he had a spare ticket for an England friendly-game being played on that same Wednesday night. I said I couldn't go and told him why.

Now, when someone sees a famous person out in public, they often ask the whereabouts of a second, somehow related, famous person. It's as if they don't want to miss this opportunity to know the whereabouts of TWO celebrities at the same time, one located by their own perception, the other by their resulting investigation. These investigations can actually transcend reality. I mean, it's one thing to say, if you see Ant, 'Where's Dec?' But is it not slightly odd to mix truth and fiction by saying, if you see Nicholas Lyndhurst, 'Where's Del-Boy?' You might argue that they are actually, in this latter exchange, asking the whereabouts of David Jason, using his character name to add a hint of humour, but Jim Davidson told me that people often asked him, 'Where's Chalkie?' – a reference to a completely fictional character, existing only in the form of an impression done by Davidson himself. Surely that is madness. Anyway, I knew that David, when people at the England game said to him, 'Where's Frank?', would take particular pleasure in being able to say, 'He's attending a poetry reading at the Swedenborg Institute.'

Furthermore, I was on Brighton beach a few weeks ago when I heard one pot-bellied guy say to another, 'Let's get some tinnies and sit here. There's tits all over the place.' Admittedly, I took the opportunity to briefly check out his observation, but I was still slightly appalled by it.

The thing is, certainly for the last thirty-odd years, I would ALWAYS have gone to the Swedenborg Institute (as long as that night's game was only an England friendly) and been unsure about that remark on the beach. I don't think I'm a massively different person to the one who hosted that King's Heath club in the eighties, but I DO think I'm prepared to show much more of the person I am, the complete picture. In the old days, I was me in public – but only the parts of me I thought were helpful to the gags. I turned the leering, laddish, in-your-face aspects of me up to ten on the graphic equaliser, and the sensitive, religious, dare I say intellectual aspects of me down to about one and a half. It wasn't a con. Grimaldi didn't put on clown make-up to be a different person; he did it to emphasise certain aspects of the person he already was, and to suppress those aspects of himself that weren't immediately relevant to his act. All comedians do the same. Writing my autobiography was a life-changing experience in that respect. I brought all my hidden bits from the back room and put the whole lot in the shop window; the public and private faces. Since then I've been loath to separate them again, less inclined to hide stuff behind the motley.

I ended the set last night with a routine that I've given more chances than most, a routine that only went OK in its first six or seven outings but one which I was determined to make work. It's about being in a new relationship and going through the horrors of jealousy, insecurity and rage that always seem to accompany that experience for me. To own up, even in a private setting, to jealousy, or the humiliation of waiting for the phone call that never comes, would have been beyond me ten years ago; now it's the culmination of my stage-act. And I was determined to make it work for that very reason: because it hurt a bit, because it was painfully true – not in its detail but in its feeling. I know that sounds grand, but the old saying that 'All comedy is truth' is not as wanky as it may seem. If I wrote a review about, say, Amy Winehouse, and said something like: 'She lived every line. You just know these songs, even the old Bessie Smith cover, are her life, her truth', you'd think that was absolutely fine. Singers, especially bluesy, souly singers, are often written about in those terms. But if I decided to do my act in an American accent, and make references to New Orleans and Miami, people would just think I was a phoney, or that I was doing some kind of character. With singers – and even more so, actors – you get your truth through a filter, through a mask. With comedy, you're often staring straight into an open wound. You can get away with just being funny, make a good living out of it, but if you're funny and true you've got a real chance to do something special.

I'm just checking the wrapper to see if self-aggrandisement and over-analysis are the usual side effects of a Lemsip overdose. Not a mention. Anyway, I have to let my stage-voice just happen; it's not just a voice, it's a presence. I have to let it be instinctive and just see what comes out. I can't be going:

And now, ladies and gentleman, I will perform fifteen minutes of knob-jokes as my alter-ego, Frank Skinner *circa* 1989. (LOUD CHEER) Please note, the views and opinions expressed in this section are those of my former self and do not necessarily relate to views I hold today. Ladies and gentlemen, I give you FRANK SKINNER 1989! (EVEN LOUDER CHEER AS I PUSH MY HAIR INTO A QUIFF) Good evening! Good evening! Football-fuck-fuck-fuck. Me girlfriend got back from the doctor's and she said, 'I think we might have to get that new washing machine we were talking about because we're gonna be washing a lot of nappies soon.' Turns out her arse-muscles are packing-up.

You know, I'm not sure anyone, other than me, would actually notice the difference.

Tonight's gig was another stormer: an even bigger welcoming cheer than I got last night, and there was more flow in me. I felt so much

FRANK SKINNER

better. I also think the old and new voices seemed to find a middle ground and become one; or maybe I'm just imagining things again. Anyway, the leering, laddish me and the cerebral, analytical me seemed to weld together nicely when I pointed out – it had literally just occurred to me, onstage – that the granny porn website Old Spunkers, which features mature women having sex with much younger men, should probably, for the sake of accuracy, be called Old Spunkees.

Either way, I did an hour and thirty-six minutes and it all went pretty well. Nevertheless, even before I'd left the dressing room after the show, I'd managed to convince myself that, despite my previous conviction to the contrary, the Birmingham crowd like me TOO much, that they're TOO pro, so I'll probably end up putting stuff into the tour-show that went well tonight and will then get a terrible comeuppance as soon as I try it anywhere else.

I got slightly mobbed outside the pub, but Adam whisked me away in our newly hired black BMW, the car that he and I will share for the duration of the tour. When he arrived in it yesterday, I casually christened it 'the Joke-Mobile' and Adam has very much taken to calling it that all the time. Our respective senses of humour are slightly out of kilter at the moment. Adam has quite a lot of what one might call 'little sayings' that he, well, says. I'm in a sensitive mood, with tour-worries, and I'm – completely unjusti-fiably – getting a bit annoyed by his avuncular manner. It's the *Ghost World* in me. I don't know if you know *Ghost World*. It's a comic book and a film about two bright but bored teenage girls who spend their days thinking that they are great and everyone else is an idiot. I find the girls entertaining but I don't want to BE them. I want to reach a stage where, when I look at someone – friend or stranger, saint or serial-killer, Jade Goody or Adam – I see God's mystical light flickering within, a flame reflected in my eyes as mine is in theirs, like that river that flows through me and Alice Cooper. However, I find this hard to sustain when the person in question refers to Westlife as Shelf-Life and began a phone call tonight by saying to the person who'd called earlier, 'You rang-utan?' These things shouldn't matter, I know. Adam honestly seems like a decent person, a straightforward 'good bloke', but when he described a strange woman in the King's Heath audience as looking a bit 'Radio Rental', a small, interior part of me died. They're just little sayings. But then there's the singing of tunes that aren't tunes. So, for example, when I got in the car – yes, the Joke-Mobile – to go to the gig tonight, Adam greeted me with an upbeat, old-fashioned-barber-style 'How are YOU, sir?' and I responded with a deliberately downbeat, 'Much better, thanks.'

'Good, good, good,' he said as we drove off, and then followed this with a 'dum-dum-dee-dee-diddle-dee' of a tune which I'm sure doesn't actually exist. I guess it's just a way of filling the silence. I sing all the time when I'm not ill. In fact, that's how I recognise the first green shoots of my return to health: when I'm singing again, I'm getting better. But I sing songs: recognisable show-tunes, rock classics, tracks from Wings' first album, all sorts . . . but always recognisable as extant musical compositions. Adam is like an Aeolian harp, those box-like instruments that people used to leave near an open window so they could be played by the wind. The tunes, gusting and indeterminate, rise up and are gone, unremembered and unrepeatable. I've only once heard him sing an excerpt from an actual song. It was Hot Chocolate's 'I Believe in Miracles', but even this rare dalliance with a recognisable work was marred, for me, when he, for comic effect, replaced 'miracles' with 'mackerels'. Another small, interior part of me died – VERY small, I'm sure, but still a part of me, dead and gone for ever. Anyway, only sixty-nine gigs to go.

PART THREE

THE TOUR

SUNDAY 9 SEPTEMBER 2007

I'm sitting in the dressing room of the Leeds City Varieties. When I was a kid, my mum and dad used to watch a BBC TV show called *The Good Old Days*. It was based on Victorian music hall, with the acts and audience all in nineteenth-century get-up: women with large bonnets and parasols; men in frock-coats and lamb-chop whiskers. People like Lulu would come on and sing music-hall classics like Marie Lloyd's 'The Boy I Love Is Up In the Gallery', followed by someone like Ken Dodd doing, essentially, his usual stuff but in a loud-check suit and a bowler. It was a massively popular show and ran for about thirty years. It was filmed each week at the Leeds City Varieties. The TV show was finally pulled in 1983. I suspect this slightly crumbling old theatre has never quite recovered. It's a proper old music hall, built in the 1860s; Charlie Chaplin and Marie Lloyd played here. It's seems an apt place for me to start the tour. I like to think of my act as a bit of a music-hall throwback, all faux innocence and saucy remarks. Marie Lloyd used to do a song called 'I Sits Among the Cabbages and Peas' with an I-can't-imagine-why-you're-laughing look on her face. I probably have a similar look on my face when I explain how, in a botched attempt to provide sexy mood-music for a hotel-room liaison, I ended up having intercourse to the very non-sexy accompaniment of Scott Joplin's 'The Entertainer':

It completely ruined the whole thing. While we were still

mid-sex I said to the woman, 'I'm sorry about this. I don't even like jazz.'

She said, 'It's ragtime.'

I said, 'You should have told me that before we started.'

City Varieties is an intimate space, a 531-capacity auditorium but with the crowd piled high and close, rather than stretching out into the distance. You can walk to one end of the stage and chat to someone in an adjacent box, like two old housewives talking over a garden wall. I like a crowd good and close, like to be able to smell the beer on their breath, to see a bra-strap through a white blouse. Mind you, any act that plans to chat to people in the boxes better watch where they're perching. I leaned against the ornate stage-surround during my soundcheck and the plaster crumbled in my hand. The manager tells me they're anticipating a large sum from the National Lottery Fund. Reading between the lines, if it doesn't come it could be curtains for the old place – and I don't mean red velvet ones.

I'd be sad to see that happen, but I can't help remembering that when the Lottery started, we were told the profits would be used to build cancer wards in children's hospitals and send the mentally ill on holiday. Instead, it all seems to get spent on new frocks for the Royal Ballet and bailing out provincial theatres that had a bad panto season. Still, maybe the terminally sick kids and the terminally untanned mentally ill will get a cut-price matinee or two by way of compensation.

Adam and I sit amidst our own broken conversation in this semi-ruined dressing room, his 'la-la-diddle-da' regularly disturbed by wandering theatre staff, as if we were co-stars in the new Samuel Beckett drama *Waiting for Lotto*. In my hand, I hold my set-list for tonight. I've probably read it thirty times since I arrived. Well, actually, I'd say four times; but it seems like thirty. I hate reading through my set-list. The memory improves but the heart aches close to breaking. The words, typed up into neatly headed columns, look cold and clinical, like an inventory of pharmaceuticals. It's impossible to imagine laughter emanating from this rigid catalogue. I have another grape. One of the exciting things about arriving at a venue is the rider, the food and drink requirements that are attached to your contract. They are supplied – laid out in the dressing room or professionally packed into a small fridge – by an allotted member of the theatre staff. My rider is a simple affair: blueberries; bottled water; Ryvita; cooked chicken; soya spread; salad; tea-making facilities. It's positively monastic compared to many. No alcohol, no sweets. The closest I get to the indulgent eccentricities that artist-riders are famous for – eight pounds of Smarties with all the blue ones taken out; sixteen white orchids; an oxygen cylinder and mask – is a request for two local postcards with first-class stamps attached: I want to let Cath know I'm thinking about her, even when the pre-show stresses are at their height. There is just one postcard tonight, the theatre's own, showing a scene from – you guessed it – *The Good Old Days*, the costumed crowd engrossed by some sort of dance routine against a Victorian drawing-room backdrop. An ageing, ramshackle shadow of its former self, still harping on about television glory days . . . like I say, a particularly appropriate place for ME to begin my tour.

This rider – one white-bread chicken sandwich, a small bunch of grapes and two oranges – is very much a pre-Lottery-money interpretation of my written requirements. Adam points this out, but, as the theatre employee explains, 'It's Sunday.' He delivers the phrase with a shrug that suggests he has stopped any further debate in its tracks. As Adam says, 'They're having a giraffe.'

The man leaves with a muttered can't-promise-anything assurance that he'll see what he can do. To be honest, the whole thing puts a downer on the tour's grand opening until, in a dramatic 'no one's gonna rain on my parade' gesture, I have an orange.

Five hundred and forty-one is a good number and every seat is sold. In fact, apart from Dundee and Plymouth, and the newly added second Hammersmith Apollo and third Birmingham NIA, every venue on the tour is sold out. Many have been sold out for months.

When I had the initial tour-meeting with my manager, Jon, we agreed I'd do a thirty-date tour, playing venues with a capacity of less than five hundred. That would gently get me back into the swing of being a theatre-tour stand-up again without TOO many witnesses to the struggle. And also, now that profit margins weren't really an issue any more, I'd be able to enjoy the non-economical luxury of working only small, intimate spaces. In truth, though I did like the idea of more-intimate gigs, my views on venue size were mainly influenced by my fear of playing to half-empty auditoriums. Thirty times five hundred . . . fifteen thousand people in total. In my opinion, I was already pushing it. Now, one could argue, with hindsight, that I was wrong about that, but the fact remains I have no idea how I've ended up on a sixty-nine-date tour, playing to nearly ninety thousand people.

Still, the omens are very good. Yesterday was a sunny day in London and I walked, with Cath, to the Courtauld Gallery, at the side of Waterloo Bridge, to see an exhibition of works by the late-fifteenth-/early-sixteenth-century German painter and engraver

Lucas Cranach. The exhibition featured a beautiful painting of
Adam and Eve. The couple are surrounded by luxurious shrubbery
and snuggle-up-close wildlife, the Adam scratching his curly head
with uncertainty as he gazes at the proffered apple already nibbled
by an androgynous but enticing Eve. If only the fruit had been
supplied by the Leeds City Varieties, Adam would have not been
even slightly tempted and all mankind would have been saved.
Anyway, Cath and I went for a post-exhibition wander and, further
east along the river, near the OXO Tower, we came across a woman
with a small wooden stall. On the counter of that stall were two
small trays containing hundreds of pieces of folded paper, some
pink, some blue. To the side of these trays stood two attendant
budgerigars. 'Would you like your fortune told, sir?' the woman
asked, in what I think was an East European accent. 'It's only one
pound,' she added. Well, it was irresistible. I gave her the pound
and she lifted a budgerigar on to her finger 'Choose the gentleman's
fortune, Brenda,' she said. Yes, I had anticipated a slightly more
exotic name, but then again, who knows what constitutes exotica
in Bratislava or wherever the woman came from?

Anyway, Brenda was quick to it. She picked, with her dextrous
budgie beak, a piece of folded blue paper from one of the trays and
dropped it on the counter in front of me. I am reading it again now,
for solace and instruction, as my three-month adventure begins:

MAN PLANET. You start several things at one time, you
are successful, even so many people hate your fate, but soon
after you'll sign some good deals. Luck will join you all
the way. Don't trust your friend. Don't be afraid of your
acts, just before death he will give you his fortune. Lotto
17-90-45-11-17-5.

It occurs to me that I should pass the last bit on to the theatre manager. I don't think he was expecting to fill out tickets but, as long as the Lottery-cavalry arrives, who cares what route it takes? The first bit, about starting several things at one time, might refer to what's in my suitcase, back at the hotel. I'm hoping to get the tour-show fairly bullet-proof within the next ten days or so. By that point, I should have quite a bit of time on my hands, mainly because I won't be spending hours and hours enticing and then fucking local women. In order to fill this sex-free vacuum, I've brought with me a chess computer, a box of eight learn-to-speak-French tapes, a book listing all the most interesting Roman Catholic churches in Great Britain (I intend to visit as many of them as possible), a drawing pad and pencils and my running gear. I also have the Bible, a book that Cath bought me, which applies Plato's philosophy to jokes, and my Mulisch. I can't play chess, speak French or draw; I've run about five times in the last year and you know about my reading habits; nevertheless, I'm optimistic that I'll utilise all these things before the end of the tour. I'm a great believer in self-improvement. I'm hoping to get really good on the ukulele too. As I HAD to bring that along because it's part of the act, I decided to leave my banjo at home. I couldn't justify travelling with two musical instruments, especially when I can't really play either of them. Anyway, all that lot should help me to use my time constructively. What happened to the good old days when comedians just played golf?

On the middle finger of my left hand, I'm wearing my Kokopelli ring. I bought it in New Mexico many years ago and I like to wear it when I go on tour. The ring is silver with an oval gold inlay that contains the silhouetted figure of Kokopelli, a hump-backed flute player used as a fertility symbol by some Native Americans. Also known as the Casanova of the Cliff Dwellers, Kokopelli is often depicted with a giant phallus, but the one on my ring is phallus-free. The ring used to be a particularly apt tour accessory. Kokopelli was a trickster-god who rolled into town, entertained everyone with his fluting and dancing, and afterwards, because the men weren't threatened by his twisted ugliness, he would sneak around, fuck selected townswomen and head off to his next gig. It was an autobiographical thing. Of course, the ring doesn't seem so relevant on this tour but, then again, I am actually playing music and even doing a bit of dancing as part of the show. The missing phallus, of course, has suddenly become particularly apposite. In three tours' time I fully expect to have my own humped back.

My mind wanders back to Brenda's predictions. For some reason, even though the prophecy was chosen for me by the budgerigar accomplice of a woman who almost certainly had to leave her homeland because the collapse of communism and resulting freedom of information act revealed her to be a secret-police informer, I have come to place great faith in these predictions. Take the last sentence, for example: 'Don't be afraid of your acts, just before death he will give you his fortune.' Could the 's' be a misprint? Should it be, 'Don't be afraid of your act'? Then the rest of the sentence could be paraphrased as 'it will cause you to die on your arse every night but it will make you a shitload of money', a sort of 'every shroud has a silver lining'. (Just getting the puns out of my system before I go on.) But what are the good deals I'll sign and who is the friend I shouldn't trust? I guess these questions will be answered as the tour pans out.

It's 7.55. I'm playing the uke and pacing a lot. Half an hour ago, some margarine and tomatoes showed up; five minutes till the tour begins and things are already on the upturn. My set-list is in my back trouser-pocket, just in case my memory goes and leaves me mouthing nothings like a goldfish at an aquarium window. Adam asks, 'Are you ready to kick some ass?' I put down my uke, have a last swig of water and head towards the stage. It's dark in the wings. If I look through the gap between wall and curtain, I can see, centre-stage in a pool of dim light, the lonely microphone in its stand. A stage-management person stands in the gloom, staring at me. People in the wings – in theatres, comedy clubs, television studios – always stare at you just before you go on. Looking for cracks, I always imagine, hoping to see a shaky hand or a tongue desperately lubricating dry lips. It's a brief, intense moment when they're suddenly glad it's you and not them, glad they are staying in the shadows and not stepping out into the bright light. Then again, this bloke is probably just thinking, 'That's the cunt who moaned about the chicken sandwich.' I turn away from him to hide my sign-of-the-cross and silent prayer; I wouldn't want my thank you to be mistaken for fear. I wonder if Chaplin prayed in this same darkness, if Marie Lloyd whispered some secret words.

I turn back and Adam, just visible in safety-light, looks at me and raises an enquiring eyebrow. I nod and the stage goes completely black. An expectant whoop goes up from the crowd; then silence; then 'Container Drivers'. The sound of it – the loud, strident guitar and drums – seems to place a firm hand under each of my armpits and raise me upward. Then, just as Mark E. Smith's barking voice says the word 'containers', a bright blast of light fills the stage and those firm hands throw me out into the middle of it.

I'm back at the hotel, post-gig, sitting at a table in the bar, eating a bowl of soup. Adam is not-very-subtly eyeing his wristwatch, his 'dum-diddle-dee-diddle' slowed to a funereal march. A two-hundred-mile drive and a long argument about lettuce has clearly taken it out of him. Also at the table is my manager, Jon – the much-feared, even hated, boss of Avalon, the company that has watched over my career for, come the day after tomorrow, exactly sixteen years. Much feared and even hated he may be, but not by me. Jon – an unceasingly driven table-thumping street-fighter of a manager, fearless in the face of broadcasters, producers and promoters who are not delivering that which he feels they should deliver – is probably the main reason I was singing 'Ah! Sweet Mystery of Life' in my bank manager's office not so long ago. As soon as I realised I was in a jungle, I decided to get myself a machete. Jon, in leather jacket and jeans, curly black hair neatly trimmed, has been trying to get me back on the road for years. He came to loads of the warm-up gigs. Sometimes, if I add a line he hasn't heard before, I hear his shrieking laugh cutting through the general guffaw. Despite the TV shows and number one records, Jon never seems happier than when I'm doing stand-up, be it in a stadium or in a sixty-seater club. He is grinning broadly, not at anything that is being said, just at life.

Completing the quartet is Emma, the head of Avalon's Live Department, the always immaculate Joan Crawford lookalike who oversaw the booking of all my gigs this year. She used to live in Max Miller's old house in Brighton. I enjoy the association, his semi-presence at the table. After the 'ghastly Frank Skinner' gig in Cannes – which, though I say it myself, was an absolute stormer – Emma and I, laughing out loud in post-gig high-spirits, went for a fag-in-gob midnight paddle in the warm, moonlit Mediterranean. No, I didn't.

Adam yawns. In his defence, I should point out that we're talking about opera. I always thought opera was boring, then as I walked through Covent Garden one sunny Saturday afternoon – a still-unknown comic killing a day in London between Friday and Saturday night bookings at the Comedy Store – I heard a sweet sound. It was an operatic chorus pouring through an open rehearsal room window of the Royal Opera House. I felt a tingle run from my coccyx to the crown of my head, raising every hair it passed on the way. By coincidence, at that time I had a friend who worked at the Opera House, in the Dyeing Shop, where costumes were gilded or distressed according to order. She had offered me free tickets to dress rehearsals but I'd politely declined. The sudden and unexpected presence of that chorus-sound in my world, like the celestial being suddenly there in Kwik-Fit, caused me to find out if the offer was still open. It was and I went to a handful of operas: afternoon dress-rehearsals, with the orchestra in jeans and t-shirts, literally reading the *Daily Mirror* or the *Racing Post* during gaps in their playing. It didn't really move me. I didn't connect. There were bits I liked but there were many more dull bits I didn't. I found nothing like the chanced-upon, tingle-inducing chorus, so I gave up on opera. I liked Pavarotti on the BBC's World Cup coverage in 1990, but that was about it.

Then, in 2003, I got myself an office in Covent Garden, somewhere to lock myself away and write: unfinished novels, un-broadcast sitcoms, that kind of thing. The Royal Opera House was very close, less than a five-minute walk away, so I thought I'd give opera another go. I chose *The Magic Flute* by Mozart; I'd heard of him. I finished writing at seven o'clock one night and strolled over to Bow Street for the show. The Royal Opera House truly is Planet Posh. I saw Baron Heseltine in a velvet jacket, for fuck's sake. I decided not to linger in the bar in case I got shot by a gamekeeper. I just bought a programme and headed for my seat, my jeans and trainers collecting sneers and whispers on the way. *The Magic Flute* was a bit long and a bit dull and a bit brilliant. There was one song – sorry, aria – which totally blew me away. There's a sort of Wicked Witch of the West character called the Queen of the Night and she does this thing when she hits notes so high you wouldn't believe they came out of a human being – and not light, flutey, falsetto notes, but strong, fleshy, split-the-air-like-lightning notes. When her aria ended, I realised I hadn't closed my mouth or, as far as I could remember, breathed for about two minutes. Something special had happened but I was still kept back, still repelled by the boring bits around the good bits, 'like diamonds set in impenetrable quartz'. Was it worth the effort?

Then, coincidentally, I got invited back to the ROH; to a gala performance of *Pagliacci*. This had three plus points: it was free; it was short; and it was Placido Domingo. I had definitely heard of him. If anything, the evening was even posher this time: a black tie job. *Pagliacci* is about an ageing clown who's driven mad with jealousy by his beautiful young partner; it was like watching a home movie.

So I'm sitting there, having a nice time, and it happens. Just before the close of the first half, Placido is singing this aria and he hits a note and there was that tingle again – a strong, physical Class-A-drug of a sensation, exciting and slightly scary, actually causing me to shudder in my seat.

During the interval, it was all off to the posh bar for champagne or, in my case, orange juice. A guy approached me, probably my age, bespectacled and clearly at home in an evening suit. 'How's it going?' he asked, in a posh accent, like Field Marshal Montgomery pretending to get chummy with a new recruit during a troop inspection.

'All right,' I said edgily, waiting to be caught out and made to look foolish when he deliberately asked me something technical about opera.

'Did you get the tingle?' he said. I was stunned. I honestly thought, at first, that I might have misheard him. He went on, 'The tingle? When Placido hit that note?'

'Yeah,' I said, slightly breathlessly. 'I thought it was just me.'

'Oh, no,' he said, 'there must have been a lot of tingles in there tonight.'

I had accidentally entered a secret world; a difficult, estranging world but one that seemed to have wondrous things in it. I don't know quite what they are or how to find them but, when I'm writing in Covent Garden, I still nip over to the ROH; often just a cheap seat tucked away, high and cosy. And the lights go down, I'm all alone and this strange performance begins; and there's always enough brilliant things and puzzling things and intriguing things to keep me creeping back. I tell Jon and Emma all this and they offer advice and recommendations and tingle-tales of their own.

But, every now and then, that broad grin lights up Jon's face. He'll lean forward and, in a deliberately quiet voice, say, 'Excellent tonight, Frank', then nod and grin some more. He's glad I'm back; glad he was there to see it.

MONDAY 10 SEPTEMBER 2007

I'm in St Anne's Roman Catholic Cathedral in Leeds, looking at a statue of Mary and Jesus. It's beautiful. This visit is the result of my first dip into the book of English Catholic churches that I brought on tour with me; *A Glimpse of Heaven* it's called. The book's a bit big for carrying around so I read the section on St Anne's this morning, and now – it's 2.30 in the afternoon – I'm consulting the crumpled bit of hotel headed-paper that I scribbled my notes on. There's no information about this statue. It looks like it's made of wood; medieval, I'd guess. Mary sits with a book on her lap and the boy, Jesus, leans across as if he's being taught to read. You'd think he would have arrived on earth already literate, but the great mystery of Jesus is how the God-bits and the man-bits mixed together. Where did one stop and the other one start? Did he know he was God from the beginning or did it slowly dawn upon him? Did he ever know for certain? It makes the whole Crucifixion thing a lot scarier if he was still in two minds, as it were. That would explain the apparent last-minute doubt. Once the nails are going in you're bound to start thinking, 'Hold on, what if I'm NOT Him?'

What I really like about this statue is that Jesus is, as I say, a boy; probably six or seven years old, rather than a baby. I love medieval and Renaissance religious art, but I've never understood why the baby Jesus always looks like Mikhail Gorbachev. It's as if the artists thought making Jesus look like a real baby was a bit disrespectful. This one is . . . oh, hold on. This one is actually a girl. Sorry, I'll start again. I'm in St Anne's Roman Catholic Cathedral looking at a statue of, funnily enough, St Anne, the mother of Mary, with – you guessed it – the little girl Mary. It's still beautiful. A little girl being taught to read by her mother: that'll do me for a timeless symbol of love. I must say, it's a fabulously Catholic thing to name a cathedral after St Anne, because she is never mentioned in the Bible; we only know about her through the Tradition of the Church. It's a real 'up yours' to the fundamentalist 'if it ain't in the Bible, it ain't nowhere' brigade.

Another fabulously Catholic thing in here is the altar. It contains the skulls of Ralph Grimston and Father Peter Snow; two Catholics who refused to accept the sixteenth-century switch to Protestantism and suffered persecution under Elizabeth I. They were captured, executed (Snow got the deluxe 'hanged, drawn and quartered' because he was a priest; Grimston had to make do with a mere hanging), and their severed heads were exhibited in York as a warning to any other stubborn RCs.

Catholics like a relic. Any bit of a saint or martyr – teeth, shinbone, clothing – always goes down well. And it isn't only the great and the good that get the relic treatment.

I went to a church in Naples where the skulls of the unknown dead are kept in an indoor cemetery, soil and all, underneath the church. Locals come in and take care of the skulls, keep them polished and in good repair, in the hope that the original owners will send them good fortune from the afterlife. This hoping can sometimes become demanding, bullying even. Next to one skull, someone had written the Italian for 'Remember my house!' Some of the skulls have become local celebrities. In a dark corner was one in its own little showcase. It wore a bridal veil and had the name 'Lucia' above it in pink neon light. The skull is visited by brides-to-be who ask for its blessing.

Grimston and Snow, for ever associated, have achieved a certain posthumous fame as Catholic martyrs. This might sound an unenviable form of celebrity but it has its upside. Take Father Peter. If he'd lived he would have had to spend the rest of his life listening to people shout, 'Where's Ralph?'

All this relic stuff might sound a bit ghoulish but I like the Old Church's dalliance with superstition and folk-beliefs. It's just another way of praying, another vivid manifestation of faith.

People like kissing statues, venerating bones – it appeals to some dark inner need that might just be a macabre container for great truth. Even in ever-more-secular Britain, straight-faced unbelievers salute magpies, cross fingers and throw salt over their shoulder, their surface reasoning undermined by some gut-deep feel for the supernatural. They offer a chuckling apology to those around them as they touch wood or sidestep a ladder but, inside, that instinct feels vital and inborn. It isn't the magpies and black cats that matter; it's the vague but nagging awareness of another world.

Christianity, certainly in England, and I include the Catholics, is prone to apologise for its supernatural beliefs, to deny its mysterious magic, for fear of being laughed at, fear that it might scare people away. The insipid pleasantness left behind – pink and clammy like a plucked and gutted cockerel robbed of its screeching, animalistic wildness – causes some people to look to the East, where religion still dwells unapologetically in its own different world. Buddhism, yoga, feng shui, those philosophical bits in David Carradine's *Kung Fu* TV series: all these offer vibrant spiritual alternatives to that cosy *Vicar of Dibley* Christianity you tend to get served up at the church around the corner.

I think this is why I've taken to Lectio Divina, that Bible-based meditation that Karen Armstrong was talking about in Edinburgh. I bought her book and, incredibly for me, read it all the way through. Afterwards I did some Internet investigations, and since then I've been using a simple Lectio Divina method that seems to work for me. I've only tried it a few times, but I reckon it could be the mystical missing ingredient I've been searching for, a life-changer. I'll keep it pithy, but if you're feeling embarrassed just skip to the next bit. I feel the need to write this down.

Lectio Divina (LD) basically has four different stages. I start by just reading the Bible. I know that sounds dull but I'm not talking about reading chunks of it or reading it in a Bible-study kind of way. You read it according to your gut-instinct. LD was developed nearly two thousand years ago by monks, face-down on the floor of stark, shadowy cells lit by a single candle, and hermits howling in echoey dark-night-of-the-soul caverns. It's not supposed to be bland and bookish; it's supposed to be scary and strange. I started with Mark because it's generally accepted as the oldest of the Gospels, the closest to the source, written, I imagine, with a feverish sense of purpose, the writer or writers gripped by a passion, a sense of great significance. I just slowly and purposefully read from the beginning until a phrase grabbed me. I didn't need to know why; something just suddenly stood out. Mark 1:3, 'The voice of one crying in the wilderness'. I read the phrase a few times, memorised it, spoke it, felt it in my mouth, completely focussed upon it.

Next comes the 'What does it mean?' stage. It's a reference to John the Baptist. Now there's a man to challenge the stereotypes of what a religious person is like. John stripped life down to the bone. He slept rough, dressed in ragged animal skins and ate locusts and wild honey. He wandered the back-roads like a wild-eyed homeless man; drunk on prophecy; indifferent to threat. He baptised people – not white-shawled babies at an ornamental font, but adults, pulled roughly down by his impatient right arm and submerged deep in the river then thrust upward, gushing and gasping, rewired and reborn. So, literally, this wasteland-wandering preacher-man was a voice in the wilderness.

On a deeper, more symbolic level, the wilderness could represent a wild and confused world-gone-wrong, and John's voice a bright light illuminating the gloom. And maybe the 'crying' was not just the shouting kind but the tearful kind as well. Maybe John agonised for the people lost in the wilderness. I just have a think about these things: the literal meaning and the, possibly many, symbolic ones.

Then comes the third meaning, the one that completes this 'What does it mean?' stage: what does the phrase mean to me personally? So I think about that and try to find a handle on it, try to dig deep into it and into me. This is a tough one to discuss in a public context, but for me, in this instance, it's all about that word 'wilderness'. That flickering flame inside us all: If, bear with me, that flame is a manifestation of God, the Truth, then it's swamped by a mass of fears, worries, insecurities, preoccupations; all sorts of distractions that make it hard to recognise and even harder to understand. It is a voice, God's voice, crying in my internal wilderness, like a lost-in-the-background, crackly radio-announcer; significant-sounding but indecipherable amidst the swirls of commercial pop. I don't think I can dig much deeper in a public place and, anyway, anyone who wants to try this thing needs to find their own relevance, their own connection. Shit, this stuff is hard to talk about. 'Where have the knob-jokes gone?' I hear you bleating. Didn't I TELL you to skip to the next bit?

The third stage is just a simple prayer, like talking to your best friend, discussing stuff unearthed by the dig, asking for help or guidance. By this stage, I feel like I'm in a spiritual place, slightly removed from my usual worldly self.

For the fourth stage, I lie flat on my back with my eyes closed, as comfortable as I can get, and take deep, slow breaths through my nose until I feel my whole body gradually slow, slow, slow down. It's like I'm barely breathing at all and then – and this is the real skill – I try to not think. I mean really empty my head and leave nothing. It's hard. I did a bit of meditation a while back so I've had some practice but, anyway, I just try my best. No past; no future; just now. The theory is that you empty yourself, like a chalice on an altar, and God fills you back up again. Some people say they experience odd feelings; hear that internal voice, even. I just lie still and disappear, stop being me and become part of the us. Then, eventually, I open my eyes and I'm back again. Though I'm not quite sure where I'm back from. With this fourth stage I think the key is not to WANT anything from it, just to be there.

You may feel all this mysticism doesn't sit easily with the dirty-comic stuff, but contradictions are healthy. The Bible's full of them. They show that the truth is multi-faceted and difficult. Does talking about sex and swearing make someone a bad person? Every now and then someone will say to me, in a condemnatory fashion, 'Tommy Cooper never felt the need to tell smutty jokes.'

'No,' I always reply, 'but he DID feel the need to drink a bottle of scotch a day, beat up his wife and have a long-term affair with his wardrobe assistant. If he gave his wife the choice, I reckon she'd have preferred a blue joke to a black eye.' I don't sit in judgement of Tommy Cooper, but it's always nice to shake someone's rock-solid certainty with a new bit of information. I'm with Dawkins on that one.

I did write some material during the early try-out gigs about being a Catholic, but most of it never even got an airing. I was worried I wouldn't be able to carry it off; not as keen to put EVERYTHING in the shop window as I thought I was. Besides, the best laughs are often in the minutiae of a subject, and the minutiae of Catholicism are things that most audience members wouldn't be familiar with. Consequently, the jokes are hampered by the need to explain everything. For example:

The Roman Catholic Church believes that, during the Holy Communion ritual, the bread we eat isn't bread any more. It has been transformed into the body and blood of Christ. OK, but where does that leave Catholics who are on the Atkins Diet?'

I suppose it says something about contemporary society, or at least my view of it, that I feel I need to explain Holy Communion but not the Atkins Diet. As usual when I write stand-up, I scribbled down the routine thinking I'd written something brilliant; it was only when I actually began to imagine doing it onstage that I realised this material would never leave the notebook:

So this bloke invited me back to his flat for a cup of tea. We walked in, he put the kettle on, we sat down, and immediately he started haranguing me for being a Catholic. 'There is no God,' he said. 'There was no intention behind creation. It was just an accidental big bang. Planets, people . . . they just happened. No mastermind, it was just a fluke. Anyway,' he says, getting up from the table, 'that tea won't make itself.'

'Why not?' I asked.

It's very easy to become one of those Catholics who act like a real bastard all week because they think an hour at Mass every Sunday will be enough to get them to Heaven. It's like driving down a road tailgating people, blasting your horn and shouting, 'Get out of the fucking way, you wanker!' Then suddenly becoming calm and smiling, doing twenty-eight miles an hour, when you pass the speed camera.

That's what God is: the best CCTV system ever. And when

you die the footage is played back to you with a slightly ethereal voice-over, like a heavenly *Police Stop!* video: 'Now, who's this young woman? At seventeen she shouldn't even be IN a nightclub. Ah, here comes Frank, like a shepherd to a lost lamb. He shows his caring Catholic side.'

FRANK: You know, you really should finish that treble vodka. There are people starving in Africa.

The voice-over continues: 'And then we cut to an hour or so later. She vomits into a dustbin in a dark and dismal back street. How kind and considerate of Frank, tightly holding her waist so she doesn't fall head-first into that dustbin. Oh, no, wait – he's not just holding her waist, he's sodomising her.'

And I'm sitting like someone just evicted from *Big Brother*, saying, 'Oh, come on. You've deliberately edited this to make me look bad.'

I quite like the tea-joke, but the CCTV bit isn't structured enough for stand-up comedy, I would say. It's too sprawling and undefined. A priest told me a joke once, so hardcore and unforgiving in its Catholicness that I laughed the joyous, exclusive laugh that only an in-joke can provoke. It went like this:

Two Roman Catholic priests were arguing. The first, Father Ryan, OSB (that is, a member of the Order of St Benedict), said that the Benedictines were the most important order in the Church. The second priest, Father Kelly, SJ (that is, a member of the Society of Jesus), said his own order were certainly superior but promised he would pray to God and ask Him for the final word on the matter. The next day

Father Kelly, SJ, arrived clutching a piece of paper. 'I prayed for the answer to our dispute,' he said to the other priest, 'and this morning I found this note on my pillow. (HE READS ALOUD) "Dear Sirs, There is no superior religious order in the Catholic Church. In my eyes, all orders are equal. Signed, God, SJ."'

The priest and I laughed heartily; delighted, perhaps, because we GOT it rather than because we found it funny. Maybe I'll try it in Dublin.

On the south side of the Leeds Cathedral they have very state-of-the-art confessional boxes. They look like two glass-fronted toilet cubicles, each containing an individual pew where one kneels to face the grid in the rear wall, behind which sits the priest. Apparently, there are small rooms behind these cubicles, where one can receive confession face-to-face, no grid required. Open Confession, as it's called.

I think confession is one of those Catholic things that non-Catholics are most fascinated by: telling someone your sins through a grid on the wall; getting absolved; the slate wiped clean; and then going away to get it all dirty again. It sounds fabulously weird. In fact, it can be an incredibly uplifting experience, like doing some really productive filing, putting disordered things straight again. You sit or kneel outside the box, thinking about your recent life, about things you'd like to do better or not do at all; or about things you wish you did, if only you had the courage or the application. Then you go in and share your thoughts with the priest and he offers counselling, words of advice or wisdom, then he says the sacramental prayer of forgiveness and you leave there feeling like John the Baptist has raised you up, wet and wide-eyed, out of the

River Jordan. When it's like that, it's a beautiful thing; but it isn't always like that.

I went to confession last April; Catholics are supposed to go during Lent, the forty days leading up to Easter Sunday. It's kind of like paying your annual fees, keeping up your membership; they used to call it Easter Duties. I went to one of the grand, high-profile Catholic churches in London. It was a Thursday morning but there was still quite a queue for the confession box and probably fifteen people queuing behind me by the time I went in. I could see the priest through the grid: bald head, intense stare – but a stare that seemed to go nowhere, like its point of focus was an imagined or remembered thing. He didn't register my arrival so I began: 'Bless me, Father, for I have sinned. It's been twelve months since my last confession.' Then I began to explain how I felt I hadn't made much spiritual progress since that last confession.

'When I made that confession I talked about how . . .'

'Look,' he interrupted, 'you're not here to talk about your last confession. Just get on with this one.'

'Yeah, but I'm just trying to explain . . .'

'Listen,' he snapped, 'there's other people in the queue. Just tell me your sins.'

'I am telling you my sins,' I explained. 'I'm just trying . . .'

'Just give me a list of your sins,' he said, with no attempt to hide his impatience.

'What, like at junior school?' I asked. This was the sort of confession he seemed to be asking me for, when we all, from the age of eight, trooped one by one into the box and said, in our breathless, childish way, 'I have told lies. I have disobeyed my parents. I have forgotten to say my night and morning prayers', the list continuing till you couldn't think of any more. Sometimes you'd accidentally double up: 'Did I say I disobeyed my parents?' I thought adult Catholics needed something more than that. Like St Paul says, 'When I became a man, I put away childish things.' Nowadays, Catholics are encouraged to avoid the word 'confession' because of its associations with shadowy Gothic confessional boxes, creaking when you kneel, and angry priests spitting hellfire. Now we are encouraged to say 'the Sacrament of Reconciliation', a term that suggests a reuniting, a loving embrace after estrangement. With this particular priest, I didn't feel a loving embrace was imminent.

'Just tell me your freakin' sins, will ya?' he suddenly barked. I was genuinely shocked. When you kneel in a confession box and start opening up about your faults and failures you feel incredibly vulnerable. It's all about lowering your barriers, laying yourself bare. You really don't feel like being shouted at.

'Just forget it,' I said, getting up from my knees. I was hurt and upset and I bit back. 'I think you need to ask yourself if you're in the right job,' I said as I left the box. I stepped out into the beautiful church, closing the door behind me. The next person in the queue stood up to take their turn. Should I warn them off?

Then suddenly the priest was right beside me; staring that intense stare but this time straight into my eyes. The box, the grid: it's all supposed to be about privacy. Of course, the priest will often recognise a regular parishioner's voice, but the sense of anonymity is still central. It takes the edge off the utter, raw exposure of kneeling to confess your sins. If you choose an Open Confession, that's one thing, but to have one suddenly thrust upon you, eye-to-eye . . . I was shaken.

He stood, bull-necked, red-faced and too close, arms at his side but fists tightly clenched; his deliberate words, aggression straining at the leash, hissed through gritted teeth. 'Get back in the box,' he said.

As I write I think of those old ventriloquist acts from my childhood where the man says to the dummy, 'Get back in the box', and the dummy says, 'I don't want to get back in the box' over and over, with much wrestling and slamming of lids and distant dummy voices from within the now-closed box. But none of those associations struck me at the time; nothing reassuringly familiar or comic sprang to mind. I had come to confess my sins, to be reconciled, but instead there was this.

'What are you doing?' I said. 'You're a priest.'

'Get back in there,' he said. He was clearly struggling to stay calm.

I looked down at his still tightly clenched fists. 'What are you going to do – beat me up?' I asked, trying to show him the craziness, the wrongness of it. I looked back at the queue. The man who'd stood to take his turn in the box was still standing, but completely still. I didn't know if he could hear us talking. Middle-aged women and old men were peering along the queue at us: what was happening? Why had the priest left the box? What terrible confessed sin could have triggered this catastrophe?

'We've started the confession,' the priest said, switching my attention back to him, 'let's finish it.' I looked at him. His eyes still raged but he was winning the battle with himself and he was determined to finish the job. I took a breath and stepped back into the box, very glad to have a wall between us again. I knelt and looked back into the grid. He too was taking a breath before recommencing.

I decided that the junior school list was probably my best option, just tell him my bad stuff and get out, but how tense would it get when questioning his vocation – a sin still hot from the oven – appeared on the list? As I put my hands together in prayer, I could see them shaking against each other. Suddenly, the priest began to absolve me of my sins, the sins I hadn't actually got round to confessing. 'Are you sorry for your sins?' he said. I said I was. 'Do you promise to try harder?' he asked. I said I did.

When I shared this whole horrible experience with a friend of mine, days later, he became incredibly excited at this point in the story. 'That's brilliant!' he said. 'All those really vile sins you've done over the years but never had the guts to confess, they're all gone now as well. It's like a blanket absolution. It's great.' I looked at my friend and he looked back at me. Slowly he began to assume the demeanour of a man who'd said too much.

It is normal, at the end of confession, for the priest to give you a penance, something to read or recite as a sign of repentance: ten Hail Marys, a selected passage from scripture, that kind of thing. 'Pray for the missions,' the priest said starkly. Having forgiven my unconfessed sins and delivered my penance, he closed with some advice: 'Next time, have a bit more thought for the other people in the queue.'

His selfless urge to defend the rights of those who waited behind me did not seem a complete justification for his behaviour. Yes, I had questioned his vocation, a poor thing to do, but his rage seemed to be there before that. I doubt I'll ever know the back-story to that Thursday morning confession, but the after-shock was with me for a long time, is probably still with me.

As I got up to leave the box, the priest said one last thing: 'Listen, don't turn your back on confession in general, just because the last priest didn't give you what you wanted.'

Over the following weeks and months, when the memory of that day nagged and niggled at my peace of mind, causing me to confront all my doubts and worries about the Catholic Church, I found some consolation in that closing remark. The priest, though still simmering in the remains of his rage, found within himself a sense of duty that impelled him to try and rescue me from my own bitter response, from any long-term, far-reaching estrangement.

I told a few Catholic friends about my nightmare confession. I figured no one else would really understand why I was so shell-shocked. They all said I should report the incident, but I never did. I didn't want to get the priest into trouble, or I didn't want to be further estranged by an unpalatable closing of ranks; I don't know which. I went back to that church another couple of times, but I felt like a stranger in a cold and foreign land. I don't go there any more.

I've been to confession since, earlier this year. I could feel my heart thumping as I knelt outside the box, waiting for my turn. I was afraid. The confession that followed was not dissimilar to the ideal confession I described earlier, like a healing embrace, but the vapour trails of that Thursday morning in April still linger. I take my share of the blame, I could have been more diplomatic, but I got hurt bad. I look now at my reflection in the glass confessional door and shudder at the remembering of it.

Great gig tonight. Even better than last night. Could the tour-shows possibly stay this good?

WEDNESDAY 19 SEPTEMBER 2007

I've just finished my first block of six tour-gigs and I'm back in London for my day off. It's the first time I've seen Cath for ten days and we're back on the drab carousel, having a row. I had lunch with her today and I was talking about people sending begging letters; there were a couple in the post this week. She said if she was in my position she'd give all her money away because being rich is just too much hassle. Cath gets quite romantic at the notion of us being broke and living in a council flat; then we'd be financial equals and my money, or her lack of it, wouldn't be an issue.

Some cynics might say this is just a double bluff to put me off the gold-digger scent, but not if they knew Cath. I'm sure she isn't just after me for my money. Well, as sure as any rich man can be when he's dating a woman with manga-eyes and an hourglass figure who's fourteen years his junior. If anything, Cath prides herself on NOT being driven by ambition or financial reward. She used to live in an artists' commune in the Welsh countryside, and I'm not sure the appeal of that life has ever really worn off. Sometimes I think Cath is too non-materialistic, too other-worldly. I'm not quite sure what that other world is but she seems to spend quite a lot of time there. Anyway, when she said the thing about giving away the money I got really pissed off. I'm not totally sure why.

Later today, after she finished work, she came to my flat to try and talk things through, but it soon escalated into a ding-dong. I was distant, she said; I didn't seem to be listening to her. The truth is, when she arrived, I was in the middle of watching England versus India in the Twenty20 Cricket World Cup. Now, admittedly, we are already out of the tournament so the game meant nothing, but it's still the England cricket team and I always care about whether they win or lose.

I love cricket. A day sprawled on the sofa, watching six-or-so hours of the Test Match on TV . . . I'm like a cat in sunshine. Smiling and purring, the occasional look of surprise, then more smiling and purring. I live quite near the Oval cricket ground and I'll often go there on my own for the day. Baseball cap and shades, good newspaper for the lunch and tea breaks, bagful of food: it's like having a day off from the world. I used to play charity cricket very badly; always living on scraps, tiny little morsels of good play. Cricket can do that. You hit one ball, sweet and effortless; you bowl one delivery, on the spot and spinning wild. Just moments, brief insights into how the really good players experience the game most of the time. A glimpse of Heaven . . . then it's gone and you're foolish again.

I played a game against the Barmy Army, England's fanatical group of travelling supporters. Their team included a guy who was known by everyone as Frank. It wasn't his real name but . . .

Let me go back about five or six years. David Baddiel and I had an idea for a new TV show to be called *First Impressions*. It was based on the theory that everybody can do at least one impression. We made a pilot show which featured videos people had sent in of themselves doing impressions, including a quite disturbing one, which didn't make the show, of someone in black gloves and a black full-face balaclava, waving two saucepans around and shouting, 'Hello, I'm Ainsley Harriot.' Not even Chris Rock could've turned that one round.

The show also included vox pops: 'Excuse me, can you do an impression of anyone?'; a sort of game-show element, hosted by me, in which people did impressions and the audience voted for the best ones. And finally, a big *Generation Game*-style sketch in which many of the amateur impressionists we'd seen, now aided by our professional make-up and wardrobe departments, did extended versions of their impressions. Now, if I learned one thing from the whole *First Impressions* experience it was this: Frank Spencer impressionists are a race apart. It's a kind of Tourette's Syndrome. The strident Spencer-genes overpower them and they don't DO him any more, they BECOME him. I remember arriving at a local arts centre for one of the *First Impressions* audition days. As I walked into the foyer alone, two strangers, one male, one female, approached. They both wore raincoats and berets. 'Oh, Mr Skinner,' said the young male, with Spencer-esque wide eyes, head-wobble and childlike voice, 'I'm glad you've made it. I heard you had a liddul bid of trouble getting in.'

'Yes,' said the female, a woman in, I would guess, her late thirties, as she stepped in front of him. They were no double act; they jostled to fill the Spencer-shaped space. 'I wondered if your cat had done a whoopsie and that had made you a liddul bid late.'

I felt like John Steed, confronted by a couple of Tweedle-Dum Tweedle-Dee eccentrics in an episode of *The Avengers*. Of course, if this HAD been *The Avengers*, I could have at least consoled myself with the certainty that they would both be found hanged with their own raincoat-belts a little later in the episode. 'It's great to meet you,' I said, and kept walking. I was interrupted, mid-sigh of relief, by the female Spencer at my left shoulder: 'Betty is a very big fan of yours. She watches your liddul chat show all the time.'

'Yes,' said the male Spencer, suddenly taking my right arm, 'but she doesn't let Jessica watch the naughty bits.' I considered simul-taneous elbows to the stomach – imagine the twin, high-pitched whimpering sound as both Spencers dropped to their knees – but instead I just said, 'Don't peak too early' and upgraded into a semi-jog. It would've been hard for them to match my pace without breaking out of their I've-just-shit-myself Frank Spencer walk. Unless they came down the stairs in a shopping trolley, I knew I'd escaped.

Anyway, 'Frank' the cricketer was another of the species. Before he came into bat – in a beret, of course – he spent about forty-five minutes on the PA system, giving a Frank Spencer commentary on the game. At no point during that stint did he slip out of character, so by the time he finally came to the wicket, my team-mates and I were pretty well Spencered-out. But not him. He began his innings by scampering a quick single and then, turning to the nearest fielder, he said, 'I nearly got myself into a liddul bid of trouble there.' Shortly afterwards, following a loud appeal for caught behind, he turned to the second slip and said, 'Oooh, I'm being harassed.' Bear in mind, none of the crowd could actually hear any of this. He wasn't playing to the gallery; this was just him luxuriating in his own Spencerness. Interestingly, he batted rather well, some deep cricketing instinct within forcing him into counter-Spencer territory. Michael Crawford's Frank could never have got forty-one runs. Apart from that contradictory prowess, however, he was still very much Spencer.

In fact, I never heard him NOT being Spencer at any point during the day. When it was our turn to bat and I was dismissed, for a paltry single-figure score, the successful LBW appeal comprised ten 'owzats' and one 'oooh Betty'.

Anyway, my point is I love cricket and I wanted to watch tonight's game. However, I had to come to terms with the fact that Cath and I don't have much time together over the next three months and we had to sort things out. I needed to get my priorities right, to make a sacrifice; so, when the talk got serious, I put the television on mute. But, unfortunately, just as things were getting intense in my flat, they were also getting intense on the cricket field. I know that sounds like a comedian for the *Loaded* generation being all laddish and immature, but I honestly felt it was possible to have this, I admit important, conversation while just keeping a sort of general eye on the cricket.

Yuvraj Singh had hit three sixes off the first three balls of Stuart Broad's over, and the Indian batsman looked pretty intent on giving the remaining three balls more of the same. I didn't know why I was so upset by what Cath had said about giving away the money, so when she asked me to explain, I was thinking on my feet. 'Well, what if we had children?' I said as Broad ran in for the fourth delivery of the over. 'Are you telling me that, if I died, you'd give the money away and let . . .' Another six.

'And let what?' said Cath, seizing on my pause.

'. . . and let them struggle, just because you don't want the responsibility of having money?'

'So we're gonna have kids?' she said. Why had I brought up having kids?

'Well, who knows?' I said, throwing up my hands at the sheer inscrutability of the universe. 'Anyway, we're not talking about having kids, we're talking about you giving all my money away when I'm dead. Fuckin' hell!' I added as the fifth ball went for six.

'Why are you shouting?' she asked, understandably.

'I just get frustrated with all this,' I said.

'All what?' she asked. I really needed to just concentrate on the conversation, or alternatively the cricket. The 'this' I was getting frustrated by was a strange hybrid of Cath's money remark and

Stuart Broad's bowling. I needed both of them to just calm down and let me think. When the sixth ball went for six I put my head in my hands and Cath said I wasn't fucking listening so what was the fucking point. She's impossible sometimes.

So now, twenty minutes later, we're still sitting in silence, telly off. I've sacrificed the England innings to get this sorted out. I need to think, to examine my feelings and consider her point of view. I find the best way to resolve a row is to sit and work out exactly what I feel, why I'm upset, then I can concentrate on discussing that and not get caught up with point-scoring. I want to sort the row, not win it, and I want to do it tonight. Otherwise a Twenty20 game could develop into a five-day Test Match.

So why was I upset by what Cath said? It's not like she has the money to give away, and if we stayed together and I died and she did get the money, I'd be dead so what would it matter? OK, if there's an after-life, they'll probably have an observation tower from where I'll be able to watch her throw my hard-earned cash away, but I'll either be sizzling on Satan's griddle – in which case the severity of my eternal torture will make me not give a shit about the goings-on back home – or I'll be in a state of blissful enlightenment, knowing that materialistic concerns like money are ultimately unimportant. Alternatively, if there is no after-life I'll just be a soil-additive, some sort of gritty powder. All that must mean my current concern is for her rather than me. If I die, I want her to be rich and strong and sorted; if the swindlers come, hoping to leave her poor and disillusioned, I want to know she'll sniff 'em out and fuck 'em off. Maybe all this is a slightly confused manifestation of true love. I'm sitting here in sulky silence next to someone I care about and care for, and who I want to care for even after I'm dead. Or is it just I don't like the idea of cunts getting their hands on my money? Oh, I don't know. I always get scatty when the cricket goes badly.

Life used to be simpler. I remember when I was just starting to establish myself as a comedian, going to see a one-woman stand-up show in Birmingham. I won't name her but she was brilliant; she did an hour and absolutely stormed it. The show was basically all about her being lesbian, so it was true and personal as well as being funny. A few months later, I stopped at a motorway services on my way back from a gig. As I crossed the car park, heading for the main building, the glow of fast-food and computer games in the wintry darkness, I saw that same female comedian standing next to a parked car. I'd met her a couple of times since her Birmingham show, so I went over to say hello. We chatted politely till I said, 'Are you OK? I mean, standing here in the dark?'

'Oh, yeah, I'm fine,' she said. 'I'm just waiting for my boyfriend.' Even in car-park gloom she couldn't miss my puzzled look. 'I know,' she said.

'Sorry,' I blustered. 'I didn't mean . . . It's just that I thought you were . . .'

'I was,' she said. 'I can't believe it either. I met this guy and, I don't know, we just fell in love. In fact, we've already talked about getting married and, I must admit, I'm really hoping to have his children.' She shrugged and grinned.

I said some 'life's unpredictable' type thing, offered my congratulations and walked away. And as I crossed that car park, I remember thinking to myself, 'Well, I'm all for love, marriage and having babies, but I wouldn't give up an hour of funny material for it.'

I would say I've mellowed since then. I like the idea of having kids in as much as I like the idea of buying one of those black baby-gros with a skull-and-crossbones on the front, or taking them to the football, or helping them learn to read like St Anne with Mary. It's the 'become totally fucking dull because all I ever talk about is my kids' aspect that I'm less keen on. I'd like to think that if I DID have kids, I'd never mention them to anyone except their teachers or, in an emergency, a doctor; although I might possibly break this rule if I was being held hostage and had to offer my captor reasons for not killing me. Then again, if any hostage of mine started going on about his kids, I'd kill him instantly. I mean, what's the point of being a captor in the first place if you're going to have to put up with that kind of shit? I would be a secret parent. If a neighbour caught me in the park or at the circus with my kids, I'd say they belonged to a friend and move quickly along. I would not describe myself as 'Proud Parent' on MySpace, nor would I fill my MySpace photos page with badly taken snapshots that have captions like 'my lovely Nathan lol'. In the past, when people have asked me if I'm going to have children, I've always said, 'Well, there's no need. I've already got plenty of stuff to talk about.'

Of course, if Cath and I did have kids and then she gave away all the money when I died, she would be, as I said during our row, disinheriting them. This has its plus points. Anita Roddick, the woman behind the Body Shop empire, died last week. Apparently, her kids won't get any of her millions because she was basically against inherited wealth. I think Anita had a point: we've all seen or read about those spoiled rich kids who don't have anything to do all day except snort cocaine and wear sunglasses. It's not earth-shatteringly original to say that money, lots of it, without the struggle, without the satisfaction of having earned it, or the resulting determination that the fruits of that hard work should not be squandered, can easily mess someone up. Besides, there is something satisfying about the idea of the Roddick kids having to buy their own vanilla bath gel. I still think that lathe operator was a twat because he'd worked hard all his life so had enough experience of sweat and darkness to be able to appreciate sweetness and light. Sweetness and light from the outset, however, will soon, I imagine, start to cloy.

What I'd like to leave MY kids is a career; something that will bring them money but money they will have worked for. I haven't actually discussed this with my publisher, but one option would be to treat them like shit throughout their childhood and then, when I die, leave them a lucrative book-deal. A couple of Mis Lit best-sellers later, they can enjoy the fruits of their labour and the knowledge that they battled on and turned their tragedy into a Tesco bestseller.

In truth, and despite all my Catholic musings, I don't give very much thought to death itself. I saw an old school friend of mine quite recently, and he said, with the approach of his fiftieth birthday, he had taken to lying awake at night, dwelling on the inevitable. My night thoughts seem to be all about re-jigging knob-jokes; mainly because if I don't sort them out, no one else will. The big plus about death, I would have thought, is that it works like a surprise party: you don't have to DO anything; it just happens to you. I probably thought about it more when I was an adolescent. I used to fantasise about being told I had six months to live. I seemed to think that, rather than great misery, it would bring me great freedom. Once I'd left the doctor's surgery, I thought, I'd set off on a six-month frenzy of drinking, telling people to fuck off and shagging a different woman every night. I put the shagging-thing third on that list, but it was probably the most important ingredient in my six-months-to-live extravaganza. Of course, when

I got a little older, I became aware of the concept of 'consent' and that put the mockers on the whole enterprise.

That reminds me, the 'not shagging around on tour' pledge is still intact. I haven't exactly had to beat them off with a stick either. In fact, the only way I was going to get laid this week was to beat them ON with a stick. Anyway, I'm not pining for it, by any means, but a large banana in the dressing-room fruit bowl at the Assembly Hall Theatre, Tunbridge Wells, last Sunday did cause me to experience something of a flashback, did make me think of my reckless past.

She, I recall, was an attractive young woman; blue eyes and short blonde hair in a fringe. She looked like she was in her early twenties. This is starting to sound like a police statement. She was part of a group who came into the dressing room – I'm not sure which theatre it was – to get autographs and say hello. My normal habit was to chat to people outside the stage door; I felt easier about inviting people back to my hotel if I was partially obscured by darkness. I've never been a ladies' man, someone who uses chat-up lines and all that baloney; I'd just sign the autograph and then say, 'Do you want to come back to my hotel for a drink?' The 'for a drink' was my concession to common decency. We would spend time in the bar, but only so I could get a look at her in bright light while there was still time to bail out with one of my mock-faints. Sometimes it seemed rude to ask only one of a group, so seven or eight people would come back and I'd use that old sheepdog technique of steadily separating one from the rest of the flock. Like the Border collie, I did this largely through eye-contact. Some dogs bark and snap at the sheep to split it from the flock, but that aggressive and alienating method isn't so clever if you're planning to try and fuck it afterwards.

Anyway, this woman – let's call her Louise – was with a group, but I soon hived her off and managed a whispered invitation. It wasn't subtle. Everyone in the room must have realised what was going on: the hushed tones; the air of pleading. As we all left, Louise turned to me conspiratorially and, gesturing towards the dressing-room fruit bowl, said, 'Why don't you grab a banana?' At first I just thought she was peckish. I figured we'd have sex a couple of times and then, like tennis players between games, we'd sit on our respective chairs – she enjoying an energy-boosting banana; me sipping a Robinson's Barley Water and checking that the last feverish exchange hadn't snapped my string. 'Not TOO big,' she added. OK, she might have just been on a diet but I was starting to put two and two together and get dildo. As I headed bowl-wards I seemed to hear a lot of squeaky little voices shouting, 'Choose me! Choose me!' I grabbed a mid-range one, put it in my pocket and escorted her to the tour-van.

As the van headed for the hotel, I started to worry about my choice: was it too big, too small, too rough at the tip? What if it was over-ripe and crumpled to mush under the onslaught? I had almost brought a second banana as back-up, but I was afraid she might think it was for me. As we neared the hotel, Louise and I sat in the back seat a distance apart. Sometimes the foreplay would begin in the dark tour-van, but not tonight.

When we got into the hotel room, I placed the banana on the bedside table. I didn't think that was too forward. Yes, it was a gesture that might have been saying 'sex toy', but, then again, it could just as easily have been saying 'breakfast'.

Then I turned to Louise and smiled. The excitement that Neil Armstrong felt as he slowly climbed down the Lunar Module's metal ladder, knowing he was about to become the first human being to walk on the Moon, may have equalled but, I firmly believe, could never surpass the excitement one feels when standing with a fully clothed, attractive stranger in a hotel room, knowing that you are about to undress and have sex with them. If, to that latter scenario, you add a banana, Neil Armstrong's excitement is relegated to the lower leagues. I didn't have my heart-rate wrist-watch in those days – which is just as well because I wouldn't have wanted me or Louise to get glass in our eyes when it exploded. She undressed and, happily, all was well. I lived in fear, during my one-night-stands period, of the eleventh-hour discovery of some terrible disfigurement: a grotesque birthmark, third-degree burns or, of course, a fat cock. Louise, however, looked lovely. If she was appalled by my own unveiling she somehow managed to keep a lid on it.

With one-night stands, anticipation is one-third of the fun; the sex itself constitutes the second third, and solitary reminiscence the remainder. Usually, at first spurt, the anticipation element becomes a distant memory, but that night it was prolonged by the presence of fruit. We lay sharing post-intercourse chit-chat – I timed it at a minute forty – and then I headed to the bathroom. I decided it would be best to pretend I'd forgotten about the banana; I felt she was keen to surprise me and, if I spent a few minutes shilly-shallying in the bathroom, I might well walk back in and 'discover' her at play. Of course, no man could have forgotten the banana – that would have been like winning the FA Cup Final and forgetting to pick up the trophy – but I was prepared to play along if it enhanced her sense of theatre. I practised my pleasantly surprised face in the bathroom mirror and listened. I had never heard the sound of a banana being used as a sex toy, but I guessed it would be a bit like someone with one peg-leg hopping across muddy ground. I waited but that sound didn't come. Maybe it really WAS breakfast.

I walked back into the bedroom and, after all that, I actually WAS surprised. She lay on the bed, her hands nonchalantly behind her head, with the banana between her legs. Only half of it was alfresco. It was as if we'd had sex and then, before heading for the bathroom, I'd bookmarked her vagina so as not to lose my place.

'Wow!' I said.

I'm not much of a one for saying 'wow', but sex – especially one-night-stand sex – has got a lot to do with confidence and, if somebody really goes for it, as she had, it's important to be a good audience, to encourage rather than to undermine. It takes guts to lie with a banana up your vagina, waiting for a virtual stranger to re-enter a room; anything less than 'Wow!' would have been a humiliation. As it was, she was clearly pleased by my response. A broad grin replaced her studied provocative pout, rendering her warm and natural again. I could tell she'd become more relaxed because the angle of the banana had lowered slightly. It struck me that, if we had waited till morning, she might have made a marvellous novelty sundial.

So, what now? I stood, naked and staring, saying nothing, just waiting for her next move. Inevitably, a pun came into my head: 'Excuse me, is this the dress rehearsal for *Bananas in Vaganas?*' but I bit my lip, knowing such patter might seem dismissive and disrespectful. I didn't want to undo all the good work done by my 'Wow!'

I'm very much a hands-in-pockets man, so standing naked for any length of time always leaves me ill at ease. I considered masturbating, but I didn't want to steal her thunder. This was her show and if she wanted audience participation, I dare say she'd ask for it. I just stood and watched. She slid her hands from behind her head and replaced them with a folded pillow. Then she took the banana in a two-handed grip, not dissimilar to that used for hara-kiri, and began slowly and deliberately masturbating with it. I had been right not to pre-empt. She pressed the banana deep inside her and then, loosening her grip, allowed it to emerge again unaided. She repeated this process several times. It was like watching someone struggling with a stubborn juicer.

I switched my attention to her face. She seemed less performance-based now; less dictated by my response, more lost in the moment. In truth, she seemed much more stimulated than she had during our sexual intercourse. I was beginning to wish I'd chosen a smaller banana; I had truly made a rod for my own back. I wondered if our second shag, which I was now more than ready for, would be, for her, a bit 'after the Lord Mayor's Show'. I anticipated the embarrassment of having to wait, once the banana was removed, for her distended opening to diminish to a point where I could, once again, hope to get some purchase.

She, however, was showing no signs of banana fatigue. In fact, she was starting to writhe and slightly whimper. I felt it was probably time for me to contribute in some way. It was a tricky one: I didn't want to disperse her rapture but, at the same time, I didn't want her to forget I was there. I was being upstaged by a banana. 'Stick it in your arse,' I said, without really thinking it through. 'No,' she replied, with conviction but no discernible dismay. She didn't even look up to check out my response. Like that Oriental woman at the Gilbert and George exhibition several years later, her refusal was, I felt, friendly but final.

Despite this knock-back, I would still maintain that it's generally a good thing, during sex, to tell the other person exactly what you want the second you want it; just anything that comes into your head. It requires a certain discipline – it's easier to say nothing and risk neither refusal nor offence – but, when it works, it can lead to an atmosphere of honesty and spontaneity, where true sexual fulfilment may fully blossom. I often started these hotel-room encounters by telling the woman concerned that she should see our encounter, removed as it was from the normal events of her life, as an opportunity to air any perversion or peccadillo she may never before have had the courage to try. 'As long as it's not actually life-threatening – borderline life-threatening is OK – I'm happy to give it a go. It doesn't matter if I like it,' I'd add, selflessly, 'the mere knowledge that YOU like it will make me happy.' On virtually every occasion the woman would say, with an indifferent shrug, 'Nah, there's nothing really', and I would turn again to my own sexual palette, with its twelve or thirteen varying hues.

Meanwhile, Louise had achieved one glorious orgasm and seemed determined to make it a brace. Since my suggestion that the show might switch to a smaller venue had been refused, the wind had somewhat been taken out of my sails, and I was loath to speak again unless the idea was a really good one. Perhaps a change of implement, I thought, give the banana a chance to cool off a little. I wondered if the mini-bar had the usual Toblerone, though maybe that would ultimately be too ribbed.

'How do you like a banana up my cunt?' she suddenly asked. It made a change from, 'Where's Dave?'

'It's great,' I said, slightly taken aback by her straightforwardness. She, however, required a more detailed response.

'Tell me how much you like it.'

'What, out of a hundred?' I asked. It was a mistake. Though an honest assessment would place the experience in the mid to high eighties, my sense of exclusion forcing me to dock ten to fifteen points, I felt I had to say a hundred; anything less might create a bit of an atmosphere. She looked at me expectantly. The banana's thrusting motion had slowed, her cauldron's boil lowered to a simmer so that she might take time out before her second orgasm – yes; both fruit-induced – to establish the exact level of my enjoyment. 'A hundred,' I said at last.

'Well, that's weird,' she said, suddenly removing the banana and heading towards the bathroom, 'considering we all know you'd rather see it up my arse.' The bathroom door slammed shut and I was, once more, alone. I decided against remonstrating with her. I felt it best to let her cool down. I lay on the bed where she had lain. 'If she comes out of the bathroom and I'm masturbating,' I wondered, 'will that make the situation better or worse?'

Her sarcastic 'Oh, thanks for your concern' when she re-entered the bedroom, two minutes later, provided an answer to my rhetorical question.

One-night stands were always throwing up episodes like this. My current set includes three anecdotes from that period of my life, and I have to ask, by closing the door on casual sex – and I'll probably never, in my life, use a more fitting analogy than this – am I depriving my sausage-machine of a great deal of raw meat? It's a worry. I don't know how many saucy flashbacks are left in the vault. That said, it would be an extremely focussed lifestyle-choice to continue these sexual shenanigans for the sole purpose of generating stand-up material, but that, I suppose, is what a true artist should do. That may sound callous, but I'm sure a lot of those women came back for a very similar reason: so they'd have a funny story to tell their friends. The thing is, it's no life for a fifty-year-old man: a night of physical union and mental separation, often with someone you don't find that attractive, done more to keep your tally up than out of any genuine desire. And then, next morning, a stilted farewell at a blustery northern town bus stop; no when-will-I-see-you-agains; no hands waving as the tour-van pulls away. Sometimes, the post-coital chit-chat turned to sad stories from broken lives, the brassy veneer melting to reveal a scared and lonely soul within. Sometimes there were tears at departure and a crumpled bit of paper, torn from a diary, with a name and a phone number and kisses or a heart or a smiley-face; worst of all, an LOL. But I never called. I was always clear, always up front: 'You know this is just a one-night stand, don't you?'

'Yeah, of course.'

But I wonder if they DID know. Was there a hope that the one-night stand could blossom into true love? I did once have what I intended to be a one-night stand that became a three-year relationship, so it does happen. Maybe for some of those women, shagging me was like buying a Lottery ticket; OK, probably nothing would come of it, and they'd still be living in Ormskirk, but maybe, just maybe, their number would come up and instead they'd be living in a celebrity pad in London, going to premieres and having their picture in *Hello!* I don't know. I never asked them what they hoped to get out of our encounter, in the long term. It was a one-night stand, not a fucking job interview.

Anyway, it's all behind me now. I have found true love at last and that's why I sit here, in complete silence, with the telly off, my stomach knotted in anticipation of the next flare-up. I'm walking away from a life of one-night stands, the very bricks and mortar of my stand-up career, and gazing at the possibility of parenthood; thus taking me into a life dominated by children, a subject I find tiresome in private and completely unacceptable onstage. Robin

Williams talking about nappies . . . please, no! It was Cyril Connolly, the writer and critic, who said, 'There is no more sombre enemy of good art than the pram in the hall.' But, fuck it, I don't read critics.

Anyway, the groupie thing is history. I'm committed to Cath – I'm going to tell her that in a minute – and I'm fifty, for fuck's sake, enough is enough. I'll write some jokes about opera instead. So far, I honestly, truly, haven't missed the casual sex. They didn't all bring bananas.

Still, all in all, it's good to be on tour again. The show still isn't quite where I want it to be, but I think it's now more a case of reordering the material rather than having to actually generate new stuff. Some shows have been nearly two hours long and that's too much. I've never seen anything – film, theatre, music gig – two hours long that wouldn't have been better if it had been one hour forty. I've dropped 'Suicide-Bomber Girl', it wasn't going quite well enough; but the Osama song has become a storming encore.

My main problem, this week, has been granny porn. This has been the centrepiece of my set since I first performed it back in March. I like its unorthodoxy, the way it speaks of old women in pornography, a phenomenon some people aren't even aware of, with genuine warmth and affection. It challenges people's accepted truths.

I sometimes, perhaps rather grandly, see my whole career in terms of a battle with Middle England. Middle England is a vague concept, but to me it refers to that great mass of people who never question or even consider anything outside of the mainstream view; people who worship at the altar of the great god Normal. Oh, they like a joke, but not if it's about old people having sex – 'Ugh, that's horrible!' – or any other subject that isn't easy, obvious or unchallenging. They tut and wince their way through my set, hate The Fall, dismiss modern art as rubbish, wear a tie with Homer Simpson on it, think comic books are just for children, like a 'few jars' at the weekend, say 'anything, really' when asked what kind of music they like, don't swear in front of women, wear baseball caps, go on and on about their kids, sneer at Goths, think Shakespeare is boring and never miss *Top Gear*. In short, Middle England is people that aren't me or Cath and a few of our close friends, and I wish they'd fuck off and stop dumbing down the world and STOP getting worked up about things that DON'T matter and START getting worked up about things that DO. So, granny porn is dead. I've given in. You have to give the people what they want, more or less. I've replaced it with the sex-from-behind routine that I dropped after King's Heath. Sex from behind: people feel easier with that; it's more normal. Ironically, I only dropped sex-from-behind in the first place because I felt the balance of the act was too heavy on the rude side. You see, my resolve has been broken down. The constant subjection to Middle England that ten years as a cuddly TV star required has made me a bit prissy and tight-arsed too. Anyway, now granny porn has gone there is a filth-spot vacant that sex-from-behind fills neatly. I tried it the last two nights and it stormed; every day a little nearer.

Of course, all this anti-Middle England rage doesn't fit with my desire to find the flickering fire of God's love in all men, the sense that we are all part of the same beautiful whole. But there is good news. Middle England has sent out a representative bearing the white flag of peace, that he and I might negotiate and find common ground somewhere between Middle England and Weirdo-Loner-land where love and mutual understanding can build a new world, where the Middle English and the Weirdo Loners might dwell together in harmony, learning and deriving pleasure from each other's apparently counter cultures. That flag-bearing representative is Adam, and he and I, this past week, on long drives and in dressing rooms, in airport lounges and motorway cafés, have slowly started to come together.

As we drove to the Brands Hatch Place Hotel and Spa last Thursday, the clouds above us were dappled purple and red. 'What a beautiful sky,' I said. Adam tensed like a man who had accidentally ended up in a gay bar. As we neared Brands Hatch, he told me he used to race cars himself. The concept was so alien to me, so relentlessly male – I am, despite the football and the filth, I think, actually testosterone intolerant – that I felt like I had stumbled into a Fight Club.

The following Sunday, as we headed for Tunbridge Wells, Adam gave me the low-down on Lewis Hamilton's performance in that day's Belgian Grand Prix, and I, always keen for English people to do well in any sport, was genuinely interested. It was probably the first conversation I've ever had about Formula One in which I didn't say, 'It's not sport, it's fucking driving.' And yesterday, as we drove from London to St Alban's, Adam craned his neck forward, looked upward and said, sort of to himself, 'That's a really lovely sky.' Who would have thought that, as I write, I'm actually getting on better with Adam than I am with Cath?

Anyway, back to the big question, the question that several friends this week have texted me: 'How's the tour going?' I wish I knew the answer. You see, the audiences are laughing most of the time, and I am working on the areas where they aren't, but I still have a nagging doubt that the whole show is a pile of shit. This theory is based on two things that happened during this first block of six gigs.

I was in the foyer of the Bull's Head Hotel in Peterborough. I had done a gig at the nearby Broadway Theatre the previous evening. As I waited for Adam to get the car, I chatted to a couple of blokes from the hotel staff. After about two or three minutes of small-talk, one of them said, 'We were at your gig last night.' I paused for the anticipated compliment. There was probably three seconds of agonising silence. 'It was what we expected,' he said at last. What the fuck did he mean by that? Then the other guy added, 'We wished you'd done more about football.'

'Anyway, best get off,' I said, and headed for the car park, all hope abandoned.

Then, in Hastings, two gigs later, I took another nasty blow. As I said, I'd been a bit worried about what effect the half-time interval would have on the tour-show. Would I lose my momentum? Would the second half be like starting the show again from cold? There was, however, an interval-related horror I had not anticipated. When I walked out for the second half at Hastings, I became aware of three sections of empty seats that I hadn't noticed before, about twenty seats in all. The show was sold out, so why were they empty? All through the second half, which actually seemed to go really well, I kept looking at these seats and wondering, were they empty in the first half and I just hadn't noticed, or, more horribly, were they full in the first half but the show was so awful the occupants left at the interval? I still don't know the answer and the doubt still nags. Is it all going wrong?

All this is a bit long for a text, so I've just replied with *Seems OK so far*. That's my version of putting a brave face on it.

Still, it's good to be seeing our beautiful land in all its autumnal glory, especially parts of it I'd never normally visit. Basildon, for example. I was happy to discover that Basildon's essential Essexness is still alive and well, that they have a nightclub called Bas Vegas, and that the headline in the local paper was '*Hit and run driver legs it, leaving two injured in road*'. How fabulous that 'legs it' has graduated from a shell-suit colloquialism to an accepted, no-speech-marks-required headline ingredient in such a short time. There is still hope for 'having a giraffe'.

SUNDAY 23 SEPTEMBER 2007

It's a long drive from sunny Torquay to Birmingham. Now it's 2.30 in the morning and I'm in bed in my Birmingham flat, feeling pretty wrecked. I say 'sunny' Torquay because, wherever in the British Isles we go, Adam describes it as 'sunny'. So, if he's on the phone to a friend, he'll say, 'We're just on our way to sunny Chelmsford' or 'We just got back from sunny Aberdeen', whether those places were actually sunny or not. I assumed it was irony on his part: Chelmsford and Aberdeen are not obvious holiday destinations and to describe them as 'sunny' seemed to subtly make this point. The word 'sunny', I think, suggests not only nice weather but also beautiful scenery, usually sea and sand, to compliment the sunniness. I imagine he'll be on the phone later this morning telling friends, with a slight chuckle in his voice, that he's in 'sunny Birmingham'; another ironic comment, you might think, on Britain's unattractive towns and cities. However, my theory was shot to pieces today when Adam described Torquay as 'sunny Torquay'. You see, Torquay IS a holiday destination, and today at least was both beautiful and sunny. Clearly Adam's vast experience of the 'little sayings' genre gives him the confidence to switch easily between the ironic and literal uses of 'sunny', like a chromatic harmonica player pressing the button to change key.

You will have noticed that Adam's 'little sayings', once a source of great irritation for me, have now become a fascinating vehicle for parsing and semantic analysis – a great way to pass an hour or so on a long car-journey. He said 'serpently' for 'certainly' today, but I've often heard this usage from other 'little sayings' users. I'm not criticising him for borrowing – Shakespeare himself was apt to see all literature as his ammunition case – no, it's just that Adam's more unusual and perhaps unique 'little sayings' will, I feel, tell me more about the man. For example, when flying to Dublin on Friday, he actually corrected me for saying Ryanair. 'No, RIOT air,' he insisted. Also, when we got to the venue in Dublin and were led to a room piled high with complimentary food and booze – there is no alcohol listed on my rider but in Dublin they assumed this must be an oversight – Adam said, 'Ah, the hostility area.' I wondered if these alternative choices – 'riot' for 'Ryan'; 'hostility' for 'hospitality' – were the subconscious expression of a mind that saw the world as essentially chaotic and antagonistic. This might sound far-fetched, but a tour manager, especially one who's worked with a lot of rock bands, might easily arrive at such a world view and then reflect it unintentionally in his choice of vocabulary. Like I say, it's a long drive from sunny Torquay to Birmingham.

When we arrived in sunny Torquay, this morning, I was shocked by its beauty. We ate fish, chips and mushy peas on the front and the sea was a deep, deep blue. I actually felt myself reddening a little in the warm sunshine. Adam and I had a discussion about whether or not we'd consider holidaying in Torquay. The fact that, in nearby Torbay, one in nine of the population are carers makes me think the click and clank of surgical appliances, the overpowering smell of Hall's Mentho-Lyptus Lozenges, and the harrowing, eavesdropped conversations about varicose veins, might start to pall after a while.

When I was in Kansas, doing the banjo doc, I spent forty-five minutes listening, as I ate my hotel breakfast, to an old American woman tell three other old American women about her numerous hospital appointments and the ineffectiveness of her subsequently prescribed drugs. One of the three listeners suddenly grabbed the speaker's spindly right hand and shook it warmly. 'Welcome to hip-pain,' she said, as if greeting her at the gates of a wondrous new world.

The locals like to call this part of the coast the 'English Riviera'; thus replacing my images of white hair and wee-stains with those of Bardot-lookalike girls carrying poodles, smoking Gitanes and letting their hair blow free in speeding convertibles. That theory, that the area is almost no longer England but rather a romantic haven of Gallic sophistication, went down the *toilette* when I saw a large sign for 'The Giant Vegetable and Scarecrow Show'. I wonder how many carers have felt obliged to take that on, wearily manoeuvring a wheelchair-bound ancient past the swollen pumpkins and hoping the poor dear doesn't recognise a dead husband's suit, now stuffed with straw.

I noticed in Torquay, and also in Hastings and Jersey, that there was a clearly recognisable middle-classness about the holiday-makers – not so much posh as Bohemian. I wonder if these people think that now the working classes have stopped holidaying in England and the Channel Isles and started going abroad, the only way to avoid them is to do the opposite. If I was a local vendor on the English Riviera I'd swap the candy-floss for tofu, and get some sticks of organic asparagus with 'Torquay' written all the way through it in quince.

One thing about being on tour is that it puts you back out there amongst the people. It's easy to hide away, lose touch with reality, when you just do telly. My weirdo-lonerness has become more and more ingrained over the last six or seven years; I'm always polite but always an arm's length away.

I did a life-saving course a few years back – evidence, you might argue, of a genuine concern for others. At the end of the course, the instructor handed out some face-sized oval sheets of see-through plastic, with a two-inch diameter hole near one end. We all looked confused. 'If you ever have to give a tramp the kiss of life,' the instructor said, 'I suggest you use one of these.' The idea, of course, was that you placed it over the tramp's face, the hole lined up with the mouth. Thus you could be compassionate and caring while still not going so far as to have a tramp's face actually touching yours. Now, in practice, I reckon you'd probably end up putting it on the tramp, as he lay flat on his back; he'd vomit, sending a jet of Special Brew and dustbin-burger through the hole, like a whale ejecting water; and you, head moving downward for mouth-to-mouth, would end up using the tramp as an unsavoury drinking fountain, hot lumpy fluid hitting the back of your throat, causing you to immediately return the compliment. The upshot would be that the tramp dies from not only inhaling his OWN vomit, but yours as well.

Despite that design flaw, the general concept behind the mask – compassionate in a close-but-not-actually-touching way – is representative of all my dealings with the outside world, especially since I've stopped fucking members of my audience. For example, the flight to Dublin included a large group of blokes, beer-cans all round, on their way to a golfing weekend. When I first spotted them in the departure lounge, they seemed to me like a Middle England SWAT Unit; I just knew they started sentences with 'I'm not being funny but . . .' and venerated all things Clarksonian. In the closed environment of the aeroplane, with the golfers now gathered just across the aisle, my testosterone intolerance kicked in. I read the paper and hoped I wasn't noticed. Even Adam, my Middle England Cultural Attaché, was deliberately averting his eyes.

One golf-guy, who'd decided to remain standing for the whole flight, started gawping over my shoulder at the newspaper. To make matters worse, I was reading a review of the English National Opera's production of *Carmen* at the time. Only Shakespeare or child pornography could have unnerved him more. To be fair, I think he felt very at home with 'English', 'National', 'Car' and 'men'; it was the 'Opera' bit he wasn't sure about. He soon stopped focussing on it and started focussing on me. 'You're Frank Skinner,' he said.

I considered saying, 'Now what would a rich bloke like Frank Skinner be doing on Riot-air?' But if the bastardisation of Ryanair got a big laugh from the guy and his now-listening friends, which I suspected it might, I would have had to cancel the tour, there and then, and given up comedy for ever. He was, I noticed, quite well spoken. I could now put class war, as well as drunkenness and golf, on my reasons-for-not-talking-to-this-person list.

He looked down at the review again. 'Why are you going to Dublin?' he asked. I think it had struck him that I might be on an opera weekend. What a conversation that would have been.

'I've got a gig tonight,' I said, not looking up from the paper. Even in the midst of this awkward encounter, I felt proud to say that.

'You don't really want to talk, do you?' he said, with sudden clarity.

I looked him in the eye. I saw a good man looking back at me; a loyal friend, a mate, someone who'd stand up and be counted if things got tough. He was probably good at golf, good at sport in general, able to drink and have fun; unlike me, who was rubbish at sport, drank till I collapsed and usually woke up in a pool of my own urine. How lovely to be off on a boozy golf weekend in Ireland, knowing you would have a great laugh in the warm, supportive and secure company of your friends; not feel estranged and distant, be in the group but not of it.

'I'm thinking I might ask the stewardess for a blindfold,' I said. He took the joke, and the hint, and turned back to his smiling, excited friends.

There was a night, back in April, when I was leaving a pub try-out gig, down the stairs and out through the crowded bar below. It was one of those places where the in-crowd gathered, the beautiful people, the cool; the sort of bar where I feel even more of an outsider than usual. Music thumped, mobile phones glowed in the darkness and shot glasses slammed hard on tables; the excited chatter of attractive people who knew they were attractive people filled the air. I swerved and side-stepped my way towards the exit, eager to be in my car, The Fall playing loud, the passenger seat empty. I was six feet from the door when someone grabbed my arm, like a smouldering sinner seeking my help as I passed, Dante-like, through Hell.

I turned, slightly alarmed, and saw a beautiful young woman. She looked like one of those eye-candy actresses from *Neighbours* or *Home and Away*: short blonde hair, perfect white teeth; a breast-hugging crop-top above a tight, tanned belly. 'Come and have a drink with me and my friends,' she said, shouting above the crowd, still clutching at my arm. Had it been the man on the plane, or any man, or any unattractive woman, I would have wrenched myself free, smiled an excuse and left, but I was single at the time, and if this woman collapsed, I would not be reaching for the tramp-mask.

She seemed to sense that I was in her magnetic field and could not walk away; I guessed it was a phenomenon she was extremely familiar with. Had Pope Benedict XVI been passing by, on a ceremonial throne carried by four Swiss Guards, even he, once he'd seen who'd touched the hem of his garment, would have stopped to have a drink with her and her friends. The prey subdued, she relaxed her vice-like grip on my arm, gently took, instead, my right hand, and led me through the crowd. The touch of her delicate fingers put everything, from my knees to my navel, on red alert. In a trice I was at her table, trying to find cola in a glass of ice and talking to a teenage DJ in a baseball cap and a dark-haired girl in spectacles who said she just wanted to go home. My new friend, let's call her Fiona, was sitting opposite me and fixing me with her Promised Land stare.

'I've got an idea I'd really like to run by you,' she said. I looked to the bar for bananas but saw only lemons and limes. That sounds like an opening line to a Marie Lloyd song. Fiona continued, 'It's a charity idea.' 'Hopefully some sexual version of Help the Aged,' I thought. 'It's called Let's Clean India,' she said.

'Oh, not this again,' said the girl in the spectacles. The DJ lowered his baseball cap and got lost in the rhythm of the bar's pulsating beat.

'The trouble with India,' Fiona continued, 'is that everyone tries to solve the problems it already has rather than prevent those problems from happening in the first place.' Oh, dear. If I did get lucky it would be like fucking Bob Geldof. She went on, 'You see, the reason there's so much disease in India is because the place is absolutely filthy.' Maybe it would be more like fucking Jade Goody. 'So here's my plan,' she said, leaning forward. I could smell the amalgam of her toiletries: shampoos and gels; lip-gloss and mascara. 'It would be expensive,' she said. I looked at the door. 'But it would save a lot of lives.'

In one last attempt to find cola, I tipped back my head till my glass was virtually upside down. I succeeded only in numbing the whole area around my nostrils and upper lip.

'We'd get a load of tanker lorries,' Fiona explained, with the confidence of someone who knew they had hatched a master plan, 'filled with water and disinfectant and drive them into an Indian village. Then we'd attach high-power hoses to the tanks and just blast away: houses, cattle, clothes . . . everything. Then off to the next village to do exactly the same thing.'

I had an image of confused villagers swept off their feet by the powerful jets; bindis washed off, turbans unravelled, in the disinfecting onslaught. 'I guess they will have all seen elephants use a similar method to keep themselves clean and healthy,' I suggested, keen to show her I was joining in. Fiona nodded approvingly. I felt this point would be incorporated into her spiel, the next time she delivered it.

'Have you ever walked through the West End at three o'clock in the morning?' Fiona asked.

I felt slightly affronted. Did she imagine I was some sad old git, tucked up in bed by 10.30? Was it that obvious? 'Yes, of course I have,' I said. The girl in spectacles was staring at the ceiling.

'Then you'll have seen those street-cleaning machines, big yellow things, spraying and scrubbing the pavements?'

'Yes,' I said, not totally sure if I had.

'My dream is that people will put the news on one night and see a long convoy of those machines trundling across the Indian mountains, heading to the next spot on the map.'

I liked the vagueness of the phrase 'the Indian mountains', it made the country seem suddenly graspable and uncomplicated; perhaps this simplicity – clarity, even – was exactly what was needed. A fresh approach, uncluttered by experience. Half of me still thought her idea was the most ludicrous thing I'd ever heard; the other half could hear that old Sinatra song about how people laughed at Christopher Columbus when he suggested the Earth was round. Was this beautiful young woman about to save the Third World? Should we Drop the Debt and Pick up the Dettol?

I wondered if I should mention the fact that India had one of the fastest-growing economies in the world and probably didn't need any outside help, but I was loath to spoil the party. Anyway, Let's Clean Africa sounded just as good.

'You know, I'd really like it if me and you could spend some time together,' Fiona said. I looked into her eyes, desperately trying to remember if I had nice pants on. 'I want you to teach me,' she added. I couldn't feel my legs. 'I want you to show me how you did it, how you channelled your energy to be successful.' Was I supposed to do this before we'd fucked, or after? She, once again, took my right hand in hers. If she was checking for sharp fingernails it was definitely a good sign. She looked at me intently. Was that sudden thud the DJ putting his pint down or my erection hitting the underside of the table? 'Have you ever seen *The Karate Kid*?' she asked. I nodded, suddenly confused. 'I want you to be my Mr Miyagi,' she said.

'You mean the white-haired Oriental guy, in his sixties, who teaches the main character about karate and life in general?' I said.

'Yeah, that's right,' she said. My heart sank and so did the table. I decided it was time to leave. I withdrew my right hand; it needed rest before the busy night ahead. 'I'm around most days if you'd like to meet up,' she said.

'Days aren't good for me,' I explained. 'Don't you work?' I added.

'Only nights,' she said. 'I'm a dancer at Stringfellow's.'

As I drove home alone, listening to The Fall, I imagined Fiona in the Stringfellow's dressing room, as other girls buzzed around in various stages of nakedness, bent over a map of India, using an eyebrow pen to mark her route. I wondered if Stringfellow's was hosed down with disinfectant at the end of each night – seats de-spunked, poles de-slimed – and this was how she'd got her inspiration.

Speaking of beautiful woman, there was one standing outside the Shelbourne Hotel in Dublin when I returned there after last night's gig. She had bright crimson hair and smoked a cigarette in a theatrical fashion. It is one of the nice things about my monogamy that I can look at a woman like that and admire her the way I might admire a fabulous painting; happy to enjoy her aesthetically, without the dreary trimmings of seduction – trying to catch her eye in the bar, the hope she'll recognise me, the hope she'll be impressed, the desperation of pursuit, the trashy obviousness of it all. This is also one of the great advantages of not drinking: the thrill of cold control.

Of course, age, by itself, brings a change in one's attitude to women. I was sitting post try-out gig in a North London pub about six months ago with a group of women, one of whom works with my manager. She had come to see the show in a professional capacity and brought a few friends along for a night out. One of these friends was a pretty, dark-haired girl who was talking about her current on-off relationship with a guy who, it seemed to me, was just, as they say, messing her around; she would get an affectionate text and then not hear from him for five or six days. She kind of agreed with my negative interpretation but explained she'd been single for a while and suggested she was prepared to put up with a certain amount of indifferent behaviour rather than be on her own.

'Listen,' I said. 'I'm a fifty-year-old man. You're a woman in your early twenties. The age-gap is clearly insurmountable. There is and never could be anything between us.' I probably did scan her face for any hint of disappointment at this statement but, having found none, I went on to make my speech. 'You are a very attractive young woman, with a kind of Jennifer Aniston feel about you, funny and cute. If I was twenty-five years younger, and thought I was in with a chance, I'd be texting you ten times a day to let you know how great I thought you were. Believe me, there are thousands of young guys out there who would kill to get close to someone like you. You don't have to take second-best, and you don't have to take shit from anyone. You – and, as I've pointed out, I have no dark reasons for saying this – are a fucking spectacularly good catch. Don't doubt yourself. You deserve someone really special. Just wait and he'll come.' A big grin went across her cute face. It felt good to be able to tell a woman how great she was without having a sly agenda behind the praise. Let's face it, I already am Mr Miyagi.

When I walked past that crimson-haired woman and into the Dublin hotel, two guys sitting near the door immediately stood up to applaud me. She was attractive, but not SO attractive that being able to walk unhesitatingly past her warranted a standing ovation. But, no. It turned out these guys were at the gig and were applauding because they enjoyed the show. They assured me they honestly weren't taking the piss, and, I must admit, it put a spring in my step as I headed up the stairs to my room.

SUNDAY 30 SEPTEMBER 2007

It's two in the morning and, once again, I'm sitting up in bed, in my Birmingham flat. It was what I would call an interesting show tonight. I played the Princes Hall, Aldershot. I must have spent at least four minutes before going in gazing at the front of the venue, fretting about the apostrophe. I'd have bigger worries than grammar before the evening was done. It had been such a lovely day as well.

I woke up in Folkestone after a cracking gig the night before; or, at least, a gig that became cracking after an initial falter. Very early on in the show, I spoke to a guy in the front row about a story in the local paper. A man had been found guilty of stealing an item worth £497, which the newspaper described as 'equipment to assist in reversing a car'.

'Isn't that a rear-view mirror?' I asked the man in the front row.

His friend immediately chipped in, 'This is Laurie. He was at your gig in Hayes last night. And he's going across to see you in Dorking.'

I knew Adam would wince when he heard that, a man referring to Dorking and no one in the theatre shouting, 'Where the fuck is that?' To make matters worse, Laurie's friend had referred to both

Hayes and Dorking without, at any time, using the word 'sunny'. Despite these blows, Adam's consternation could not have equalled my own. I know it's a great compliment that anyone would see me three times on the same tour, but it hits me hard on that 'sorry if you've heard this before' level I wrote about in Edinburgh. I saw The Fall seven times on their last tour, but, as I've said, music is different: you want to hear it again and again. Not so with jokes. 'You know it's basically the same stuff,' I told Laurie, in an apologetic tone. I was ashamed to admit that to him and, indeed, to the audience in general. He looked at me like he really didn't believe me, like he fully expected to hear a completely different show from the one he'd heard the previous night.

Once I'd got the local stuff out of the way, again breaking Jerry Seinfeld's rule about never starting with untried material, I moved into my usual set. There were some changes – I'd woken up at four o'clock that morning and scribbled down a whole lot of restructuring ideas and some new lines that seemed to come to me in a dream – but it was still, basically, about ninety minutes of stuff Laurie had heard before. The worst bits – the moments that made me feel genuinely ashamed, were my un-ad-libbed ad-libs; I just couldn't look him in the eye.

The whole un-ad-libbed ad-lib phenomenon is an interesting moral dilemma for the stand-up comedian. I once stood at the back of the Comedy Store in Leicester Square, watching a comic completely mess up a *Star Trek* joke and then get good laughs as he squirmed his way out of the, by then, ruined routine. He eventually just gave up and collapsed into a laughing fit. The audience applauded this touching moment. I joined in. 'He does that every night, word for word,' a comic next to me whispered. Sure enough, I saw the same act two months later, with exactly the same cock-up and laughing fit. I was unimpressed. It somehow seemed dishonest, phoney. There is a difficult distinction here. As I've said, when I went through my post-gig check-lists, I would often add lines that I'd improvised that night – this is simply the writing process occurring mid-performance – but to retain a mistake, something that one would never sit and write, seems to fit into another category: a sort of cheesy falseness.

Let me offer an example from my own set. At one point I talk about visiting an African village with some people from Comic Relief. When telling the story one night, I said, with no comedic intentions:

When we got to the entrance of the village, it was very moving. The village people had lined up and were forming a sort of . . .

By now the audience were laughing and it took me a while to realise it was because I'd said 'the village people', the name of the iconic seventies gay band who did 'YMCA'. It was a simple slip of the tongue, but I ran with it:

No, no, not the VILLAGE PEOPLE; they weren't there. If they'd have been lined up, who knows, I might have been tempted. After all, I was on my holidays, sort of.

The crowd then seemed to laugh at the idea of noble Comic Relief work in Africa being described in such flippant terms. This led into a mime of me sunbathing and saying to someone, in a dismissive tone, 'Look, I must do another twenty minutes on this side. Just give them some more rice.' And, again, laughter ensued.

I wouldn't want any of this stuff to be sealed in a time-capsule containing representative examples of my work, but laughs is laughs so I was tempted to repeat the process the next night. The writing-onstage idea justified the latter end of the material, but the real problem, for me, was having to 'accidentally' use the phrase 'village people' and then, worse still, 'laugh' when I 'realised' what I'd said. That isn't stand-up comedy, it's acting. Nevertheless, the lure of the laughs took me through the shame barrier and I've been accidentally saying 'village people' ever since.

With Laurie in easy eye-shot, I considered not saying it in Folkestone. Why grind my poor, disillusioned now-ex-fan into the dirt? But when it came to that point in the act, I just gritted my teeth, averted my eyes and said 'village people'. I couldn't resist a quick peep at him one second after my phoney laugh. He had the look of a man who'd just discovered his father got paid to suck cock.

Adam, of course, hears my repeated ad-libs every night – unless he turns the dressing-room speaker off when I'm not there – but he has never mentioned it. He has worked with other comedians and, I'm sure, accepts it as part of the game. Maybe he regards such moments as my 'little sayings' and smiles with affection at a kindred spirit. I don't know why it troubles me so. It's not exclusively a stand-up thing. I was in a shop recently, and the young female assistant, funny and flirty, suddenly said, 'I bet you're glad it isn't raining, like yesterday.'

'Erm, yes,' I said, not sure why she'd brought it up.

'Still,' she said, with a cheeky grin, 'it's good to get wet sometimes.' I felt sure she had made this remark yesterday, and probably on several other rainy days, and it had gone down well. Now, totally drawn in by the positive customer reaction, she had, on dry days, when the joke was not apposite, taken to back-referring to previous wet days in order to crowbar in the gag. Comedians are not the only ones who keep their ad-libs in formaldehyde.

What tinkering I had done with the set seemed to be successful. I resisted the temptation to conduct a check-as-I-went ongoing workshop with Laurie after each change, making a mental note of his thumbs-up or thumbs-down gestures and agreeing to re-convene in Dorking for a final de-briefing.

Anyway, back to today. This morning, Adam and I went for quite a long walk around Folkestone's 'creative quarter', an area where artists are encouraged, mainly by the offer of reduced rent, to live and work – another example of the British seaside resorts' Bohemianisation. Adam told me, during our art-based wandering, that he collects images of the Virgin Mary, anything from stickers to statues, prayer-cards to paintings. I'm intrigued by this. I put it to him that this could be more than just an ironic appreciation of kitsch religious iconography, that it might suggest some deeper subconscious yearning. He seemed sceptical but didn't dismiss it out of hand. I wondered if he'd doctored the lyrics of Hot Chocolate's 'I Believe in Miracles', replacing 'miracles' with 'mackerels', because he DOES believe in miracles but is loath to admit it. Then again, in saying that he believes in mackerels, is he declaring his faith in all fish symbolism and thus Christianity itself? As I say, it was quite a long walk.

On the way to Aldershot, we saw a sign for Jane Austen's house. I like a literary place of interest, but when we arrived it was shut. We got into the garden and a couple of nondescript outhouses, even looked through some ground-floor windows, but the actual house – even the shop, where, I imagine, we could have bought a souvenir eraser or some *Mansfield Park* fudge – was barred and shuttered. Probably just as well. I've never got into Jane Austen, but when I visit a birthplace or home or even graveside of a literary or historical figure, I often get completely obsessed with them for about a fortnight, checking websites, buying books and DVDs, and then the fad passes and my *Pride and Prejudice* is for ever bookmarked at page fourteen, my half-grown Mr Darcy whiskers shaved and forgotten. And these obsessions, literary or otherwise, don't need to be tied to anything as concrete as visiting a historical site. I can see a picture in the paper, hear something on the radio or even just have a thought come, out of the blue, into my head – and then there's a mind-altering moment and the obsession kicks in. They're not all short-term. Some take root and last for years, maybe for ever – The Fall, baseball, Breugel – but even the two-week wonders always leave a trace, a bulging dossier at the back of my mind, always there to flick through if the obsession returns.

Luckily, Jane Austen's house having been such a flop, I saw a sign for Selborne. I had vaguely heard of the Reverend Gilbert White's book *A Natural History of Selborne*, but didn't really know anything about it or him. I had an image of an eighteenth-century country vicar crawling around his village pond and pastures with a magnifying glass and a notebook, drawing quick sketches of cuckoo spit on burdock and scribbling long descriptions of newts, the locals tutting at his muddy stockings and sniggering at his wayward hair. This is how the thing starts with me: a vague yearning for knowledge – of astronomy or Gandhi, Tarzan or drawing, Buddha or chess – and then I feel a sort of wave wash across me, like I'm being photocopied, my brain seems to ever so slightly wobble and I know the obsession is upon me, fixed like a limpet for as long as it takes. Suddenly I was desperate to visit

Gilbert White's house, to read his book. I imagined becoming an expert on him, getting into nature, being able to recognise insects at a glance, to know their Latin names, to recognise bird cries and footprints, to get a cottage in Selborne, to sit drinking tea in my herb garden watching a spider dance across a dew-spangled web in the early morning sunshine. Bear in mind, I get bored in the country, detest gardening and am frightened of spiders. Suddenly, none of that matters. Whenever the obsession hits, a new year-zero begins. Gilbert White's house was going to be life-changing, I just knew it.

Of course, it was fucking shut. But now the hooks were in, it would take more than that to put me off. Across the road from the house was St Mary's, Selborne. Everything you'd want from an English country church: the feel of cold grey stone, the smell of candle-smoke; stained-glass dappling across the rows of wooden pews. The stained-glass in question was a large window showing St Francis of Assisi surrounded by dozens of multi-coloured birds – at his feet, cradled in his arms, encircling his halo. St Francis is often shown in the midst of nature; some Catholics like to portray him as an early environmentalist. He used to preach to the birds and, so the story goes, on his deathbed he thanked his donkey for years of carrying him and his associated loads. Legend says the donkey wept. I would love to have heard what that sounded like.

Anyway, Gilbert White was the vicar of St Mary's and the comparison with St Francis, their shared 'each little flower that opens/ each little bird that sings' approach to Christianity, seemed to be what the window was hammering home. As I, with my new-found love of nature, studied each pane of plumage, I suddenly realised that at my feet was Gilbert's grave: a simple flat black stone with just his name and dates. Even though I still wasn't sure exactly who Gilbert White was or what he'd done, I felt extremely emotional. The obsession always races ahead; the facts come much later. Adam looked at his watch. The gig was nigh. I said a prayer for dear old Gilbert – not easy with such scant knowledge of his life. Half an hour ago he was a vaguely remembered name; now, suddenly, he was at the centre of my universe. Still, for now, I had to put the obsession on pause. There was work to do.

The Aldershot gig didn't start that well. They never really went for the local material. As Aldershot is an army town, I thought I'd better talk about the army. I referred to the commonly held view that 'our boys in the Gulf' are under-funded and therefore short of equipment. I said that army surplus stores will soon go through a complete role reversal and civilians will be taking in their old combat trousers and camouflage-print t-shirts so they can be distributed to the troops. The local stuff has gone pretty well this week. In Folkestone, thieves had been stealing copper from the town's roofs and I suggested it was being used to supply local pensioners with black-market arthritis bracelets. That got a good laugh. They like a pensioner joke at the seaside. Aldershot weren't having any of it, though, so I moved on to the tried and trusted opening. They laughed, settled in, and all was well.

Now, as I've explained previously, during the building of this current act I tried a few paedophile jokes. It's a hot topic in modern Britain and, as with apposite subjects like street performers in Edinburgh, or the army in Aldershot, to NOT include it seems to me to be a glaring omission, a cop-out. Thus, those few paedophile-related jokes that survived the journey are still very much in the set. There is one joke which seems to particularly upset Middle England and I've come to see it as my test-joke. If it goes well, I know the show will rock; if it goes badly, and they get uncomfortable, I have to back off, be a bit gentler, and the show isn't quite so much fun. The joke comes about ten minutes in, which is way too early for that kind of joke, but I just can't wait to see how it goes.

So what I now have, set-wise, is an opening of five or so minutes of local stuff I've just written in the dressing room, which is inevitably hit and miss, then ten minutes of fairly certain laughs, then the test-joke.

Now, as I've said, paedophilia itself is obviously horrible and wrong blah-blah, so I avoid the actual act and concentrate on less-upsetting periphery things. This particular joke works differently. The idea is it sounds like it's going to be a really horrible joke but then, at the last minute, it turns into a silly one. Here goes:

I've often wondered, when a new paedophile arrives in town, does he seek out an older, more experienced, local paedophile and say, 'So, where's the best places round here to pick up kids?' And does the old paedophile look at him, blow out his cheeks, shrug his shoulders and say, 'Well . . . swings and roundabouts, really.'

The night after my Canadian gig from Hell I was standing in the wings, a little shaky to be returning to the same stage. Five or six minutes into the act, they were laughing and I'd regained my confidence. Canada liked me. I was back. So what did I do? I told the swings and roundabouts joke. There were no laughs, nor were there heckles or boos; there was just an uneasy silence. Now, to silence a whole crowd in the middle of a good gig is quite a task. The line had been getting big laughs in England so I didn't quite know what had happened. I left the stage, puzzled, and bumped into one of the Canadian guys who'd organised the show. 'Shit,' I said, 'they really didn't like the swings and roundabouts joke.'

'I didn't get it,' he said.

'Well,' I said, even more puzzled, 'you know that saying, "swings and roundabouts"?'

'No,' he said, 'I've never heard it. We don't have that saying in Canada.' He left me to process this new information. What the fuck did the audience think I meant, then? Did they honestly believe that, in the middle of a comedy show, I'd stopped to tell an anecdote in which a young paedophile asks an old paedophile, 'Where's the best places round here to pick up kids?' and the old paedophile just TELLS him? 'If I was you, I'd try swings and roundabouts.' 'Thank you very much. That's most helpful.' Why the fuck would I do that?

Anyway, they got the joke in Aldershot; they just didn't like it. This was tour-gig number eighteen and the first time that joke had gone badly. 'You are a sick man,' shouted one guy. Another, slightly oddly, yelled, 'This is not good.' I have to admit, my replies weren't exactly from the heckle-response top-drawer. I told the first guy to 'fucking grow up', and I said to the second, 'You look like the kind of bloke who has twelve pints, drives home and then slaps your wife; now you're here, moaning about jokes.' Inside my head, of course, it was more stagger than swagger. There was a general hubbub, a break in the audience–performer relationship; I sensed that I might lose them.

Coincidentally, a few nights before, while watching the darts on late-night TV, I became acutely aware of how much the players' throwing was affected by their mental state. An experienced darter could be going really well, but then a miss, or the realisation that he was near the finishing line, any minor disturbance, would suddenly change everything. They couldn't throw; their body-shape, even their faces, seemed different. They were the same player with the same ability; they just seemed to have forgotten that obvious fact. It didn't make any sense. Now, I'm not claiming this is an earth-shattering new discovery that will rewrite sports-psychology, but it was a helpful thing to have at the back of my mind when it all went a bit Middle England in Aldershot. I took a breath, resettled myself at the oche and made sure the three darts after the swings and roundabouts joke were just as steady and sure as the three jokes before it. The audience, apparently reassured by this, quietly dismounted their high horses and started laughing again. There was no need for me to change anything. They continued to laugh, and laugh heartily, to the end of the show. Just for old times' sake, because it was Aldershot, I took my heartbeat in the dressing room afterwards: 80 bpm; still alive.

Unless you're doing a sanitised stand-up act, with one eye on a mainstream TV presenter's job, you always run the risk of upsetting people in the crowd. Almost every joke has the power to offend someone. There will be a woman out there whose parents were killed in a car crash as they swerved to avoid a chicken that was crossing the road; a man whose wife was electrocuted changing a light bulb; a couple whose cancer-stricken dog has got no nose. You have to make your own judgements and allow for a certain number of casualties. If the upset comes from a collision with Middle England, I'm rarely filled with remorse. I don't, by any stretch, see myself as a shock-comic. I see myself as a comic who, in the pursuit of a laugh, might occasionally slightly shock; but you forgive him because he's more naughty schoolboy than holier-than-thou taboo-basher. If what I say onstage upsets anyone, it's an accident, but obviously there are some jokes which, I know, make that accident a bit more likely. Sometimes, however, I don't see the accident coming at all.

Folkestone was, as I said, a good gig, but there was a moment in that show that is still in my thoughts, sitting here in Birmingham, more than twenty-four hours later – a moment, unnoticed by most of the crowd, which troubles me much more than tonight's moral indignation.

Whenever I'm on tour, I become aware of other shows that are touring at the same time. When I arrive at the theatre, I always ask for a 'what's on' brochure and I'll often talk about the previous or forthcoming attractions at that theatre, during my act. For example, The Black Dyke Band are touring at the moment. Well, it's hard to resist, isn't it? I just say The Black Dyke Band are touring and then mutter, 'It's political correctness gone mad.' If only it was always that easy.

Plays, bands, comedians, these are the staples, and if you tour this time of the year there'll be a panto as well – usually featuring, as the poster proudly boasts, someone like Southern FM's Danny Pike. But this tour I've noticed a new phenomenon: the rise of the theatre spiritualist. I know these kinds of shows have been around for years, but suddenly, in secular Britain of all places, it's boom-time. Everywhere I've played there is always at least one dead-disturber in the listings. I was talking about this during the Folkestone show, about how Derek Acorah is the king of the spiritualists, but it seems ironic that his shows are on Living TV. Then I told a story that a friend had told me about a spiritualist show he had been to see:

There's five hundred people packed into this little theatre and this spiritualist guy comes onstage and he seems really normal.

He says, in a calm and friendly voice, 'Thank you so much for coming. We are going to go on a strange journey tonight. We will explore worlds that are largely unknown and . . .' Then suddenly the spiritualist starts holding his head and saying, in a feverish manner, 'The letter D . . . does the letter D mean anything to anyone here?' Nothing; not a whisper from the crowd. Five hundred people, none of whom have had any experience of the letter D. The spiritualist is pacing the stage, holding his head but occasionally having a sly peek at the crowd, clearly desperate for a raised hand. At last he says, 'It's D . . . D for "Dad".'

What a masterstroke; what a fabulous piece of damage limitation. I really wish, though, that just for that night the crowd had been from some single-mothers' organisation, out for a bit of light relief during their locally held three-day convention. Child and adult looking at each other and saying, 'Dad? Doesn't ring any bells with me.'

Pretty soon the spiritualist guy would have been on his knees, holding his head and saying, 'It's D . . . D for "dead relative".'

I asked if anyone in the crowd had been to the theatre's recent spiritualist night. A young girl near the front raised her hand. I quizzed her on the event and asked her if she believed in all that stuff. She admitted she did. 'But surely it's all bollocks?' I said. She smiled and nodded but it was a sad smile, a smile that seemed to take her into herself, that caused her head to drop. The bloke sitting next to her, I assume her boyfriend, put his arm around her. Clearly the subject was a raw one and I was happily drilling holes in that fragile little boat which, it seemed to me, was just about keeping her afloat on a dark sea of despair. What right did I have to let the water in? I believe in a lot of unbelievable things myself.

The thing is, I worry about the whole contacting-the-dead phenomenon. There are three possible explanations: one, it's true; two, it's bollocks but the spiritualist THINKS it's true; three, the spiritualist knows it's bollocks but they pretend it's true. I'm OK with the first two possibilities – either could apply to my religious beliefs, for all I know – but the third is surely unforgivable. Of course, my current concern with spiritualism is all about whether it's funny or not, but what about that girl in Folkestone? If the spiritualist who gave her solace was from the third category, a pretender, he deserves to be ridiculed and dismissed. However, in undermining him I also end up puncturing her fragile little boat. Did she leave the theatre last night suddenly doubting that very thing which, over the last few weeks, had given her consolation? If the crowd continue to laugh at the steadily expanding spiritualist routine, will I keep doing it, despite its potentially unsettling effect on the bereaved – probably a weaker and less-able-to-defend-themselves group than the assembled troops of Middle England? Yeah, I probably will. Just like that dodgy spiritualist, I have to give 'em a show; I have to make them marvel at my special gift.

I wonder if the spiritualist ever looks at the front row and thinks, 'Oh, shit. That guy was in last night. I'll have to choose a different letter.'

What a strange job stand-up comedy is. Up there onstage for nearly two hours, telling my stories, hypersensitive to their responses: their disappointment at my sleight-of-hand faux-spontaneity; their outrage at my taboo-tilting; their sadness at my sneer. 'You are a sick man' is fairly easy to interpret, but the rest . . . how much of it is actually true and how much is my neurotic imagination? That bloke might have put his arm around the girl because he thought I was trying to chat her up; Laurie might suffer with Alzheimer's disease and honestly have thought it WAS a completely different show. The woman outside the stage door in Buxton last week who said, 'Can I hug you? I love people who've triumphed over adversity' might not have meant I'd gone well DESPITE my act. I could, of course, have asked her to clarify her statement, but I'd rather have nagging doubt than nagging certainty.

How many of my bad gigs have been objectively bad gigs; how many good gigs objectively good? Apart from the individual debriefing option, it's very difficult to tell. Even when I used to fuck representatives of the crowd, I NEVER asked them what they actually thought of the show. If they had praised it, I would have dismissed that praise as sycophancy – foreplay, even. If they had criticised it, I fear it might have transformed the ensuing sex into a snarling, pinching, cervix-pounding act of revenge.

It is, more or less, a sell-out tour but what does that prove? Maybe they're here out of curiosity, have got their answer and will never, never return. *How's the tour going?* That's what all the texts say, but I just don't fucking know. My manager wouldn't give me an honest answer, nor would Adam; their professional obligations forbid it. I don't read reviews; but then, even if I did, I've heard a million stories about reviewers that praise or condemn for covert, ulterior reasons. I never ask people who've seen the show because they might politely praise me or jealously tear me down.

I hear the crowd laugh or not laugh. That has always been the only response I ever trusted. Even that now somehow – through heightened cynicism or growing paranoia – seems to be up for grabs. I don't know and I can never know, never truly know, how the tour's going. There is no objective answer. Its success, or lack of it, lies in the eye of the beholder, of every individual who's seen the show. If they loved it, the tour's going great; if they hated it, the tour's going shit. And then there's the thousand shades of grey in between. Judging by the laughs I hear, the ayes have it at the moment. I'm working hard to get as many votes as I can.

Perhaps none of this really matters. Perhaps the mere doing of the tour is its glory – and I am definitely doing it, as well as I possibly can. I am a stand-up comedian but I simply don't know, can't know, what adjective should go between 'a' and 'stand-up'. I must be content to leave it blank.

A siren wails in the street below. I bookmark my agonising and check my watch. It's almost 3 a.m. Where I live, in London, I hear so many sirens I don't really hear them at all. They're so common-place they melt into city-noise; an alarm that no longer alarms. Terrible accidents, violent crimes, heart attacks, rape: someone's talk-about-it-the-rest-of-their-life moment zips by half-ignored. Even out there in the street, where the speeding vehicle flashes and screams, passers-by just pass by, the blue lights lighting and un-lighting their oblivious, preoccupied faces.

There is a story from Greek legend about a father who makes wings for himself and his young son, Icarus. He warns the boy not to fly too close to the sun because the wax which holds the wings together will melt and he will fall. Of course, the boy disobeys and drops into the sea. The Flemish painter Breugel painted his own version of the legend. In it there is no spectacular fall, no horrified expression on the boy's face, no distraught father vainly swooping to save him. There is, in the foreground, a man ploughing; behind him ships sail by and a shepherd looks to the sky at something strange he saw, or thought he saw. Where is Icarus? In the bottom right-hand corner of the picture, you can just catch two flailing legs, disappearing beneath the waves. The picture is called *The Fall of Icarus*, but Icarus barely appears. As W.H. Auden pointed out in his poem 'Musee des Beaux Arts', that's how personal tragedy often goes: unnoticed and uncommented upon. YOUR life-defining moment is someone else's incidental backdrop.

Downstairs in the street tonight, someone's crisis is screaming for attention. Perhaps a blurred medic in a smell-of-disinfectant ambulance is someone's last view of the world; perhaps a man kneels in his own blood and wonders when they'll come; perhaps a frightened mother, lost in smoke and smoulder, cries quietly so she'll hear the rescuers' approach. But it isn't ME the sirens scream for, not tonight. No, I'm sitting, ten storeys high, in my nice warm bed, getting dramatic about stand-up comedy. It's important, but not sirens-and-blue-flashing-lights important. I'm not Icarus. I'm the guy with the plough – always in my own foreground, no matter how many people are dropping from the sky. The shepherd's asking me, 'How's the ploughing going?' and I'm struggling to sort out my reply: 'Is ploughing ever objectively good or bad, or is the mere act of ploughing all that counts? I am a ploughman, but I don't know which adjective . . .' The shepherd turns away, mutters, 'Cunt' and heads back to his sheep.

I need to get things in perspective, to enjoy the journey, embrace this whole rich and varied tour-experience. In fact, what I really need, I see now, what will truly change my life and make me, at last, completely content, is Gilbert White's *Natural History of Selborne*. I'll buy it tomorrow.

FRIDAY 5 OCTOBER 2007

We're on our way to Dorking. That argument seems a long time ago now. Adam and I are getting on fine. Last night, after the Bournemouth gig, we walked down the dark beach at Boscombe till we reached the ragged edge of the sea, and stood staring up at the swirling masses of un-light-polluted stars, their grandeur almost scary; Adam and me and our half-forgotten argument, very, very small.

When we checked out of our Bournemouth hotel this afternoon, I said to the owner, 'This is the coolest place I've ever stayed.' From his expression, I think he may have guessed that, coming from me, this was not necessarily a compliment. The hotel was called Urban Beach; I think you get the picture. When we arrived, in bright autumn sunshine, it was like an episode of *Home and Away*: lots of pretty teenagers, of both sexes, sat in the outside bar, all surf-gear and tousled sun-bleached hair; the Arctic Monkeys' 'Fluorescent Adolescent' was playing loud. Being a fifty-year-old non-swimmer carrying a ukulele in a black, battered old case, I decided not to join them. In reception a teenage boy offered to carry my bag upstairs. I wondered if they'd brought back bob-a-job week, but no, it turned out he was the manager, in flip-flops. Despite his footwear, and the fact he was carrying my heavy bag, the helpful youth had to wait a good eight or nine seconds at the top of the stairs for me to finally complete my ascent.

I've almost given up on communicating with the young and beautiful, following an incident in a West End bar back in February. I had recently turned fifty and, in order to celebrate my golden jubilee, I'd decided to have a gold tooth fitted. I already had a false tooth, a white one, right at the front, so it was a simple case of replacing that with the gold one. My dentist advised me against it, as did the dental technician whose job was to make the new tooth. This latter fellow said gold teeth were very unfashionable and all those people who'd had them fitted in the nineties had since had them removed. Nevertheless, I'd made up my mind. The very second the tooth was fitted, I fell in love with it; it seemed to blend much better with the surrounding teeth than the white one ever did. I also thought it made me look quite 'street'.

A couple of days later, I was meeting a friend in a very fashionable bar in St Martin's Lane. It was early evening. My friend hadn't arrived yet, so I sat on a barstool and chatted to the barmaid. She was, I would guess, early twenties and very attractive. I could tell she had no idea who I was, but I noticed her checking out my new tooth. She was, I guessed, probably thinking I was some kind of hip-hop dude. Then she spoke. 'Do you work on the waltzers?' she said.

I felt my estrangement from all that is young, pretty and fashionable even more strongly in Bournemouth, because my ganglion had returned. A ganglion is a vile cyst that swells into a lump – usually, like mine, on the joint of the wrist. It is fucking painful and also, to make matters worse, seems to be very much an old person's ailment – a sort of lumpy, inflamed, puss-filled messenger of mortality. There is something slightly medieval about the word 'ganglion'; I wouldn't be surprised to discover that the Venerable Bede had one. Anyway, I doubt it's a subject that crops up very often at Urban Beach. I would guess any blemish on that crowd outside could only be sun- or skateboard-related.

My ganglion made its first appearance at the beginning of the year, just in time for my fiftieth birthday. Some men have a half-naked woman jump out of their birthday cake; I had a puss-lump jump out of my wrist. I only discovered the ganglion by accident. I had been suffering with back pain – at my age it never rains but it pours – and was having weekly sessions with a cranial osteopath, a very charming Oriental man whose gentle, almost ethereal, method seemed to make no fucking difference whatsoever. He didn't even touch me that much; he just held his hands about six inches above my back and looked like he was really concentrating. I half expected to levitate, and felt, when I didn't, I'd slightly let him down. Cranial osteopathy, recommended by a slightly hippyish type I knew, seemed to be all about emotional stress and body-rhythms. What I wanted was Deep Heat; or at least, in deference to the practitioner, Tiger Balm. One day, as my Oriental non-healer waved in the general direction of my lumber region, I thought I might as well mention that my wrist had been hurting. He looked at it, said two things were 'jammed' and suggested I made another appointment. I suppose cranial osteopathy is too trendy to even register a ganglion.

A couple of weeks later, I gave up hope of a cosmic cure and went to see a physiotherapist, a sporty, no-nonsense Irish woman whose personality was as strong as her fingers. She, after laughing out loud at my mention of cranial osteopathy, massaged and manipulated my back till, wrapped in a cloud of reassuring embrocation, it started to feel normal again. When I showed her my wrist she took one quick look and said, 'You have a ganglion. Hit it with a Bible.' I smiled edgily but she insisted. 'That's what you do with a ganglion. Get a really big old Bible and give it a whack. It'll go splat and no more ganglion.' I could smell the Venerable Bede all over this remedy. It must have been his idea. If the only thing you OWN is a big old Bible, it's obviously going to feature in your home remedies. I wouldn't like to have gone to him with testicular cancer.

I decided to take a slightly more sophisticated approach to my own ganglion problem and went to see my doctor the next day. He is based in fashionable Sloane Square and, despite the fact that his general manner is not dissimilar to that of Roger Moore in *The Persuaders* – I once arrived at his surgery to find him discussing, with Ronnie Corbett, the best places to buy silk pocket-handkerchiefs – the occasional well-fingered medical journal on his desk suggests that, professionally, he is at the cutting edge.

'You might want to try hitting it with a Bible,' he said, rolling his thumb over my lump.

'How big a Bible would I need?' I asked, deciding I might as well go with the flow. I own a few Bibles but they're of a size more likely to produce a doink than a splatter.

'Well, now,' said my doctor, clearly feeling he was being painted into a medieval corner, 'it doesn't actually HAVE to be a Bible. Just use the heaviest book you've got. Or, alternatively, you might want to bang it up against a wall. If that doesn't work,' he added, as he adjusted one of the ornately framed eighteenth-century oil-paintings that hang above his desk, 'we'll send you off to a specialist and he'll cut it out.'

Back at my flat, I opted for the *Collins English Dictionary* – hardback, of course. Luckily the ganglion was on my left wrist so, being right-handed, I was able to give the book a mighty swing before bringing it down on the back of my hand. The ganglion is sore at the best of times; hitting it with a heavy book caused me to actually cry out – an 'Aaaaaaaaaagh' that lasted for about five seconds. No wonder the Venerable Bede lived alone on an island. Even medieval neighbours wouldn't have put up with that on a regular basis. The lump really, really hurt and no hint of a splatter. By the time I'd hit it a third time, I was actually in tears.

I put down the book and suddenly, without even looking, I slapped the wall hard with the back of my hand, like a Nazi trying to surprise a tight-lipped interrogatee. Aaaaaaaaaaaaaaagh. The back of my hand was already showing signs of bruising. I gave up. I wiped my eyes and called Jenny, my PA. She said she could still hear a slight tremble in my voice. I asked her to sort out my appointment with the specialist.

I sat looking at my battered hand. Despite what my doctor had said, was it possible that the Bible was a crucial element in the cure? Was some randomly chosen big book doomed to failure because it lacked the Bible's magical curative powers? Had I diminished Bede's remedy by secularising it? 'Ganglions are also known as Bible bumps,' I said to myself. 'The clue's in the name.' Maybe I was still in shock. When I calmed, I decided, for once, to adopt the Dawkins approach: to turn my back on the Bible and look to science.

A week later – yes, I go private – I was sitting opposite the genial, besuited specialist. 'I tried hitting it with the Bible,' I said, 'but it didn't seem to work.'

'Hitting it with the Bible?' he said, aghast. 'This is twenty-first-century Britain! You need to hit it with a series of books representing ALL the world religions.' He slapped his thigh with delight. Everybody's a comedian.

Anyway, he didn't cut it out. He stuck a big hypodermic needle, filled with a steroid cocktail, into my wrist and the ganglion went away. But now, ten months later, it's back. It's the archaic nature of it I hate. It would be nice to have an illness that was at least up-to-date. Bird flu or C. difficile – that's what they want to hear about at Urban Beach.

A couple of years ago I went to see a doctor about a black dot near my lip. 'It's nothing to worry about,' he said, putting down the eye-piece he'd used to examine it. 'It's what in the old days they used to call a beauty spot.' Of course, I always knew I'd get more illnesses as I got older, but I still expected them to be MODERN illnesses, not something Nell Gwynne would get. What next? A lazy eye . . . trench foot? What happens to all those old illnesses? Actually, that would make a good television series; a sort of medical version of Where Are They Now?

I don't mind, generally speaking, getting old. It's the little surprises I don't like, the unpleasant markers on the road to old age that you should be prepared for but never are. Fucking hell, I'm starting to sound like Denis Norden. It's true, though. I was in the hairdresser's a few months back, and when he'd finished cutting my hair, he said, 'Do you want me to do your ears as well?'

What was I supposed to say to that? 'Yes, please. Can you leave it quite long on the lobe but crop it short around the actual hole?'

Even more humiliating than that, I was making myself lunch a few weeks back – just a simple cheese and ham on Ryvita – when I had to make a last-minute change to my choice of relish because, wait for it, I couldn't get the top off the piccalilli jar. I was going red in the face – I could hear the thumping pulse in my neck – but I could not get that fucker off. The next day, having laid awake, fretting about the stubborn jar, I got up early and, after several attempts, spaced about twenty minutes apart so I had the chance to rest in between, I finally did it. I placed the open jar on the work surface and then gave it a heartfelt V-sign, my thrusting fingers just a couple of inches from the label, like I was giving the piccalilli an aggressive form of cranial osteopathy.

For years, whenever I've been faced with a stubborn lid or bottle top, I've always said, 'How the fuck do old people manage?' Now I know the answer. I also know the answer to that other much-asked senior-citizen-based poser 'Why do old people get up so early?' Quite simply, they HAVE to get up early – six-thirty or seven o'clock – otherwise they wouldn't have the relish jar opened by lunchtime. Then a nice cup of tea, an after-lunch nap and it's time to start work on the ketchup, or it'll be a dull breakfast in the morning.

To complete this hat-trick – or should I say this geri-hat-trick? – of signs that I'm growing old, last Tuesday I went to my doctor to get a flu jab. I only did this because it recently occurred to me that, at my age, if I get the flu, it could actually fucking kill me.

Bournemouth has made me more aware of the age-thing than ever. We went out for a walk along the beach this morning, Adam and I, and saw lots of old men in tiny Speedos, enjoying the surprisingly warm October sun. They looked, with their mega-tanned, leathery, wrinkled bodies, like the pictures you see in Roman Catholic books about the incorruptibility of saints: ghoulish faces, dried and drawn out in a rictus grin. I didn't get too close to these ancient bathers in case one shook my hand and said, 'Welcome to ganglion pain.'

We lunched at a place called Funki Sushi. One member of staff was wearing shades, indoors. The coolness army was gathering its troops on all my fronts. It launched another sortie when a beautiful young woman – a slim brunette with ice-blue eyes, a denim micro-miniskirt over brown, patterned tights – came to sit, with a not-quite-so-attractive female friend, on the table beside us. They ordered three lettuce leaves and a segment of satsuma before getting down to the job at hand: dismantling the characters of a few close mutual friends.

Meanwhile, I asked Adam about the possibility of stopping off at Stratford-upon-Avon when we headed for our next free day in Birmingham. As soon as I uttered the name of that Warwickshire town, Adam raised a hand to silence me: 'Stratford-YEW-PON-A-VON' he said (with a rhythm like 'O'Donovan'). I actually smiled.

Despite this bonhomie, my eyes, naturally enough, soon returned to the brunette. I was suddenly struck by her tight, brown t-shirt; not for the obvious reasons, but because it had emblazoned across its front the phrase 'Beautiful Forever'. Suddenly I didn't feel so bad about getting older. It has at least brought with it a certain amount of wisdom and humility, and made me think twice before using the word 'forever' about anything. In the old days I would have been falling over myself to get friendly with this woman, but at my age, falling over is a much bigger deal than it used to be. I felt no desire to speak to her – not even to inform her that, despite her optimism, 'Rough winds do shake the darling buds of May'. I considered getting a t-shirt printed up that said, 'Very average-looking, and not anticipating any improvement between now and the grave', but it was too wordy for a t-shirt and only really worked in conjunction with hers.

I looked out of the window at the street two floors below. Opposite the restaurant there was a disused crazy golf course – all the mini-helter-skelters and open-mouthed clown-faces faded and overgrown with moss, the laughter and excitement now derelict and forgotten. Speaking of my career, I've been asked to be a contestant on a one-off panel show that celebrates twenty-five years of Channel 4. I'm not usually keen on these things but, to paraphrase Dean Jones, I have to start wanting the ball to come to me again. Besides, Cath works at Channel 4, she's an assistant in their comedy department, and I like the idea of being stormingly funny on the show so she can feel proud of me at work the next day.

The not-shagging-around thing is still going fine. I ghost into town, get my fix of comedy glory then ghost back out again, like Martin Peters at a free-kick. Of course, if, shortly after the tour, Cath and I split up, I will be crippled with bitter regret at the opportunities I might have missed. Still, I'm sure I'll put a good Catholic slant on it and come to see Cath as a visiting guardian angel that saved me from my bestial self; leading me not into temptation as I roamed from town to town, spreading laughter and joy instead of my usual laughter, joy and chlamydia.

By the way, Cath and I are now officially back together and have been for nearly a month. I've managed to see her about once a week since the tour began, but I don't know if the schedule will allow me to maintain that average. I saw her on Tuesday, though. It was one of my nights off so we arranged another of our couple-counselling sessions. One of the things I suggested, during my persuasive phone calls from Canada, was that we had couple-counselling to try and get us back on track. I got Jenny to do a bit of research and she finally found us a guy who, for the purposes of this journal, I'll call Kurt.

Before I start, I know a lot of people think all counselling is nonsense – I used to think the same – but 'psycho-babble' or not, it seems to be helping Cath and me. If, ultimately, it fails, I'll have to go back to my original plan and hit her with a Bible.

I'd only ever tried counselling once before: when trying to save my marriage in 1991. My wife and I went to see a middle-aged lady from Relate, the relationship counselling agency. She was nice enough, diligent and caring, but nothing like Kurt.

Kurt is German, probably mid-thirties. He dresses all in black and has a shock of punkish black hair, its wayward quiff stopping just above his intelligent blue eyes. We've had five two-hour sessions with him now. We sit in a sparsely furnished room, a chair for each of us and a small table upon which sits an ominous box of tissues. When we're all settled – bags and drinks put down, coats off – Kurt smiles and says, 'So, how is it going?' and we're off. Honesty is the thing. Cath and I have to dig deep and lay it all bare: fears, suspicions, doubts. Things we DON'T seem able to say when alone together, we DO seem able to say with Kurt. At the first session, Cath asked me how I felt the last time we split up, about twelve months ago. I said I was angry, frustrated: 'I felt I'd spent years trying to make something work that was never going to work. I felt I'd wasted all that time, been flogging a dead horse.' Cath winced but said she understood how I felt.

'Now, that is intimacy,' Kurt said with a slight tone of celebration in his voice. We both looked at him, confused. 'To be able to say that, to be able to hear it and accept its validity, that is true intimacy. If you've got that you've got hope,' he said calmly. He says everything calmly. Before we left that first session, Kurt gave us a new approach, a sort of homework, to try out: 'If the other person says or does something that upsets you, tell them, honestly and openly, but not in an accusatory way. Don't blame them or demand a response. Try saying this: 'I'm going to tell you about something that I'm feeling, but you don't have to respond unless you really want to. I just want to let you know how I feel.' Then you, very calmly, tell the other person what's pissing you off, and that's it.

It sounded a bit clinical, inhuman even, but maybe that was just the German accent. Anyway, we decided to give it a try. By that stage, one session in, we were already seeing Kurt as the oracle. He was so fucking bright, so sharp. I really enjoyed our two hours in that room. It was exhilarating to hear a new voice talking about our old problems, inviting us to get off the drab carousel and start again. It was intellectually stimulating as well. I never realised how fascinating relationships were – their rituals and hidden messages. We were taking ours apart and seeing how it worked. We both felt we were being pro-active, no longer just letting things drift. Transforming our relationship would be a bit like editing the chat show – trying to keep all the good bits and lose most of the shit – but the rewards were much bigger . . . which is saying something considering I was on fifty-five grand a show.

Cath and I tried the 'this is what I'm feeling but you don't have to respond' formula over the next few weeks and it did feel slightly inhuman at first. One thing I discovered, when I examined my attitude to the constant arguments, was that although I hated them and all the damage they did, I was also, on one level, reluctant to let them go. I had to dig very deep to find this out, but constant arguments, when they're not just breaking your heart, make you feel like you're part of something passionate and exciting. The shouting, the slammed doors, my head in my hands: I was that tragic hero again. But it wasn't just me any more – James Dean in New York – this time there were two characters for me to dramatise. We were Richard Burton and Elizabeth Taylor: fiery, complicated, alive. Not Rock Hudson and Doris Day: happy, simple, dull. It was, of course, a chicken-and-egg job. I didn't know if I was subconsciously creating the arguments to make sure I stayed in the right film, the Burton and Taylor fight-fest; or if the arguments were, as it had always seemed, beyond my control and I was retrospectively glamorising them to make the best of a bad job.

Anyway, the new formula, though it wasn't easy to stick to, definitely helped. Cath saying, 'Just to let you know, I'm feeling distant because you snapped at me for being late this morning, but even so, I don't need you to respond' did seem to feel less confrontational than, 'OK, I was fucking late. If you don't want to be with me just fuck off!'

Over the next sessions Kurt slowly deconstructed the basic building blocks of our personalities. Apparently I'm something of a control freak who hoovers up knowledge and information to give me the reassuring feeling that I've got a grip on the world. I'm never down for long because I am constantly stimulated, constantly moving on. As Kurt put it, I feel that I DO to the universe.

Cath is more of an escapist who likes to spend time in a sort of La-La Land where troubles and pain aren't allowed; otherwise she feels blown around and out of control. She feels that the universe DOES to her.

According to Kurt, statistics show that roughly 50 per cent of people have this general sense that they DO to the universe; the other 50 per cent feel, like Cath, that the universe DOES to them. But these, of course, are generalisations. From what I saw of the darts players, it's possible to flit between the two.

Still, Cath and I do seem to fit into the 'opposites attract' bracket. Kurt says – and when Kurt says we listen – that it is my nature to question everything; nothing is fixed for me. The me I show to the world, however, is ordered and solid. (Well, it was until this was published.)

Apparently it's something to do with Jung's shadow. Cath always gets those technical references because she has a degree in psychology and used to work in that field. She gives me the footnotes on the way home. Her personality, it seems, is just the opposite of mine. She needs absolutes and fixedness while displaying chaos.

The one psychological trait we do, apparently, have in common, is not that helpful on the relationship front: we are both quite flaky when it comes to commitment. No matter how well things are going, we both like to keep one hand on the door-handle. As long as we accept that, in ourselves and each other, it's fine.

As I say, I'm sure this sounds like hokum to a lot of people, but I'll try anything to make Cath and me work out. I'm not expecting a pain-free zone. I once said to Kurt I felt like Cath and I were on a tandem and I was doing all the pedalling. He said if I needed an analogy, a more helpful one would be the image of the dance: two people in a warm and loving embrace, gliding across the floor together, both facing in opposite directions, seeing everything from a completely different perspective. Unfortunately he chose the tango as his example.

Cath and I recently agreed that our relationship is 70 per cent good-to-brilliant and 30 per cent shit. I think every couple should sit and work out their own relationship's score. Cath and I are basically happy to live with the 70/30 average while slowly chipping away at the shitty bit. It may get smaller; it may not. If it gets bigger, and outgrows its cage, we're in trouble.

Seventy/thirty, favouring good-to-brilliant, is a decent average, I think. As I've said before, I'd settle for that split in any area of my life. Except, of course, my stand-up. Warm-up gigs, yes; but the tour-show, definitely not. This is one of the problems of trying to rebuild my relationship while I'm on the road. Whatever I'm doing, saying or even thinking, gig-days or days off, the show is always with me, my tour-head is always on.

When we were in that counselling session last Tuesday, Kurt warned us against comparing our relationship to other ones that don't actually exist. I think he was referring to a sort of Platonic ideal. Plato, the ancient Greek philosopher I was reading about at the beginning of the tour, believed everything in this world was a slightly crappy version of a perfect, abstract idea. So there's a sort of Heaven, Plato thinks, where, for example, the perfect version of a horse is trotting around; and all the real horses on earth fall short of that ideal horse. That other world also contains the perfect wheelbarrow, the perfect bow-tie, the perfect everything – including, of course, the perfect relationship – but it's mad to compare OUR relationship to that perfect one; we can never hope to match it. So, if we agree we're all stuck with earthly, imperfect versions of the ideal, where are the REAL relationships that make ours look so bad?

Kurt asked us to name five relationships we would regard as inspirational – relationships we knew about that really seemed to work. We struggled.

I probably could have named two or three, but by then my tour-head was starting to intrude on my thoughts. Was I comparing my show to the Platonic ideal of a stand-up show, setting a standard I couldn't possibly hope to meet? I thought about the stand-up shows I'd seen other comics do over the years. As with the relationships question, I struggled to think of one that was actually THAT great. Good – very good, even – but still flawed. Nothing is 100 per cent. I found that thought rather cheering.

Anyway, I'm in my very lovely suite at the Forbury Hotel in Reading, sitting on my sofa in my big white hotel-robe. There is a three-foot-deep copper bath in the room – not in the bathroom, in the actual room. I just treated myself to a long, hot, post-gig soak. At home I only ever use my bath on a Thursday morning. The rest of the week I use the shower. What's more, I only ever use my juicer or my George Foreman Lean Mean Grilling Machine on a Thursday morning. You guessed it: my cleaner comes on Thursday afternoon. All three are lovely to use but a pain in the arse to clean afterwards.

My hotel bed has got six cushions on it. I'm not talking about pillows – there are six of them as well, two-deep across the top of the bed. No, I'm talking about eighteen-inch-square cushions. Nice hotels always have them on the bed. Very firm ones, in slightly stiff covers, with a tasselled edge. I assume they're for Pharaoh-style lounging but I never use them myself. In the course of my sordid past I've been glad of additional pillows, just to raise and widen the target a little, but I never used a cushion for that purpose. Well, I did once but there was spillage, and once you've seen a matted tassel, you never want to see another one.

There are always way too many pillows for me. I'd love to know the health gurus' official line on this. How high should the head be raised when sleeping? I only sleep with one pillow under my head; two gives me a stiff neck. As there are six pillows and this is a double bed, I can only assume that most people sleep with their head three pillows high. That just sounds impossible to me: suddenly you're not a person, you're a ramp.

And then there are the towels. Virtually every hotel I've stayed at on this tour had a little card displayed in the bathroom, dealing with the subject of towels. One typical example read like this:

Many towels are washed unnecessarily, every day, in hotels worldwide, resulting in needless water-pollution from cleaning chemicals. Please consider if you need your towels washed today.

The usual drill is, if you leave your towel in the bath, it'll be taken away and washed – pollution unleashed, electricity wasted –

otherwise, it'll just be folded up and put back on the rack. Now, I'm all for saving the planet. I never leave my towel in the bath, and I wouldn't be so cynical as to suggest that the hotels are just trying to penny-pinch on labour and detergent while dressing it up as environmentalism. But if their intentions ARE honourable, if they really DO care, they need a more consistent ecological programme. In the vast majority of hotels that display these help-us-save-the-planet cards, I return to my room post-gig and find at least five separate lights switched on and Classic FM playing on the plugged-into-the-mains hotel radio. The room is set up like that during the house-keeping rounds at about six o'clock and stays like it, illuminating and entertaining no one, till I finally return around midnight. Then I brush my teeth, dry my mouth on a towel I've previously used to dry my arse-crack, and go to bed convinced we're winning the battle with climate-change.

I really enjoyed the Dorking gig. In Cambridge, four nights ago, I decided to see what would happen if I removed all swearing from the show, other than that which seemed absolutely necessary. When I say 'necessary', I mean helpful to the joke. This was not a moral decision – I'm a big fan of swearing – it was a sort of less-is-more experiment. I wondered if I'd been diffusing the impact of key 'fucks', etc. in the set by sprinkling them too liberally in less-essential areas. Having gone through this process and decided it WAS beneficial, there's now only one 'fuck' in the whole of the first half. I hope I'm not letting anyone down. I think the swearing is all some people come for. I need to be strong, though. I don't want to end up like Oliver Hardy, unable to lose weight even when it was damaging his health, because everyone saw him as 'the fat one'. The filthy one is still filthy; I've just honed it a little.

The place-specific stuff was enjoyable tonight. I found an article in the paper that described a local scout group, Eighteenth Dorking, as 'a group that like to put the OUT in scout'. I read it aloud, commended Eighteenth Dorking for their openness and moved on. My spiritualist routine continues to expand. It said in the Dorking Halls brochure that there was an evening of mediumship and psychic art at the theatre two weeks ago. I asked if anyone present had been there. An usherette with a sonorous voice – I sensed some am-dram experience – explained to me, from the back of the hall, that the event had been cancelled. I said I was sorry to hear that and wondered aloud what the show would have been like. The usherette, now operating like a Greek Chorus, again intervened. In normal circumstances, she explained in her bell-like tone, the male medium contacts the deceased relatives of people in the audience and then his female assistant does a drawing of each deceased person. It sounded brilliant, but the usherette, like most Greek Choruses, had a tragic twist in her tale. She explained that the female had recently fallen off a stage and broken both her ankles.

I took this opportunity to tell the audience about a telephone conversation I'd had with a friend at the end of last year. I was telling the friend about a news story I'd heard that morning. I said, 'Did you know Jimmy Krankie was taken to hospital with head injuries after falling off a beanstalk in pantomime?' There was a brief pause and then my friend said, 'Do you think that sentence really needed the "in pantomime" bit on the end?'

I thanked the usherette for her help and said that if the theatre could get the male medium back, I myself would volunteer to take over the sketch-pad – then draw every spirit exactly the same, arms outstretched with a big white sheet over them.

When I got to the hotel tonight, there was a large brown

envelope waiting for me on reception. Inside were several pictures and estate agent specifications for country cottages. Jenny, my PA, has been working on it all week. She's heading off into the countryside on Monday to check some cottages out. Cath, who loves the countryside, has got really excited about the whole idea. I told them both I desperately wanted to buy a country cottage. This is all to do with my new Gilbert White obsession – or should I say my OLD Gilbert White obsession. Having finally got hold of *The Natural History of Selborne*, I found it to be deathly dull. I only got to page twenty, which sounds good for me until you realise the text doesn't actually begin until page seven. The limpet has released itself and moved on. Thank God I didn't stop off at Isambard Kingdom Brunel's house when I was in Torquay. Jenny would have been driving round the country trying to buy a bridge.

WEDNESDAY 10 OCTOBER 2007

We're in the Joke-Mobile, driving round and around Blackburn. We usually get to the theatre about six for an eight o'clock show, but I like Adam to get us into town an hour earlier than that. Then we have time to cruise a little and check the place out. If I see anything that has comic potential, I scribble a note on one of my two dozen hotel notepads with one of my two dozen hotel pens. As soon as we get into range, I switch on the local radio station and comb that for little gems. Tonight it's 107 The Bee and their drive-time competition to win a CD. All you have to do is guess who's taller: Gary Owen or Jamelia. We continue listening until we pull on to the theatre car park but I never find out the answer. We used to cruise the towns listening to an album called *Oneiric* by Boxcutter. A friend bought it me to, as he put it, 'get me through the tour'. It's an hour and a bit of slightly discordant, staccato spookiness; the sort of thing C3PO would listen to if he lived in a terrible bedsit and did heroin. It seemed to be the perfect soundtrack for driving round British industrial towns but, with the possible exception of Bolton, everywhere turned out to be too nice. It might be a trick of the memory, but it seems to me that Britain is much lovelier now than it was when I toured ten years ago, and there seems to be more and more ongoing development wherever we go. As far as I can tell, it's the water that attracts them. Around the coast, on the sides of rivers, along canals, there are luxury apartments, restaurants, fancy shops, hotels, arts centres – all constructed, it seems, so the towns and cities can, like Narcissus, admire their own beautiful reflection in the water.

When I get to the gig at six, a local paper and the theatre's brochure are waiting for me to dissect. I also bring a print-off of the town's Wikipedia page. As we say on the Tesco ads, every little helps. I've always felt that the audience appreciate a bit of local stuff, it shows you've made the effort to tailor the show specifically for them, but even if I'm wrong about that, writing and performing the local stuff each night is good for my head – something new and fresh to add to the mix. Even if the jokes aren't as strong as the tried-and-trusted stuff, in content or performance, I enjoy their disposability. At six o'clock, I see a big British Home Stores at one end of Reading Football Stadium; at eight o'clock, I'm onstage asking if they've got a British Away Stores at the other end. Then, laugh or not, it's gone. Unless, of course, I put it in a book, pretending it's disposable but obviously thinking it's good enough to repeat.

My old friend Roger came to the Reading gig. Though he's younger than me, he's recently retired and plans to live alone in a cottage in rural France. Compared to him I feel like Weirdo Loner Lite. He's not a rich man, he'll rent the cottage, but he's desperate to leave Britain. 'I just want to be somewhere they appreciate wine,' he said. It reminded me of that film when Peter Sellars plays a left-wing shop steward who dreams of going to Russia: 'all them cornfields and ballet in the evenings'. Roger and I sat talking, back at the hotel, till half past midnight, mainly about comedy and a French nihilist author he's recently discovered. For all our lonerness, we hugged heartily when saying goodbye.

I hit a bit of a milestone this week. After each gig, I text Jon, my manager, my score, out of ten, for each half. For example, the paedo outcry at Aldershot made the first half a seven, but the second half stormed up to a nine. I could never give a ten. On Sunday, after the gig at the Lowry Theatre, Salford, twenty-five gigs in, I texted my first nine and nine. I've been tinkering with the show every night: shaving bits off, rewriting gags, changing the order. All of my previous tours developed organically in this way, every slight dip or clumsy segue eventually ironed out. Now, I think, it's more or less spot-on. My friend Rosemary, who moved up North last year, was at the Salford gig with her new bloke and a couple of other friends. In the dressing room, me quietly elated by my first nine and nine, one of the friends said, 'So, have all the gigs been this good or was tonight exceptional?'

'Oh, I'd say it was about average,' I nonchalantly replied.

Having at last reached this stage, I was looking forward to taking my foot slightly off the pedal. Obviously, I'd still be doing the local stuff but, with the body of the show in good shape, it meant my next day off could be just that – a completely relaxing day off.

Consequently, when I arrived at my Birmingham flat in the early hours of Monday morning, after a block of six consecutive gigs, I was looking forward to a long sleep and a lazy day to follow. I went into the kitchen to put the remains of that night's rider – plums, salad, chicken breast, soya spread and a pint of skimmed milk – into the fridge; that would save me having to shop the next morning. A fly buzzed around my head as I unloaded the carrier bag. A fly in October – that's global warming for you, I thought to myself. We must stop washing those towels. In fact, two flies; there was another one on the microwave. I tell a lie, there were TWO flies on the microwave so that was a total of three fat, hairy houseflies in my kitchen. Suddenly, I felt uneasy.

I looked at the kitchen window. It's probably about three feet by four. Even against the night sky, I could see that almost every inch of it was covered with these fat, black flies. I shuddered and then tiptoed out of the room, stooping slightly, making myself smaller so the flies wouldn't notice me. On seeing them, lining the window, I'd immediately closed my mouth, tight shut. My first thought had been that they would all suddenly fly into it; I mean, all really cram inside it so my jaws hurt at being forced open so wide. I would eventually have to place one hand on top of my head, the other under my chin, and force my mouth shut. I imagined the result of this desperate measure: the terrible crunching sound; the sudden warmth of the creamy fly-innards as they filled the space between my teeth and gums and puke-provokingly agitated my tonsils; the squirming of the survivors and the resulting second, harder bite, assisted by a muscular raising of the tongue, to finally finish them off. Then the terrible spitting and throwing up, the obsessive rinsing with tap-water, the toothbrush dappled with wings and legs, the dogshit belches the following morning.

I stood outside the kitchen, with my back against its carefully closed door, and slowly unclamped my mouth. It was 2 a.m. Too late for Rentokil. Above my kitchen door is a small glass panel, about one foot high and as wide as the door itself. The light in the hallway where I stood was shining through that glass panel into the dark and, now, slightly buzzing kitchen. It must have formed a rectangular light-source in the corner of the room. And if there's one thing flying insects like, it's a light source. I could hear the buzzing increase as the flies, jockeying to get at the glass panel, swarmed and seethed directly above my head.

Checking one more time that the door was securely shut, I walked into the lounge to sit down and let my heart-rate return to normal. I flopped on to the sofa and said 'fuck' several times. I had a vague memory of seeing a can of fly spray somewhere in the flat. Then I remembered it was under the sink – the sink that is, of course, in the kitchen. I bit my lip nervously as I considered the prospect of going back in there. Then a fly crossed my line of vision; then another. Shit! I'd forgotten the serving hatch. The light in the lounge had diverted the flies' attention from the one in the hallway, and they were now piling in through the little wooden sliding door to my left. I threw myself across the room and slapped the hatch tight shut, but by now there were about twenty flies in the lounge. I could retreat to the bedroom, but no, this was it. It was time to face the flies, eye to compound-eye.

Now, I like to pride myself on being an original thinker, someone who doesn't just follow the crowd, who questions and innovates, takes the alternative route. What I did next, however, was, in the field of fly killing, about as route-one as you can get. Yes, I rolled up a newspaper. For the next ten minutes I swished, swatted and swore at the little fuckers till I was genuinely out of breath. Having my jaws clamped tightly shut again for the duration of the attack didn't exactly help. I figured even twenty flies in my mouth, sucking at the food between my teeth and careering off down my windpipe in search of an escape route, would still be quite unpleasant. It did strike me, mid-swish, that the flies could, theoretically, get into my mouth through my nostrils. At this point, I stumbled on one of the rare plusses of getting older. No fly, I realised, unless it carried industrial secateurs, could possibly get through the wiry undergrowth that my nasal hair had become. This realisation gave me new courage and I swished on and on. You can keep your kick-boxing and exercise bikes. Just spend ten minutes a day chasing twenty flies with a newspaper and within six months you'll have a heart like Paula Radcliffe. No wonder spiders keep so slim.

I never really settled on a method. I began my attack using mainly forehand but then developed a sort of backhand sweep. For some reason, during the whole attack I hummed 'The Final Countdown' by Europe. A patriotic '633 Squadron' or a high-spirited 'Those Magnificent Men in Their Flying Machines' . . . lots of stuff would have been more appropriate, but it was 'The Final Countdown' that came into my head. To be precise, it was the opening riff, which I repeated over and over in a very high-pitched hum because I'd read somewhere that flies are repelled by high C. I never progressed to the verse.

Sadly, after ten minutes of vicious combat, my final countdown was two flies, both of them killed, in quick succession, as they took a sly breather on the lounge window. Interestingly, for the brief time it took me to kill these two, my 'Final Countdown' morphed into 'Eye of the Tiger'. But when the killing was done, I reverted to Europe's glam metal classic for the rest of the attack. Splatting a fly in mid-air seemed virtually impossible. I did manage to hit one as it flew; there was a lovely, skeletal clicking sound at the point of impact. The stunned creature slammed into the wall and dropped on to the carpet. Now, I may be imagining this – I was over-tired – but it seemed to me that as I went in for the kill, the other flies deliberately flew closer to my face, causing me to shield myself with my arms and do a closed-mouth hysterical scream. It was as if they were trying to give their stunned colleague a few extra, life-saving seconds to recover himself and return to the air.

I collapsed back on to the sofa in a humiliated heap. I'd never felt so old. I must have looked like Yoda, out-manoeuvred in a light-sabre duel by younger, sprightlier opponents. I thought of C3PO, doing heroin in his horrible bedsit. Oh, how the mighty had fallen.

My only hope was the fly spray. Let's see them dodge and dive through that. When I could no longer hear the pulse throbbing in my head, I stood up and walked towards the kitchen door. I seized the handle, clamped my jaws even tighter and went in, closing the door behind me. The flies, in the now brightly lit kitchen, seemed to be employing the same dive-bombing tactics they used to protect fallen colleagues; anything to stop me getting under that sink. Not only was my mouth shut tight but I was seriously squinting too. Suddenly, it was like a low-rent version of *I'm a Celebrity . . . Get Me out of Here*; I know that's hard to imagine. Despite the aerial assault I bravely marched on and then squatted to the level of the cupboard, the flies deliberately losing altitude to stay in my face. I flung the door open and there was the aerosol can. I looked at the colourful flowers on the label, and the words 'pine' and 'heather'. It was fucking air-freshener. I was too far in to go back. I grabbed the can and started shaking it violently. Looking back, I probably imagined the high-pitch sniggering that seemed to emanate from all corners of the room. Pine and heather . . . it was either a reference to the air freshener's scent or a brief description of what happened to Paul McCartney after Linda died. Either way, I needed, for morale reasons, to convince myself that air freshener would do the job. I had to get rid of my hairy-legged intruders – which is what, I think, Jan Leeming said, when asked about those lesbians that invaded the *Six O'Clock News*.

Air freshener, let's face it, is for dispelling the smell of shit. Flies are basically made of shit. Therefore, air freshener will dispel flies. It didn't. It just made the window white and the kitchen smell like a scratch-and-sniff episode of *Take the High Road*.

Eventually, at about 4 a.m., I gave up and shut myself in my dark bedroom, anxious and upset. Within seconds, I had to get up and put the light on. There was a fly in there. It took me twenty-five minutes to kill it, eventually squashing it against the wall with an anthology of Elizabethan verse. I switched the light off and tried, again, to get to sleep. As I lay in the dark I wasn't sure if I could see flies flying around or if the repetitive patterns of their trajectories had burned themselves into my mind's eye: 'Dost thou desire my slumbers should be broken/ While shadows like to thee do mock my sight?' I just put my head under the duvet and willed them to go away. I dreamed about flies all night.

The next day I lay in bed considering my options. I couldn't face the prospect of the people from Rentokil coming round. I decided I'd rather have the flies. The little shit-scoffers may well have been carrying killer diseases, but at least I didn't have to speak to them. I needed to sort out the problem myself. I didn't fancy making breakfast in the fly-infested kitchen so I went straight to the corner shop, utterly famished, and shouted a loud explanation of the fly problem to a very friendly Indian lady. She shouted back the name of a fly spray she recommended and I shouted my agreement to buy it. She wasn't deaf. It was just that the shop's fridge had gone crazy and was making a loud, horrible noise throughout our conversation. It was not the relaxing day off I had dreamed about.

I returned to the flat and crept silently into the kitchen hoping the flies, after last night's activity, had decided to have a lie-in. Instead, the pine and heather had put them in a rambling mood; they were all over the kitchen. I carefully put away cutlery, crockery and the chopping board to avoid contamination and then, after pausing for a few seconds, like a conductor about to begin a symphony, I sprayed those flies like there was no tomorrow. For them, of course, there wouldn't be. After about three minutes of spraying, the besieged insects, having spiralled into blind panic, buzzed and banged into the window. I calmly put down the can, stepped through the chemical mist and left the scene of carnage, flies spinning on the kitchen floor, as I closed the door behind me. I had a quick bath and then Adam and I combined lunch with a bit of shopping. I bought a brush and pan for the corpses, and a Bible. I wasn't taking their deaths THAT seriously; I just needed one for my Lectio Divina.

Despite spending most of last night sweeping up the dead, when I got up this morning the air was, once again, thick with flies. The terrible thing is I'm starting to get used to them.

Like the previous morning, I visited the corner shop – this time to get a newspaper, for reading and keep-fit purposes, and some tea-bags. Despite the fridge's racket, I had enjoyed my time with the Indian lady twenty-four hours earlier. There I'd been, in my local shop, having a bit of a chat. I usually go into complete weirdo-loner mode when I stay at my Birmingham flat. Now, suddenly, I felt like I knew someone, like I was part of the community. I walked into the shop, all smiles, and, as I paid for my goods, I decided to chuck in a bit of friendly banter, just to cement our neighbourly relationship. 'The fridge sounds healthier today,' I said, with a chuckle. The Indian lady just looked at me, straight-faced. 'You know,' I said, her stare sapping my confidence, 'the . . . erm . . . the fridge.' I pointed at the fridge. She gave me my change. I muttered my thanks and left. Maybe she was just having a bad day. Maybe the loud fridge had affected her hearing. Or, horror of horrors, maybe I'd made the unforgivable white liberal mistake and it was a different Indian woman. I was glad to get back to work.

MONDAY 15 OCTOBER 2007

I'm home in London, sitting on a cushion on the floor of my flat. I live near enough to Big Ben to hear the chimes. It just struck 2 a.m. I got back from the television studios about half an hour ago. I was recording *The Big Anniversary Quiz*, a two-hour, one-off panel show to celebrate twenty-five years of Channel 4.

I got the train down to London this morning. I played York last night. Adam and I did the Minster in the afternoon. It was fabulously dark inside; the glass in the massive windows is grey with age. One of the things I'm loving about this tour is the opportunity to visit great churches. Adam likes them too. I don't know if he always did or if it's another example of our cultural exchange programme. He has actually got me interested in the Rugby World Cup that's happening at the moment. If this continues, at the end of the tour I'll be off to the DVD shop to catch up on all those series of *Top Gear* I was too un-male to appreciate, and Adam will be worrying his mates by talking about beautiful skies.

We did Winchester Cathedral before the Dorking gig. Jane Austen's grave is in there, a flat black slab that's a lot wordier than Gilbert White's but makes no reference to the fact she was a writer. If anyone forgets to mention that I was a comedian on MY slab, I'll be straight on to Derek Acorah. Ms Austen is becoming an enigmatic theme on this tour. No obsession ensued, though.

Speaking of which, Jenny called to say she didn't like any of the country cottages she went to see. I told her not to worry. I didn't tell her the whole country-cottage project was a stupid whim based on a book I hadn't read and which, when I did read it, turned out to be extremely dull; thus putting me off cottages, and the countryside in general, for ever. No, I just said, 'I've decided to leave it for a while.' Four or five weeks ago we had a similar conversation about hot tubs.

I took a picture, in York Minster, of a beautiful Virgin Mary, about ten inches high, carved in wood above the entrance to the choir stalls. It's now the screensaver on my phone.

On our York drive-around I noticed a place with painted-out windows that had the phrase 'Adult Shop' over the door. It was written in a sort of gothic font, clearly trying to blend in with its more respectable surroundings. Onstage, shortly afterwards, I wondered how far this establishment had gone in its attempt to integrate. Did they sell gothic condoms with gargoyles around the base that remained alfresco throughout the act to cope with any sudden overflow? It didn't get a big laugh but the image pleased me.

Anyway, back to tonight. When I arrived at the television studio, there were gifts in my dressing room. A lot of production companies do this nowadays but it's usually just a bottle of champagne or some Jo Malone. (Wasn't that a Macaulay Culkin movie?) Tonight's gifts were exceptional. There was a Paul Smith scarf (it's just getting cold enough to need one), a mini camcorder and, best of all, six mint condition back-issues of *The Phantom* comic book from the early sixties (I love *The Phantom*). They were undoubtedly the best TV show gifts I've ever received.

The show started recording at 7.15. It was hosted by Jimmy Carr, a sort of twenty-first-century Bob Monkhouse, professional and prolific. There were three competing teams with two on each team. Jack Dee, a contemporary of mine, deadpan and dapper, was paired with one of the new crop of television comics, Alan Carr – a traditional camp comic, very loveable, with thick spectacles and a cheeky smile. Two other comics of the new breed formed a team: Richard Ayoade from *Garth Marenghi's Darkplace*, probably my favourite comedy TV show of the last ten years; and David Mitchell, posh and very bright. All these five are genuinely funny and in the midst of success. Jack Dee started out in comedy about the same time as me, but his new sitcom, *Lead Balloon*, puts my own sitcom efforts to shame. It's got the joke, character, plot balance just about spot-on. The other four are flavour-of-the-month hot. I was paired with Carol Vorderman. We were, I guess, supposed to represent Channel 4's earlier years. She's been on the quiz show *Countdown* virtually since the channel started. Carol isn't a comedian but she is much loved and happy to muck in. So, nice gifts, good guests . . . it was all set up to be a cracker.

I've been doing panel shows for years and virtually always do well. My first appearance on *Have I Got News For You*, in the early nineties, probably did more for my profile than winning the Perrier Award. If you're funny, panel shows are very straightforward: you just blast away and have a laugh. Having said all that, I hadn't actually done one for a while, the last one being my Jade Goody encounter in December of last year, so I was aware I might be a little rusty. Still, being onstage virtually every night for the last two months had to count for something. I was certainly match fit.

But not for this match. It was a fucking disaster. The recording lasted till 11.35 – four hours and twenty minutes in total – and I don't recall getting a single laugh. At one point I actually became convinced that my mic wasn't on. The four new guys, Jimmy, Alan, Richard and David, totally stormed it; the crowd seemed to love them as much as they hated me. That late-night quiz in Edinburgh turned out to be a warm-up for tonight. It's as if I'd adopted the same, try-out gig approach to it as I did with the tour: 'I've got to die on my arse on a TV quiz show in October; be made to look old, unfunny and obsolete in the presence of younger, more talented comics. I don't just want to go into it without a dry run. I'll try it out in a little late-night venue in Edinburgh a couple of months before, just to be sure. That way, if I'm slightly funny, not completely over-shadowed by the young comics in Edinburgh, I've got a couple of months to un-polish my sense of humour and make sure I'm totally and utterly shit by the time we get to the big night.' If I'd actually done that, if I'd actually worked as hard to be SHIT on the quiz as I have to be GOOD on the tour, I still couldn't have been any MORE shit than I was tonight.

It wasn't just that the audience didn't laugh at my jokes; it was the 'Unnngh!' of annoyed impatience that followed each punch-line. There was even some tutting, some disgruntled head-shaking, some dismayed rolling of eyes – not because I was rude but because I was THERE. I felt like Eli Wallach, telling the Hawaiian pizza joke over and over and over again. This wasn't me challenging the sensibilities of Middle England. These people used to be my crowd, the alternative TV comedy lot. Now I was their fifty-year-old wife, dumped for a younger, prettier woman. After a while I realised I was keeping my left hand under the desk, desperately hiding my ganglion. I thought of the sixteenth-century poem by Sir Thomas Wyatt, the one I always think of when I encounter someone whose response reminds me I'm not flavour-of-the-month any more: a cold PR girl at a premiere, scrutinising my invite with an air of disbelief; indifferent paparazzi outside a restaurant, scurrying past me to photograph a girl from *Britain's Next Top Model*. The poem begins, 'They flee from me, that sometime did me seek'. It's become an incantation, a leitmotif for this aspect of my life. Builders in the street don't say, 'Oy, Frankie' any more. Mind you, that's not necessarily a sign of my declining popularity; I never was that big in Eastern Europe. I suppose the grim truth REALLY hit home when I got a 'Sorry I Missed your Birthday' card from my stalker. If I've slid that far down HER league table, times really are tough.

I have to say, though, the loss of fame thing sounds a lot more traumatic than it actually is. I spent the first half of my life being more-or-less ignored by people. Going back to that, for a weirdo loner at least, is a bit of a treat. But tonight was different. I felt like an intruder, and it wasn't just the audience. In the middle of one slightly desperate, no laughs, point in my performance, I looked across at David and Richard, both glowing with the love the audience was pouring on them. They looked back at me. They seemed exasperated and genuinely puzzled, like they were saying, 'Why are you here? It's our turn now.'

And that was what lay at the core of my experience, that nagging sense that the carnival was over, the game up. Comedy, comedy performers, comedy crowds, had all moved on. I wasn't quite sure where they'd moved on to – it still seemed to be mainly knob-jokes – but they'd moved on without ME. I'd been watching the telly in the dressing room, before the show. Ming Campbell, the leader of the Liberal Democrats, had just resigned, pressured out of office because he was perceived, aged sixty-six, as being too old to compete with younger party leaders like the Conservative's David Cameron. Cameron is nearly ten years younger than me.

Every person I looked at in the Green Room after the show seemed to avert their eyes. The pretty young things that flitted around the new comedians would sneak a quick look at me and then mutter something behind a conspiratorial hand. The toughest thing was having to face Cath.

She smiled and hugged me and tried to say, 'That was great', but it just came out muffled and wrong. I know, on one level, it's just a stupid, disposable television programme, but I wanted so much to be good for Cath. I had imagined her at work the next day, saying things like, 'And did you all see my extremely funny boyfriend last night?', laughing, being happy and proud. As it was, she probably wouldn't mention the show at all; and no one would mention it to her. Too embarrassed; too polite. When I kissed her goodbye in the car park, she looked so beautiful and – unbelievably – still happy, still proud, despite the night's events.

A couple of years ago, I went to see the American singer Patti Smith performing the live version of her most celebrated album, *Horses*. Towards the end of the set, her grey-haired drummer, who's only five years older than me, leaned a little too far forward on his stool and fell, awkwardly, into his drum kit. It was a sort of a slow-motion fall: he was so horrified, so aware of the humiliating nature of the spectacle – an old man, with a drumstick in each hand, slowly collapsing, by instalments, on to and in between a hostile collection of snares, cymbals and spiky metal poles – that he seemed to try, by sheer willpower, to defy gravity and resist his fall. The drum kit, not made for being stage-dived on, looked fragile and collapsible under the assault. It provided nothing solid, nothing fixed, that he might grab in order to save himself, but a whole array of sharp, metal things, with which he might do himself great harm. He decided, for some reason, to make his whole body completely rigid, faced fixed, arms at his sides, resisting impalement like an Indian fakir on a bed of nails. The drum kit ever-so-slowly collapsed, the first tumbling cymbal alerting the rest of the band to his plight, but no one could help him; they could only watch. Another cymbal went over; a high-hat crashed to the floor, weakening the structure enough for him to come through, still stiff as a board, like a swaddled corpse falling through a crumbling funeral pyre. A dozen roadies raced to his aid but it was too late. The drummer knew what everyone was thinking: 'Aren't you getting a little bit old for this?' He looked desperately ashamed and upset. His excruciating fall, from initial over-reach to first bodily contact with stage, lasted about twelve seconds. Mine lasted four hours and twenty minutes.

When I got back to my flat, I went on to my computer to see how the papers had reacted to Ming Campbell's departure. An article on Times Online described the attitude of Ming's colleagues: 'They appear not to have told him to his face to quit, but he had not detected enough support to stay on.'

As Big Ben strikes 2.15 I have, for some reason, rolled off my cushion and am lying on the floor, flat on my back, laughing out loud. Mild hysteria, I expect. The difference between me and Ming Campbell is I'm not resigning. I'm going be like one of those old footballers who plays on when his glory days are behind him, turning up, grey-haired and grinning, at insignificant football grounds to play insignificant games, except they won't be insignificant to me. I'll still want to win, still want to please the crowd, an occasional flash of the old magic amidst the muddy toil.

Having said all that, I'm beginning to wish I hadn't spent thirty quid on that 'Forever Funny' t-shirt.

SUNDAY 28 OCTOBER 2007

There is a joke, not one I wrote but one I love, about two comics who meet in the street. The first comic says, 'Hey, how are you doing? I haven't seen you in the clubs for ages.'

'Well, I live in America now,' says the second comic. 'I moved there about six years ago, to do stand-up, and it went really well. I did national tours, *Letterman, Leno,* HBO specials, the lot.'

'Really?' said the first comic. 'I never heard about that.'

The second comic is shocked. 'I don't like to brag,' he added, 'but then I starred in a sitcom out there and it was a smash – we've just filmed our fifth series. And I did a movie with Adam Sandler . . . I got great reviews. You must have heard about that?'

'No,' said the first comic, 'I didn't. But that's fabulous news. I'm really happy for you. So, how come you're in England?'

'Well,' said the second comic, 'I thought it would be nice to do some stand-up in the UK – you know, three or four big stadium-shows – so I'm over here doing a bit of a recce, trying out some new stuff. I did a little room above a pub in Hammersmith last night. To be honest, it didn't go that well.'

'Yeah,' said the first comic. 'I heard about that.'

I'm in the dressing room at the Theatre Royal in Newcastle, remembering that joke. This has been a golden weekend: Friday in Southampton, Saturday in Llandudno and now tonight – all brilliant shows that I've really enjoyed. I felt the love and I think the audiences did too. In fact, the last two weeks have really rocked. My horror night at the quiz seems to have given me a whole new momentum: a need to prove to myself that I'm not completely shit.

I accidentally caught a sort of review this morning, just a sentence in the *Sunday Times*. I was in their 'things to do this week' section. It said my tour has 'proved a surprising success' – praise with the usual hint of poison. It only hurt for a couple of hours. By then I was in Durham Cathedral, another of the tour's great churches, this one my favourite so far.

Because my father was Catholic – my mother converted from the Church of England when they married – and he came from County Durham, I feel that Durham Cathedral is somehow the source of my own Catholicism, the home of my faith. Walking around it this afternoon was very emotional for me. St Cuthbert, who they call 'the Great Saint of the North', is buried here, in a quiet corner, next to a statue of himself which was beheaded by anti-Catholic protestors in the sixteenth century. It occurred to me, as I stood at his tomb, that were it not for gutsy, determined individuals like Cuthbert, the Church in the North East might not have survived and the chain of faith, which eventually passed through my father to me, might have been broken when it was just a few links long.

Last night, after the gig in Llandudno – a gig which I began by saying 'the clocks go back tonight, but, let's face it, in Wales they never really went forward' – there was a group of people waiting outside the stage door. I chatted and got my photo taken, but one guy held back. When everyone else had gone he told me that, on the strength of reading my autobiography, he had stopped his heavy drinking – in fact, stopped drinking completely – and started going to Mass again. He shook my hand, said thank you and disappeared into the night. When, on Judgement Day, I'm watching my CCTV lowlights, trying to justify banana night and the swings and roundabouts joke, you never know – having that bloke from Llandudno in my ticks column might just turn things around.

The Venerable Bede's tomb is also in Durham Cathedral. I rubbed my ganglion against it in a show of solidarity. Then a young guy stopped me and introduced himself as the son of the Irish comedian Jimmy Cricket. He is training to become a priest (only six years to go) and I wished him well.

There's a bit in the Catholic Mass when the congregation all shake hands and say, 'Peace be with you'. I was in a Catholic church in London earlier this year and, during that 'sign of peace' interlude, an old guy who was sat in front of me turned to shake my hand. I knew I'd seen him somewhere before. With me in church that morning was the TV presenter Adrian Chiles, a fellow West Brom fan and Roman Catholic. I whispered to him, when the penny dropped, 'I think that's Blakey from *On the Buses.*' Sure enough, it was Stephen Lewis, the bloke who played Blakey. I went up to him afterwards and introduced myself.

I tell you these two stories because I don't want you thinking that Scientology and Kabbalah have cornered the market on celebrities.

When we arrived at the theatre in Newcastle tonight, there was a bunch of about thirty autograph hunters outside, the biggest gathering so far. Don't get me wrong, this is by no means a compliment. Autograph hunters are interested in autographs, not the people who sign them. They represent a true democracy. Whoever turned up at this theatre, be it Madonna or Southern FM's Danny Pike, they would be accorded the same respect. All they have to do is sign: old-fashioned autograph books; pictures from newspapers and magazines, cut out and glued on to A4 pages, with an autograph-sized space left below; rectangular pieces of white card, carefully cut to size; leaflets advertising the show; photographs of the autograph hunter with said celebrity, taken at a previous gig; all kept neat in ring-binder files crammed into battered carrier bags with an array of biros and felt-tipped pens. Often you're asked to sign multiple leaflets or pieces of card; then you know you're going to get swapped. Those that gather outside theatres, waiting for the act to turn up, might occasionally nip into the foyer to buy a souvenir programme, but they rarely go in to see the show. No one can sign a night out.

One guy told me he'd got 27,000 autographs 'indoors'. Are there that many famous people? Mind you, I got a thrill when I signed his traditional autograph book and noticed that Petula Clark was on the facing page; Pet and me for ever joined. I saw her on a poster a few dressing rooms ago – she toured in the spring – and I remember thinking, 'Oh, I hope she was treated with due respect on her arrival at the theatre.' Not by the local autograph hunters; they, for all their strangeness, are always friendly and polite. No, it was that theatre's grungey crew I was worried about.

When Adam and I walked in, they were seated around a table, reading red-tops and rolling cigarettes, and didn't even bother to look up. The snub barely registered with me. We often arrive at theatres like children evacuated to the countryside during World War II; the villagers, their cosy lifestyle disrupted by these intruders from the big city, brooding and resentful, and wearing their spleen on their sleeves. But I didn't like to think of Petula being treated that way. The crew probably didn't know who she was and hadn't bothered to find out. I bet they couldn't have named one of her songs. Ironic, because they looked to me as if they probably DID sleep in the subway.

The crew were all right at the Theatre Royal. Newcastle's unfriendly greeting came from outside the theatre. As I signed the books, cards and pictures, I heard a sound like somebody gargling in a Geordie accent. Eventually the words 'West', 'Brom' and 'shite' seemed to emerge. I looked beyond the autograph gang and saw an enormous fat man, with a massively bejowled head, sitting outside a pub. Some of the autograph hunters seemed to know him – as if this was his regular habit, the abuse of arriving artistes. I concentrated harder on his gargling and managed to pick up a couple of sentences, most notably, 'Come over here or I'll mash your head' and what may well have been 'I'll spark you out'. He waved – considering the rest of his bulk – a surprisingly skinny arm, gesturing me to his side. Sitting there, with a few shadowy cronies, he looked like Jabba the Hutt after a run of bad luck. His Huttese accent had been replaced by a Geordie one, but that could well have been the result of a heart-to-heart phone call with his agent: 'Jabba, the bad news is the *Star Wars* franchise is all washed up. The good news is that, if you're prepared to work with a voice-coach, I can get you your own strip in *Viz*.' The Hutt protests but his agent goes in for the kill: 'Look, Jabba, you want to think yourself lucky. C3PO's in a bedsit doing heroin and Yoda couldn't hurt a fly.'

After the show, I had surprise visitors in my dressing room, Ross Noble and Dave Johns, two very funny comedians and, in my experience, very likeable blokes, both from the Newcastle area.

When they arrived, along with Ross's wife, I was genuinely pleased to see them.

'Good work,' said Ross.

'"Good" as opposed to "great"; "work" as opposed to "entertainment",' I thought to myself.

'Are you enjoying it?' he asked.

How could I not have enjoyed a show like that? It was an absolute stormer . . . or was it? Now, I wasn't sure. Of course, his 'it' may have referred to the whole tour. Maybe he'd read some terrible reviews. Suddenly, the weekend wasn't quite so golden; it was a grey, heavy lump of lead, covered with a thin, flaky layer of easily removable gold leaf. Sure enough, my comedy colleagues easily removed it.

'I wasn't in tonight,' said Dave. I waited for him to say why. He didn't. Either, I reasoned, he wasn't in because he couldn't face watching something he knew would be shit, or he WAS in but hated the show so much he said he wasn't; thus cleverly avoiding having to comment. I really liked these two guys, as comics and people. Why had they come to torture me so?

I thought about asking Adam to go and get Jabba from across the road. The *banderilleros* had placed their twin barbs in the old bull's back; let the matador come and deliver the final thrust.

We sat and chatted and, after a while, I calmed a little and began to realise I'd imagined the earlier slights; my twisted, paranoid alchemy turning the golden weekend into base metal. We swapped anecdotes and old times.

'Mickey Hutton said you had a tough time in Canada,' Dave suddenly said.

Jabba's help would not be required. I had dropped my guard and my old comedy mate had administered the final blow. It was my own fault. 'Don't trust your friend' . . . that's what the budgerigar had said.

I blathered a disclaimer, then an excuse, then gave up. Tonight, onstage, for almost two hours, I had made wondrous comedy magic, spraying punchlines and patter like a wizard juggling stars. Now, instead of being chaired, shoulder-high, around Newcastle city centre, I was sat in my dressing room trying to justify a twelve-minute gig I did three months and 2,500 miles ago.

'Yeah,' said the first comic, 'I heard about that.'

MONDAY 12 NOVEMBER 2007

I'm on a small Eastern Airways aeroplane, heading for Birmingham Airport. West Brom play Coventry tonight and, as it's my day off, I'm going to the game. I've only seen six Albion games since the tour began. That's painful for me, but the show must go on, blah-blah. I sometimes fantasise about giving up work and watching every game: home and away; overseas pre-season tour; the lot. If, as a kid, you'd said to me, 'You're going to be rich, what will you spend it on?' that would have been my plan: every game; every season. Now I COULD do that, I go to work instead. Oh, the lure of the lathe.

I was up at 6.30 this morning at the Roker Hotel in Sunderland. At last, it was my turn. I was that person who walks around hotels first thing in the morning, slamming doors and having loud conversations in the corridors. I enjoyed being on the other end of the experience, not being the fuck-muttering victim shaken awake by the noise. When I set off on this tour, I brought earplugs with me to soften the blow of noisy hotels. They are the tubular foam style of earplug, though a friend told me the wax ones are much more effective. The ironic thing is I only brought one pair of earplugs with me and, two months and several noisy hotels later, I now have the best of both worlds: foam and wax. Each inch-long tube of foam has a thick coat of earwax completely covering one end. I don't go to sleep with them in; I have them, instead, ever-ready at my side. They stand, like two little brown-topped toad-stools, near my bedside light each night. I might get some wicks and a couple of ornamental candlesticks for them when the tour is over. I like the idea of meditating in the musty half-light of my own self-generated glow.

The Roker Hotel is right on the seafront. I sat in my room yesterday afternoon, reading the Sunday papers and watching massive grey waves explode into spray as they hit the coastal wall. Norman Mailer, the American writer, died on Saturday. He had an interesting analogy for diminishing fame which made me think back to the Channel 4 quiz. He said, when his flavour-of-the-month period subsided, it was like being a child who suddenly had a new little brother or sister who everyone wanted to kiss and cuddle and generally pay attention to. He had clearly been hurt by the whole experience. I understand the pain of neglect, but there's a pleasure that comes with it too: the pleasure of being left alone to sit in the corner, reading a comic book, while everyone coos and google-oos around the pram. I love that feeling, but you can't explain it to people. They don't believe you; they don't WANT to believe you. Non-famous people need the loss of fame, the crumbling of celebrity, to be unremittingly dreadful or there's no justice in the whole fame process – no down to balance the up; no hangover. Celebrities have got the lot: easy job, money, plenty of room at the Velázquez exhibition. They have to pay for that somehow: alcoholism, drugs, cellulite . . . something, anything, to unsweeten their soufflé. That is why Shakespeare wrote tragedies. He knew people like to see the rich and mighty – kings, princes, warriors – brought down to their knees by some character-flaw or a humbling twist of fate. If any celebrity does manage to have a good run of fame combined with happiness, they should at least have the decency to wail and whimper when the spotlight slowly fades. Well, look, you have me mourning my unshown sitcom and falling through my drums at the quiz. It's just gonna have to do.

Even if my sparkle has faded somewhat, I can still get starry if I need to. Adam and I checked into the very lovely Hotel du Vin in Bristol last week, and as we chatted in the bar, two hours later, I aired my disappointment at the size of my room. 'Oh, I think the rooms are quite spacious,' Adam said, hurriedly adding, 'well, not spacious, maybe, but a good size. Not small anyway.' A silence ensued. We were, I'm sure, both considering the possibility that Adam had been accidentally given the nicer room. I mean, it's only one night, but the deal is, if there's a nice room and a not-so-nice room . . . well, it stands to reason, doesn't it? Some comics stay at a five-star hotel and put the tour manager in a bed-and-breakfast down the road. If we had equally fantastic rooms, that would be fine. Well, actually, no, it wouldn't, because I don't see why I should pay for two fantastic rooms when a fantastic room and a quite nice room would clearly suffice. Oh, look, I've done *The Karate Kid*; I'm not doing *Trading Places*.

I couldn't look Adam in the eye as we passed in the hotel corridor, mid room-swap, each accompanied by a member of staff who carried our half-unpacked things. I just kept walking, feeling petty and ashamed of myself. When the hotel person opened the door to what was now MY room, I didn't even stop to appreciate its size. I walked straight into the bathroom and put all the towels in the bath.

Speaking of perks, I got a free book in the post a few days back: *Three Lions: The Unofficial Story of the England Team Since 1966*. I always like a freebie and this one seemed particularly appropriate. I know the England team's badge has had three lions on it since the nineteenth century, but I doubt the book would be called *Three Lions* if David Baddiel, Ian Broudie and me hadn't written a number one song with that name. There was, as is usual with a freebie book, an accompanying letter from the publisher. It began:

Dear Frank Skinner

In an effort to cheer you up in the light of England's sad defeat against Russia, we thought you might enjoy Brian Beard's *Three Lions* . . .

Adam and I had watched that Russia game in a pub in Gillingham. It was an afternoon kick-off, so, at a squeeze, we could stay till the final whistle and still get to Chatham in time for that night's gig. One-nil up at half-time; everything was looking great. Second half: a dodgy penalty, a quick goal and the game was lost. Russia had now only to beat Israel and Andorra and we were out of Euro 2008.

As we dashed, gig-bound, from the pub, a rustic sort of guy raised a halting hand. 'Can I show you something?' he said.

'I'm really in a rush,' I explained. 'I've got a gig in . . .'

'It won't take a minute,' he said. 'I think it'll cheer you up.' Adam looked anxiously at his watch.

'Come on, then,' I said to the guy, 'but it'll have to be quick.' He led us back through the pub and into the garden at the rear. The headline '*Quiz Debacle Comic Disappears*' came to my mind, but I think it was just post-match depression blackening my thoughts. Finally, as we reached a wooden enclosure, the guy stopped and proudly pointed inside. The enclosure contained an aggressive pure-white billy goat, almost clambering over the wall to get at us, and an enormous, fat black pig, covered in thick wiry hair. The guy turned to us and held his outstretched arm in the animals' direction, like a magician's lovely assistant, drawing the crowd's attention to a marvellous trick. He grinned broadly, a mixture of delight and pride.

'Brilliant,' I said. Adam agreed. And the guy looked prouder still. We stood like that for about eight long seconds. What did he want us to do? Sing 'Ebony and Ivory'?

'Anyway . . .' Adam said.

'Yes,' I agreed, and we headed for the car.

When I opened Brian Beard's *Three Lions* book, I immediately turned, of course, to the chapter on Euro '96, to see if our song got a mention. The section began:

'Football's Coming Home' (Baddiel and Skinner)

The expectation that England had lived with for thirty years was finally about to be fulfilled with Euro '96. Or so we were informed by excessive media hype, and the chorus of that irritating chart hit by those irritating comedians, Baddiel and Skinner.

Now, OK, slag me off if you must but don't then send me a complimentary copy of that slagging, with an accompanying letter that says it's part of an effort to cheer me up. Give me billy and the pig any old time. And these people even have the audacity to name the book after our 'irritating song'. Anyway, there you are, you player-haters, a lovely example of how a celebrity perk, the unsolicited freebie, can be a sugar-coated vehicle for personal abuse. Enjoy.

Now, as you know, I've been deliberately avoiding my once-favourite celebrity perk throughout the course of this tour. There was a girl outside the stage door in Sunderland last night, her tiny crop-top exposing the silky curvature of her hips, who made my Kokopelli ring slightly twitch on my finger. The girl carried a dog-eared copy of my autobiography in her hand. 'I'm probably too young for you,' she said, 'but if you wanna call me . . .' She handed me a business card and smiled, her eyes twinkling beneath her dark beret. I took the card and moved on before she said, 'Oooh Betty!'

According to the Samurai code, we can learn much from the sparrowhawk. When he flies into a flock of pigeons, he has his eyes fixed on the one he wants. Though others fly past in easy reach, some even brushing his wing-tips, he is not distracted from his target; he does not change his mind. It's a bit more picturesque than 'eyes on the prize' but, either way, that's how it is with me at the moment.

Continuing the pigeon theme, it turns out it was a dead one that caused my fly infestation in Birmingham. It was outside the window and the flies got in through an air-vent. There's no real escape from the nasty outside world, is there, even for the weirdo loner? You can hide yourself away in a barred and shuttered flat, a ghostly presence on the upper floors, but the bad stuff will always get in: smarmy remarks in a football book, dropping through your letterbox; dispersed pigeon, wriggling through your wall.

I was back in Edinburgh on Saturday night, at a big fancy theatre this time. The gig was good but, as any comedian will tell you, no matter how well you're going, no matter how hysterical the crowd, you'll always spot one person who's sitting there stony-faced. In Edinburgh, it was a young woman in the front row with spectacles and black hair pulled tightly back. It wasn't just the fact that she didn't find me funny. Obviously that always hurts, but over time I've learned to cope with it, sort of. No, with this woman, it was more than that. She hated me. I tried directing a few lines straight at her, delivering them with a cheeky, ice-melting smile, but she just glowered back, daggers dipped in bile. How she'd ended up on the front row of one of my shows I couldn't quite imagine – unless the ticket was a spot-prize at that nightmare gig in Montreal, and she'd flown over especially, just to have one last loathe.

On the surface, I grinned my usual grin and frolicked merrily through my usual set; but always I was aware of her. I was Dorothy, dancing down the yellow brick road with a sharp stone in my sparkly bright-red shoe, unable to stop and shake it loose. Eventually I got to the routine that closes the main body of the show before I return with my ukulele for the encore. It's the bit about jealousy and insecurity in new relationships. It's developed into a fully fledged rant now. I end up flat on my back screaming at the ceiling, a fine spray of saliva showering down, cool against my face. I didn't remove any of the swearing from THIS routine; it's frenzied and obscene. And all delivered at pace. No gaps for laughs. I hear them laughing but I've already moved on:

... and I phone her up and there's no answer and I think, 'Her phone's off; she's obviously fuckin' someone else.' And then the ansaphone kicks in and she says, 'I'm sorry, I can't take your call right now . . .'

'No, you can't take my call but you can take someone else's stiff cock. Well, I hope he's dripping with Aids.' And then I realise I left that last bit on her ansaphone . . .

. . . and people say to me, 'Jealousy, it's like a cancer, isn't it?' Well, in a way, it's worse than cancer. At least with cancer you get some sympathy. If I'm out with a friend and I say, 'Look, I've been dating this girl for about a week and I think she's seeing someone else, so when she went to the toilet last night I went through her handbag and started reading her diary', he's just gonna look at me. I know I'm not gonna get a phone call from him a few days later, saying, 'Listen, I was telling some of the gang about your jealousy and we've had a bit of a whip-round and we're gonna send you to Disneyland.'

It's never going to work on the page. You'll just have to trust me. Anyway, unlike anything else I do in the set, it needs to be fuelled by rage; spat out. In Edinburgh the rage, thanks to the bespectacled stone in my shoe, was already just below the surface, so I decided to utilise that. I doubt I've ever done that closing rant better. I became aware of a whole new level to the material. I could see my bespectacled opponent out the corner of my eye, po-faced and disapproving. Suddenly she became every finger-wagging, sour-expressioned tut-tut disapproving person whose ever told me what I should or shouldn't say. The sort of person who gets upset if you hit them with a spoon, so you might as well hit them with a shovel. I belted out every unpleasant remark, knowing that her mean-spirited self-righteousness would prevent her from realising that the whole routine is about fear: fear of failure and humiliation; betrayal and loneliness; my fear. I bet she doesn't have that look on her face when she hears 'Love Hurts', even though it expresses, basically, the same sentiment. Because the song is a bit more obvious, it requires a bit less work, it's sugar-sweet and safe.

Bloody hell, listen to me, all up myself and angry. The poor dear might have been profoundly deaf, or have facial paralysis from the nose down, or have seen the show before. Still, it doesn't really matter if I got her completely wrong. The personality I sensed, even if I imposed it upon her, was incredibly useful when I did the rant. At this stage in the tour – last night was gig fifty-five, or gig seventy-three if you count the Edinburgh Festival and King's Heath – anything fresh or different is good. The routines have been pruned to remove the B-sides, while the A-sides have been extended and re-mixed, but I don't know how many new places this material has to go. As I've improvised, the successful ad-libs have remained, the organic growth has continued. But I feel like a painter now, standing back to look at the canvas and saying, 'I think I've finished. There's nothing else to add.' The real challenge, for these last fourteen gigs, is to say every line, some of which I've said a hundred times, like I've never said it before. 'The village people had lined up . . . Hold on a minute. Why's everyone laughing? Oh, no, not the VILLAGE PEOPLE! If they'd have been there . . .'

WEDNESDAY 21 NOVEMBER 2007

I'm back in my Birmingham flat having just completed three consecutive nights at the National Indoor Arena; that's an audience of about 13,000 people in total. The first two nights were filmed for a DVD of the tour, to come out in autumn 2008. Knowing a show's being filmed gives it a whole different ambience, a new significance. You feel the pressure to make it perfect. Creating a stand-up show is like making an ice-sculpture. All that effort – writing, trying out, polishing – a three-month tour, then it's gone. Once he's carefully carved his ice-sculpture, getting every groove and graceful line spot-on, the artist, I imagine, must at least want a few snapshots to remember it by, something to prove it existed before it drips and drains away. That's how I see the DVD. The problem is you don't want an average night immortalised; you want the time-capsule version to be the show at its very best. And once you get that idea in your head, you're in trouble.

It's like someone once said: breathing is the easiest thing in the world until you start thinking about it. You see it a lot with the England football team. Players who instinctively, unthinkingly, do the same excellent things week after week for their club side put on an England shirt, and suddenly it all goes wrong: they try too hard; become desperate to get it right. And 'desperate' is never a good mindset for a performer. Maria Callas, the opera singer, said she tried to treat every performance as if it were a rehearsal. She wanted to get it right, but relaxed and easy right – not tense and self-conscious right. In the latter case, the performer puts their talent in an immaculate but too-tight suit – every button buttoned-up, the necktie tight as a noose. It's a very neat outfit but the talent can't breathe, can't move; can't be itself. That little bit of loose and scruffy freedom, that place between effort and intuition, is where the magic lives.

The knowledge that you are being filmed – that the specific intonation of each word in the joke you're currently telling, the particular facial expression you wear while you're telling it, are being recorded and will represent this joke, this show, this tour, this comedian forever – is not necessarily conducive to a laid-back, go-with-the-flow performance. Part of me would like to let the ice-sculpture just melt away, to live on only in the memories of those who turned up to see it, to not do the DVD at all. Then again, the money's not bad – possibly one of those 'good deals' the budgerigar predicted.

When Adam drove us down the M6 in the early hours of Sunday morning, it started to snow. By the time we reached Birmingham, the world was swirling white. We've taken to listening to Radio Three in the car. I hadn't listened to Radio Three since they lost *Test Match Special* in the early nineties. If I happened across it accidentally, blindly twirling the dial while trying to not crash my car, it was always classical music or jazz, neither of which I much cared for. However, my opera obsession made me brave and I decided to give Three another shot. Adam was less keen to experiment, but, as with hotel rooms, I get first pick on the dashboard radio, so he had to take my hand on the terrifying journey into Beethoven and Brahms or Beiderbecke and Basie.

By that stage of the tour, Adam had developed some slight trust in my judgement. He seemed to genuinely enjoy my five-CD Fall box-set; thus adding a new, musical, element to our cultural exchange. HIS musical influence on ME had been a much more subtle one. I noticed, during one of my later and thus more con-fident skirmishes with the Birmingham flies, laying down the spray-can and once more, for old times' sake, taking up an old *Times*, that I had unintentionally swapped 'The Final Countdown' for a non-specific dee-diddle-dum-dum-dee. The tour-fusion continues; two apparently very different men swapping and sharing their differences and surprising themselves as they stumble across more and more common ground.

Anyway, we began our Radio Three journey like Hansel and Gretel, lost in the forest. At least with The Fall, one of us knew roughly where he was going; with Radio Three it was just tune in and hope. We started off with very short bursts, ten or fifteen minutes at a time, unless it was jazz, in which case we'd do four to five seconds. Sometimes I'd feel a twitch of enjoyment but mostly I was just bored. Adam and I would do a brief post-match analysis after each listen, scratching about for plus points, but we were both getting close to calling it a day. The turning point, incredibly, was a programme about mathematics and Bach. Neither of us had a clue what the bloke was talking about, but he was so fucking enthusiastic, we found ourselves being drawn in. And that was the thing with Radio Three, the thing that finally won us over. Everyone on there was so mad about music – so knowledgeable and keen to instruct. OK, it wasn't really OUR kind of music, but we loved how much they loved it, and wanted to hear what THEY could hear. It was what Radio One could be, if it didn't see its target audience as a thirteen-year-old girl with ADD.

Adam and I soon took our Radio Three helpings in thirty- or sixty-minute lumps, branching out to include world music shows as well as classical. We also finally confirmed that neither of us liked jazz, another patch of common ground. Now Three gets us through entire journeys: Purcell's contemporaries or Somalian drums. As we drove into snowy Birmingham (even Adam couldn't hang a 'sunny' on this one), we were listening to an hour of religious choral music: a heavenly choir to guide us through the storm. Oh, dear, I'm passionate about radio. My TV career must be fucked.

Monday afternoon, a few hours before the first gig, I bought the *Birmingham Evening Mail* from the shop near my flat. I didn't take any chances with the Indian woman. I was polite but with no back references. The fridge purred but did not roar. It would be my last chance to read a Birmingham paper safely, this week, with no possibility of being ambushed by a review. I opened it up, all relaxed and unsuspecting, and there was a picture of me; and next to that, a picture of Heather Mills.

She was angry. I've been doing a routine about her and the word had spread. You see, this is the irony of my latest anxiety, the fear that being filmed will fuck up my performance. I've actually BEEN filmed for most of the tour. Rarely a gig goes by when there isn't at least one little light shining in the crowd, one home video being recorded. And I know if I follow that little light, let it lead me into the darkness, I will soon reach that magical land where all roads lead to YouTube. Of course, I haven't looked myself, but I hear the tour shows are all over YouTube like a rash. Apparently the entire Basildon gig is on there in ten-minute lumps.

The DVD company's initial idea was to record a tour-show in early October and put it out in time for Christmas. I mean Christmas 2007. In other words, the DVD would have been in the shops by early November. Thus, I'd have been doing a show for the last three weeks of the tour which was already available on DVD. I had to say no. Some comedians are apparently fine with this, but my phobia about people having heard the jokes before would have gone through the ceiling. It turns out now that people have been able to watch the whole show on YouTube since mid-September. I've had a go at a few people in the crowd – asked them to stop filming – keep comedy live – but it just disrupts the show and makes me look like a cunt. Suddenly you're Metallica picking on poor little Napster, just because they want to give your work to the people. 'Hasn't he got enough money?' The thing is, it's not about money – my DVD payment isn't based on sales – and it's NOT like Metallica, or any other bootlegged music. Once you've heard a joke, no matter how much you love it, you'll never laugh at it again. It's a used joke, and a used joke is like a used condom: any pleasure is in the past. Like I've said a million times, I want to put on the best show I can. If half the crowd's already seen it on YouTube, it's unlikely to be a great night. I want laughs, not nods of recognition.

Anyway, it seems Heather Mills' associates have also been watching YouTube and have taken exception to some of my gags. Ironically, the routine is more or less on her side. It's about how people, when it comes to the Mills–McCartney marriage, automatically assume that Heather is the bad guy, even though they've never met either party. I always think any opinion THAT widely held has a very good chance of being wrong. Some of the Mills material came from a chat I had with two guys in the audience of the Comedy Café, at one of my warm-up gigs. One of them had said he hated Heather Mills. I asked him if he'd met her and, of course, he hadn't. I admitted a similar lack of first-hand knowledge:

> I've never met her either – a situation that will no doubt be remedied in a couple of years' time, when we both arrive to disappointingly lukewarm applause at the *Big Brother* house.

But how could this guy have such a strong opinion about Heather? I asked him to at least consider that he could be wrong about her, but he was off on another tack. 'I don't understand Paul,' he said. 'He could have had anybody. Why did he go and marry a woman with one leg?'

'Ah, well,' the other guy chimed in, 'people will do anything for a parking spot.'

It was the jokes about Heather's disability that her people were angry about. I have to take that on the chin. I tried to write a routine that was a new angle on the Heather Mills story, but on the way a few one-leg jokes did slip in. I did suggest, for example, that the only way Heather could have got the public on her side was to produce video evidence that Paul had treated her badly:

She needed one of those things they use on the cricket coverage: the stump-cam.

I went on to demonstrate her secretly filming Paul in this way. Maybe that was wrong, but if I lose a limb, I hereby give people permission to make jokes about it. During the routine, I talk about how surprising it is that, in the light of her disability, people still feel OK about slagging her off.

Usually we give disabled people the benefit of the doubt. Even if they don't seem to be very nice we respect them because they have battled against the odds. You take Abu Hamza, the Muslim cleric. Now some of you may think he is a bad person, someone who preaches separation and hate; but surely you still sympathise with his disability. He lost both his hands in an accident in the 1990s, and now has two hooks instead. Imagine having to go through life with two hooks for hands. Luckily, he likes corn-on-the-cob.

Anyway, the *Evening Mail* article quotes the stump-cam gag and includes a response from 'a spokesperson' for Heather. 'Is that the best material he can come up with?' the spokesperson asks. This is quite a big question, centring on the subjectivity of comedic appreciation and a semantic analysis of the word 'best', but, all that considered, I would be inclined to say 'no'. There are, in my opinion, much better jokes in both my current set and my back-catalogue. But, having said that, I do quite a good whirring and clicking video-camera impression, I enjoy the specialist-knowledge cricket reference and I can't get away from the fact that the joke always gets a good laugh. It may seem difficult to justify the gag on moral grounds – it is essentially making fun of someone else's misfortune – but Heather's success, aura of strength and impending wealth seem to take the edge off the cruelty. It's like when some comics lay into Americans: the victims seem too powerful to BE victims. It's hard to see Americans as an oppressed minority and it's hard to see Heather as helpless prey.

The spokesperson goes on: 'I wouldn't wish having one leg on my worst enemy.' Well, who would? People like me, who are compassionate and see God's eternal flame flickering in the soul of each individual, don't wish disability on anyone, including our worst enemy . . . whoever that is. But even people who DO have such malicious thoughts would be unlikely to wish having ONE LEG on their worst enemy. Their worst enemy, I'd imagine, qualifies to have AT LEAST death wished upon them, probably slow and painful death. 'Having one leg' would be wished on a foe much further down the Enemy League Table – maybe just someone who'd cut them up in traffic or spilt their drink. To complicate matters further, one might actually wish 'having one leg' on a dear friend, if that dear friend had no legs at all.

The spokesperson's final point is that 'comedians are a different species'. Though the statement is biologically unsound, I suspect the spokesperson is making a point along the lines of 'Comedians are from Mars, one-legged people are from Venus'. This seems to suggest that one-legged people can't possibly be comedians and I find it much more monopedist than my stump-cam joke – the latter being, after all, a suggested method by which Heather might have got a fair hearing.

I was a bit pissed off by the Heather Mills article, but only, if I'm honest, because, for any *Evening Mail* readers in the Birmingham audience the stump-cam gag is now a 'used' joke. There were 5,500 people in the arena on Monday night, the first of the three Birmingham shows. The two great loves of my life were represented: Cath was there, and so were forty players and staff from West Bromwich Albion. It went pretty well but, despite my attempts to ignore the cameras, to make it feel like a normal gig, I did still have that sense of being filmed. I felt a bit like I was an actor playing the part of a comedian. I wondered afterwards if this self-consciousness had stopped a good gig from becoming a great one. Still, people rarely film one show for a stand-up DVD. The usual method, the one we were employing, is to film two shows and use the best of the pair in the final edit. So, if my internal angst did show up on camera, at least I had another bite of the cherry to come.

There was an after-show party at the NIA and I duly mingled. Dean Keily, the West Brom goalkeeper, said he'd enjoyed the show, and I, of course, said it could have been better. 'You got eight out of ten in the *Sun*,' he said.

'Oh, did I?' I said, gloomily.

'That's good,' he insisted. 'Eight out of ten will usually get you in Team of the Week.'

I didn't know if he was joking or referring to an actual review, and I mingled away before he could tell me. Then I spoke to a couple of staff members from West Brom, repeating to one that I really wasn't sure about the show. The other looked crestfallen.

'Oh, I thought I'd just seen a really brilliant gig and now you've put doubt in my mind,' he said.

After that I decided to keep my opinions to myself. It was a strange night on that front. I started to wonder how good I am at judging my own gigs. I did the granny porn routine as a second encore that night. As I've said, I dropped it early on in the tour and hadn't done it since. People seemed to stop getting my point of view on the subject – that, in the unlikely setting of granny porn, I often felt genuine warmth and affection for the old ladies involved – and instead just seemed to see it as a bit sick. I thought I'd do it tonight so I at least had a record of it for future reference. It seemed to go really well and it was the routine that got the most compliments in the after-show chat. Cath thought it was 'fantastic', but, then again, love is blind. As Adam drove me back to the flat, I wondered again how many routines I had abandoned too soon, how many ticks, crosses and question marks I had allotted incorrectly.

When I saw Adam on the afternoon of the second Birmingham gig, he handed me the *Evening Mail*. I could see that half a page had been ripped out; I'd asked him to remove any reviews beforehand. My manager called and I mentioned this precaution to him.

'Oh, I haven't read it,' he said, 'but I heard there was nothing bad in it.' The old madness kicked in. What did he mean, 'nothing bad'? If it had been a good interview he'd have just said it was good. By the time I was sitting, pre-gig, in my NIA dressing room, I'd written the review in my head:

'He's lost his edge . . . the granny porn routine was embarrassing

... summer has turned to autumn ... Birmingham's love affair with Frank Skinner is over.' I sighed deeply. Then there was a knock on my door. It was show-time.

Adam and I walked across the gloomily lit, football-pitch-sized backstage area. I could hear the expectant hum of the crowd. I walked with my arms at my sides, twirling my hands clockwise and anti-clockwise. It was something I saw Elvis do as HE walked through the gloom, towards the stage of the Las Vegas Hilton, in the movie *Elvis: That's the Way It Is*. My obsessions come and go, but Elvis, even his smallest gestures, seems permanently imprinted on my consciousness. 'The Container Drivers'. I was up the steps and, fuck the cameras, let's do it. And it just sort of happened. The coy expressions, the rim-shot punchlines. It felt good, good enough for the time-capsule.

Tonight, the third and last of the Birmingham gigs, was always going to be strange. England were playing Croatia in the last Euro '08 qualifier. My manager, Jon, had a great idea. I do the first half of the gig, then they show the second half of the game on the big screens, by way of an extended interval, then I come out and do the SECOND half of the gig. England only needed a draw to qualify. If they did it, the second half would be a thing of beauty, a cross between a stand-up show and an open-topped-bus, ticker-tape welcome.

I didn't get to sleep till 4 a.m. this morning, the morning of my comedy-football rally. I'm guessing it was a post-DVD adrenalin thing. I woke at nine. I did my Lectio Divina, on Mark 4:40, 'Why are ye so fearful? How is it that ye have no faith?', the perfect meditation to precede an England game, and then I had a bath, in total darkness, listening to Verdi's *Il Trovatore*. I even, in my latest show of down-to earth independence, cleaned the bath afterwards.

Adam picked me up at 5.45 and handed me tonight's *Evening Mail*, with another half-a-page missing. 'That'll be the disappointed punter's mailbag,' I thought to myself, 'a dozen or so letters saying I've lost it and that living in London has de-Skinnered me for ever.' 'Why are ye so fearful? Why is it that ye have no faith?'

The first half of the gig was good, but when I walked down the steps into the backstage gloom, Adam said, 'We're two-nil down.'

I can't say my immediate thought was, 'Oh, no, this'll ruin the rest of the show', or even 'Oh, no, *The Times* newspaper won't send David Baddiel and me to do three weeks of podcasts from the European Championships, like we did in Germany for the last World Cup, seeing loads of live games and generally having a real laugh.' No, I just thought, 'Fuck, England aren't going to be in the European Championships.' I sat in my dressing room, watching the second half on television. We pulled one back, then we equalised. I decided I needed to be in a crowd. I sneaked out into the darkened auditorium and found an empty seat. No one seemed to notice me. It was the football that mattered. There were people screaming and swearing all around me, kicking every ball, pleading with the players, folding over, head in hands, at every near miss. We only needed a draw and we'd be there; just a draw, that was all. We lost.

The second half of my gig was a bit flat. When England lost to Portugal in the last World Cup, David Baddiel and I spent the seventy-five-minute drive back to the hotel in complete silence; we should have had big white mugs of tea, and blankets round our shoulders, like rescued ferry passengers fresh from the cold, grey waves. But shipwreck self-pity wasn't an option tonight. I felt obliged to be all 'we'll bounce back' about it, when all I really wanted to do was sulk.

I'm married to West Bromwich Albion, in sickness and in health. I accept the dull days and disappointments, the stretch-marks and the smells, but England are supposed to be my glamorous extra-marital affair: the designer-labelled, Lamborghini-driving, multi-millionaire world-beaters who I meet in exciting, exotic locations for sexy floodlit thrills. But, as usual, I'm sitting in the swanky restaurant, all suited, shaved and gelled, looking at the door, then looking at my watch, knowing it's the same as it always is: when it comes to the special occasion, they never fucking turn up.

I hate the England team tonight; I resent their misplaced arrogance. Not so long ago it was us, the fans, who took all the shit. You'd hear players moaning about fans in interviews – they were too violent or too corporate-prawn-sandwiches soft; they sang personally abusive chants or they didn't sing at all and were too quiet – but now the tables have turned. The fans are appalled by the players' behaviour: owning up to violent vendettas against their fellow professionals or feigning fouls and injuries; cheating their way to success. Greedy wage claims and secret meetings; seedy gang-bangs and allegations of rape. The tabloids are full of it. When I was at the World Cup last year, every England game was a monument to our supporters. I know we've got our share of drunken, mouth-breather yobs, but as a whole the fans were incredible. Every game became a home game; crosses of St George covered the stadiums wherever we played; every opposition was completely out-sung. It wasn't the fans that didn't deliver in Germany, and it wasn't the fans that didn't deliver tonight. At this precise moment, I hate those fucking England players. I never feel like that about the West Brom lot, no matter how badly they play. But that dark feeling will pass. Maybe I shouldn't write this journal when I'm so worked up.

Still, even though, for tonight at least, those players feel like my worst enemies, I have at no time since the final whistle wished having one leg on any of them. Heather's spokesperson was spot-on.

To be honest, the second half of the gig wasn't so bad. We all held hands and walked through the darkness together until we eventually saw light. My now-near-bullet-proof set kicked in and we put our despair on hold. They laughed and even applauded, but the clouds never truly cleared. If only I could have returned to the stage for my encore, leading that pig and that goat.

I wasn't feeling too bad till I got back here and put Sky Sports on. They showed a list of the teams who will be in Euro '08: France, Germany, Italy . . . on and on went the list, scrolling downwards until it reached the end: Holland, Greece and Spain. I was all right till I saw that list. Everyone seemed to be on it except us.

The last time Adam and I were in Birmingham – it's been a regular stopping-off place on the tour – we shopped at Selfridge's. It's housed in a high-concept building that looks like a whale in bubble-wrap. I tried on a charcoal-grey overcoat. I really liked it but I already have a few overcoats – the Frank Skinner Tragic Hero Collection – so I took it off and moved on. Then I went back and tried it on again. I still liked it. When I looked in the mirror and squinted, in order to deliberately blur my vision, I thought it made me look a bit José Mourinho. When I say 'squinted', I mean 'completely closed my eyes'. But did I really need it? Adam, probably wondering why a millionaire would be doing quite so much soul-searching over a two-hundred-quid overcoat, urged me to splash out but, after examining it, and me in it, from an array of angles, I finally handed it back. When the tour is over, in seven gigs' time – I don't really think in days and weeks any more – I'm going to buy that overcoat, a congratulatory gift from me to me. Shit, I broke the rule. I vowed to myself that I wouldn't speak, write or even think about the end of the tour until, well, you know. When I used to have swimming lessons, I could just about manage to front-crawl a length of the pool (it was a small pool). As I neared the end of that length, my stroke would noticeably deteriorate, not because I was tired or breathless but because I was thinking about the end. 'Just concentrate on making each stroke as good as it can possibly be,' my teacher would say. 'The end will come when it comes.' When I stuck to that I swam pretty good, right up to the end. I lived in the stroke I was making; there was no world outside, no anticipation, no goal. That's me with seven gigs to go: living in the stroke.

FRIDAY 30 NOVEMBER 2007

It's been hard not thinking about the end of the tour while planning Adam's end-of-the-tour present. I wanted it to be just so. In one of our four million late-night drives together, I happened to mention a meal I'd eaten at the Fat Duck in Bray, reputedly the best restaurant in Britain. I'm very much not a foodie; I only eat to avoid malnutrition. When I was a kid, I used to read about astronauts eating a meat-and-two-veg dinner compressed into a tiny green pill. I dreamed that, when I got older, that pill would be the norm and I'd be able to spend my lunch break going for a walk or drawing, rather than wasting my time cutting, forking, chewing and swallowing food. I still dream about it. The pill with a swig of water, an hour of banjo then back to work.

I haven't really played banjo since the tour began. For the last three months, I've basically just written jokes, told jokes and read the newspaper. I'll have a spare twenty minutes on the uke, but that's still work-related. My plans for personal development haven't quite worked out. Each time I stop off at my London flat, I leave behind another dream. The chess computer was the first to go.

I've been wanting to learn chess for about ten years. The urge first came upon me when I saw old men playing it at outdoor tables in New York's Central Park, and it was rekindled when I read a book about Bobby Fischer and Boris Spassky a few years later. I have four or five very nice chess sets that patiently wait for me to learn. My most recent I-must-learn-chess moment came during my Canada trip. In Toronto's main square, I saw a weird old Peruvian guy called Raul. I knew his name because he had written it on an A5 piece of paper, reinforced the paper with sticky-tape and fixed it to the back of his waistcoat; he also wore a home-made badge that said 'Commander'. He sat on a low stool with a four-foot-square chessboard on the floor at his feet. He challenged all-comers, for five dollars a game; a sort of intellectual version of the boxing booth. A pretty black girl, about fifteen, had a try, moving the eight-inch-high pieces around the board. She concentrated hard but Raul won. Then her cool-dude boyfriend tried and also failed. I must have watched six or seven games, six or seven challengers; Raul didn't take long to finish each five-dollar job. I was enthralled but mystified; not being a chess-player, I couldn't decipher his skills. But I admired Raul. He got his money on the street, with ingenuity and finesse. It was way more impressive than just sticking out an upturned palm. Maybe chess could be my New Year's Resolution? On the next trip home, I left behind the Learn French tapes and so it went on. Even my Mulisch is home in London. Only my running shoes remain, in a side pocket of my bag, and not one step have they taken. Still, I've lost half a stone – apparently, just from doing the gigs. I used to think I shagged myself slim on tour, but it turns out that telling jokes is a diet in its own right.

Anyway, speaking of weight-gain, when I went to the Fat Duck I had the tasting menu. I think it was fourteen courses, but it was more like going to the theatre than having a meal. Each course was introduced by the waitress and was a little event in its own right. There was snail-porridge, egg-and-bacon ice cream and a seafood platter you ate while listening to an iPod that played sounds of the sea. My favourite course was hot and iced tea, which doesn't sound that remarkable until you realise they are in the same cup but the hot tea stays hot and the iced tea stays iced. It was like a magic trick.

I told Adam all this and he was enthralled. He said the Fat Duck's super-chef owner, Heston Blumenthal, was a hero of his and he'd dreamed of eating there. I was, I'll admit, slightly shocked that a man's man like Adam would make a 'hero' out of a cook and that, this time, the airing of his feminine side had nothing to do with me. I had actually met Heston Blumenthal, as I tucked into my fifth course, the liquorice-coated salmon, and thought he seemed a very sweet bloke. I was relieved at the time, because I'd heard tales of Marco Pierre White throwing people out of restaurants and Gordon Ramsay telling people to fuck off, and, considering that Heston is a big, broad-shouldered skinhead of a man, I was half-expecting my fifteenth course to be a kick in the bollocks.

I sat next to Gordon Ramsay at a birthday party once. He was friendly but, goodness me, he was very alpha male. He began by telling me he'd been battered to fuck in a rugby game the previous weekend and then said he would soon be off to the Ironman Triathalon where he would swim 2.5 miles, run 26 and cycle 112. At this point my quickly diminishing penis joined my testicles in a hastily arranged hansom cab and they fled into miserable exile. Gordon asked me why I didn't have a crack at the Ironman Triathalon myself. I explained that, as I could barely swim or ride a bike, it would be a bit of a shambles. Shortly after that, he went and sat somewhere else. To be fair to him, the party was at Elton John's villa in Nice, and a lot of the heterosexual male guests were talking, in a deeper-than-usual-voice, about stuff like stag-shooting and World War II. When the Scissor Sisters turned up, even I was beginning to wish I'd brought my pipe.

Anyway, I've arranged for Adam to have lunch at the Fat Duck, food and wine all paid for, and also got him a local hotel room in which to sleep it off. I told him a few days back and he seemed very pleased; ironic, really, because only last night we had an argument about food.

We were in the dressing room, before the gig at Sheffield City Hall, and there was a packet of sliced chicken on the rider table. The contract just says 'chicken' and this has been interpreted in many ways. We've had whole roast chickens, party-food chicken-legs and a variety of processed chicken treats; but tonight was a first. Tonight it was those circular slices of chicken with a smaller circle of stuffing in the middle – an unexpected pleasure, but only four slices, barely enough for one person. While Adam was doing his Dr Doolittle bit with the crew, it would have been the easiest thing in the world for me to eat the lot. But no, I thought I'd be polite. I listened on the dressing room speakers to him diddle-diddle-deeing his way through the preliminary soundcheck, and then, when he finally returned to the dressing room, I gestured towards the food. We both stared at the table, with its fruit juice and soya spread, its blueberries and ham. But I suspect all Adam and I saw were the chicken slices staring back at us with their come-to-bed eyes, stuffing-coloured pupils and irises of pinkish-grey.

'Are you thinking of having any of those chicken slices?' I said.

'Yes,' he replied. I was severely fucked off. Clearly I was just being polite. Most performers wouldn't even ask.

'What is the advantage of being the turn on this tour?' I asked him.

'How long have you got?' he replied.

Though I would, on one level, have been interested to hear Adam's full-length reply, with all its rage and resentment, I didn't think it would be an ideal preparation for the show. Thus, as if the two contesting mothers had said to wise Solomon, 'Of course, cut the baby in half. That's a great idea', we ate a profoundly unsatisfactory two slices of stuffed chicken each, seasoned with umbrage and bile.

Sheffield was a great gig, one of the best on the tour; I caught myself saying, onstage, 'I love this job.' I haven't done that since the early club-gigs when I was so happy to be back. To be saying it during the sixty-seventh gig of the tour surprised me somewhat. It just came out, unpremeditated, like I had forgotten and was reminding myself.

I could say it was a great crowd, it certainly felt like one, but what does that actually mean? Comedians talk about good crowds and bad crowds, lively and quiet, quick and slow, but does it really make sense that a large group of unconnected strangers would all feel the same way on any given night? What could cause that – room temperature? Atmospheric pressure? Isn't it more likely that each crowd, at the beginning of the evening, is essentially a blank page and it is something in the performer that dictates their joint response? That scenario would require only one person, and a person that everyone is paying attention to, to be good or bad or nervous or tired or whatever. If it's a club night, with several performers on the bill, you'll often see an individual comic make a 'bad' crowd 'good' or, tragically, vice versa, which suggests that the mood is defined by the comic, not the other was round. Having said all that, some nights, like that warm-up gig in Aldershot, you walk out onstage and feel the muted response straight away, which suggests the tone has already been set before you were added to the mix. But maybe just your walk on stage, some indefinable this-isn't-going-to-be-funny body language, can kill a gig before you've even spoken. Well, I must have got my walk right in Sheffield because the whole gig was a beautiful thing.

Adam and I are in the Joke-Mobile, driving back from Salford, and I'm not giving any thought whatsoever to the fact that there's only one show left. It's been a great week this week, and not just the gigs. On Tuesday, we were in Dundee. I mentioned to Adam a few weeks ago that Dundee is the home of the publishers D C Thomson and Co Ltd. That name represents a magical world to me. When I was a kid, it appeared at the foot of the back page in every *Beano* and *Dandy* comic. D C Thomson's was the home of Dennis the Menace and Desperate Dan, Korky the Cat and the Bash Street Kids, and dozens of other characters who accompanied me through my childhood. I'd first discovered them as just pictures, before I could read the words, following the comic strips in sequence, frame by frame, trying to make sense of what I saw.

Then, when I started school aged five, I quickly learned to read and the comics suddenly started to grow in my hands, the pictures sprouting words and meanings. I was like a deaf person who'd been used to a silent world but now, at last, was beginning to hear.

There is a story about the American rock 'n' roll star, Eddie Cochran. He was killed in a car crash in 1960, in Chippenham, while on a UK tour. They say he was found face-down in the road, his right-arm outstretched, reaching, as his life ebbed away, for his Gretsch 6120 guitar that lay on the ground nearby. The guitar and all its associations were obviously at the centre of Cochran's universe and he didn't want to die alone.

Seven or eight years later, as my family, in their council house in Warley, West Midlands, prepared for a day-trip to Rhyll, I ran off to the nearby newsagent's to get a *Beano* to read on the coach. I'd be seven or eight. As I ran back home, clutching my comic, a car hit me on a zebra crossing and thudded me to the ground. As I lay in a daze, face-down, half on the zebra-crossing, half off it, I reached out for the fluttering *Beano*; Billy Whizz, General Jumbo and Lord Snooty, each appearing as the pages turned in the wind; trying to grab it before it blew away. It's nice to have your friends around you when you're feeling scared.

Adam, unbeknownst to me, made a few phone calls and arranged for us to have a private tour of D C Thomson's Dundee HQ. I was as excited as that kid, running to get his comic, when we drove into the public car park and saw a Billy Whizz mural on the wall. Shortly afterwards, we turned a corner and discovered a massive statue, more a tableau, of the *Dandy*'s Desperate Dan, striding purposefully forward, not noticing the *Beano*'s Minnie the Minx, catapult raised, just behind him.

Way back at the beginning of this tour, I watched an interview with Leo Baxendale, the Michelangelo of British comics, the artist who, back in the fifties, created Minnie the Minx and several other classic strips. He said something about his creation which I've thought back to several times, whenever the tour, on- or offstage, has caused me to tremble or doubt. 'I didn't give Minnie superhuman strength,' he said. 'I gave her an intensity of will, and that carried her through.'

I think I was expecting D C Thomson's to be like the U.N.C.L.E. headquarters in the *Man from U.N.C.L.E.* TV series: a secret organisation hidden away behind a misleading shop-front, the local residents unaware of its existence. It turned out the *Beano* and *Dandy* characters were local heroes, celebrated in public art. Unlike prophets, they were very much NOT without honour in their own land.

When we finally turned up at the enormous old red-brick building, and saw the D C Thomson brass plaque on the wall, the hairs stood up on the back of my neck. I met the editor of the *Beano*, a smiling Andy Williams lookalike, who introduced me to a smartly dressed old guy, the *Beano*'s resident artist. Very friendly and gentle of manner, he sat at a desk on which lay, pushed to one side, an enormous pile of his own drawings in various stages of completion. He picked out a few and showed me how the work developed: from an initial rough sketch which concentrated on movement and energy, the characters depicted as a series of coiling lines, to a neatly polished final draft. He said, interestingly, that his favourite stage lay somewhere between the two, where the raw energy of the original still dominated, had not been contained by the pernickety search for perfection, and a few remaining rough lines only added to the immediacy of the piece.

Of course, still having my tour-head on, that mindset that feeds everything through a stand-up comedy filter, I found myself applying this to my own work. What was my favourite stage in the process? Maybe it was the early club-gigs, the ascent. Once you've climbed to the top and stuck your flag in, the job feels done. After that you're just admiring the view. I asked the artist if he ever drew for pleasure. He smiled at me as if puzzled by my enquiry. 'I draw all the time,' he said.

In the *Dandy* office, which used to be the *Beano* office, I was shown a view from the window, looking down on to the main entrance of an old school. Leo Baxendale, more than fifty years ago, used to gaze down at these gates as the kids poured out each evening, surveying the scene as he absent-mindedly scribbled on his pad. That outbreak of children, their bustling escape from captivity, was the inspiration for another of his great creations, the Bash Street Kids.

I stood in the archive room, picking my way through untidy piles of comic genius: cow-pies and slipper-wielding fathers; mortar-boards and sausage-studded mash. As I said onstage that night, 'A roomful of faded old comics – I've never felt more at home.'

Since we left Salford tonight, I've had six or seven phone calls from Cath. She is in Cricklewood, North-west London, watching The Fall, and every time they play a new song she phones me up so I can listen to it. It's always exciting when a new song appears in The Fall's live set. That first appearance is often chaotic; the Fall's leader, Mark E. Smith, is happy to unveil a song when it's still in embryo form. The regular Fall gig-goer can then watch the song develop, watch several songs develop simultaneously, until the new album is born. Maybe most bands do this, I don't know. I don't study other bands closely enough, don't go to the required multiple gigs. I suppose it's not unlike my own method for developing material, but I'm not as courageous as Smith. He'll present a song when it's still just a thought wrapped in noise, a growling anti-riff of guitar and a dark thudding rhythm raining down as he spits out indecipherable words read off a scrap of paper.

Detractors will say all The Fall's stuff sounds like that, but they don't understand. They'll never know how beautiful it is to watch that thought, that noise, grow into a Fall song, and yet not grow too much, never be allowed to complete, always remain a man shouting in a storm. One of Smith's great gifts, I think, is that he knows when to halt the development, knows when the song is at its rough and reckless best – like that *Beano* artist's favourite stage in the drawing: caught between raw, coiled energy and polished expertise, deliberately unfinished, rough lines and immediacy still intact.

The Fall have been around since the late seventies, but I am a new member of the congregation, with all the zeal of the convert. Like most people, my first experience of The Fall came through John Peel's radio show. I was driving one night, about twelve years ago, when Peel played a Fall song called 'Spoilt Victorian Child'. I absolutely loved it and resolved to buy it the next time I was in a record shop. For some unknown reason, it took me ten years to get round to it. I wonder now if a deep survival instinct was telling me to save The Fall for my twilight years, a spitting, sparkling beacon to illuminate the gloom of a world turned predictable and stale. It was certainly odd how fate kept us apart.

In December of 1989, I was doing a gig at Glasgow Students' Union. The plan was I'd open the show with a twenty-minute set and then reappear through the course of the evening to introduce each of the bands, notably Bad Manners and The Fall. When I turned up, the union's nervous little Ents Officer told me there'd been trouble during the soundcheck. Apparently a knife had been pulled, and The Fall had refused to go on if Bad Manners were doing the show. The ensuing chaos that surrounded Bad Manners' exit lasted so long that I ended up doing my twenty minutes and then dashing off to get my train. I never saw The Fall.

Then, finally, in a Brighton record shop, on 16 April 2005, I bought 'Spoilt Victorian Child'; on a Fall Greatest Hits album called *50,000 Fall Fans Can't Be Wrong*. Cath bought a My Bloody Valentine album at the same time. When we got back from shopping, we went into separate rooms to listen to our new purchases. Five tracks later, Cath walked into the room.

'How is it?' she asked.

I turned to her, shallow-breathed and shaking. 'This is the music I've been searching for my whole life,' I replied.

A couple of months later, I was on holiday in Portugal with David Baddiel. It was another one of my dark-walk-on-the-beach experiences. The resort we were staying in was strangely synthetic – none of the buildings pre-dated 1980; it was like Legoland – and we'd gone down to the beach at midnight to escape. As we walked and talked beside the moonlight-dappled waves, I told Dave about my new obsession.

'The thing is,' Dave said, with a slight hint of concern, 'The Fall are one of those bands that cunts say they like, in order to sound cool. I'm not saying you DON'T like them, I'm just saying keep it to yourself.' The ocean swished into the shore and we moved on to another subject.

I know what Dave meant. I hate those celebrity questionnaires when every answer seems to be saying, 'This is who I want you to THINK I am.' Men are the worst. Every try-too-hard trendy male celebrity seems to like Japanese movies – well, Japanese anything, really – snowboarding, and a football team they don't get much chance to see because of work. And they always, when asked about music, choose reggae or hip-hop; thus establishing not only that they're cool but also that they're NOT racist. Maybe they ARE completely sincere and do really like these things, but I'm always very suspicious, always think their PR person has told them what to say, always wonder what part of their public persona they're trying to sell me. Consequently, it makes me self-conscious about expressing my own likes and loves. If only I could have held on to Gilbert White; that would have been monumentally uncool.

Anyway, I love The Fall. When 'Container Drivers' kicks in before I go on stage, it isn't meant to be a badge of honour; it's because the song always makes me feel excited and sends me on with a rocket up my arse. And Cath loves The Fall too – and I mean REALLY loves them, not just tags along with me to be loyal. Hence her going to the gig tonight, when I'm away on tour. Our shared love for The Fall is one of the pillars of our relationship. It's like that bit in the Wheatus song 'Teenage Dirtbag' – except for the Teenage bit, obviously – when the guy finds out the girl he's been hankering for likes Iron Maiden as much as he does; that she, after all, is just a freaky, geeky weirdo loner too. I must be the only person in the world who cries at that song.

PART FOUR

AFTERMATH

MONDAY 3 DECEMBER 2007

The tour is over and I'm in my London flat. It's four minutes past midnight; you just missed Big Ben. The last gig was in Harrogate. I walked off stage, shook hands with Adam and Jon, but had no sense of a dramatic ending, no feeling of freedom, sadness or relief. I just put my ukulele in its case and had a nice cup of tea.

There have been times during this tour when I've decided I will never tour again, and times when I've decided I'll tour and tour forever and, even if the tubes up my nose and drips in my arm make me look more *Starlight Express* than stand-up comedian, still I will abide. As I sat drinking that nice cup of tea in Harrogate, it didn't feel like a full stop; it felt like a dot-dot-dot.

I was in church that morning, the morning of the last gig, and I saw a Down's Syndrome guy pass another Down's Syndrome guy in the aisle. I felt strangely disappointed that they didn't acknowledge each other; no nod, no smile, nothing. I thought it should have been like when one Volkswagen Beetle passes another, and the drivers toot their horns, a little gesture of solidarity between two kindred spirits. I instinctively reached for my pencil, and wondered if the 'you are a sick man' section of my NEXT tour was already beginning to form.

I don't know if the priest saw that brief encounter in the aisle but, if he did, he didn't mention it in his sermon. He talked about people's sense of individual self and how it has increased in importance over the centuries. He used art as a means of illustrating this. He said the medieval artists didn't even sign their work because it was the subject-matter that was important, not them. But eventually, the priest said, things started to change. During the Renaissance period, the cult of the artist rose up. By the late eighteenth century, Romanticism was reflecting the artist's complete self-obsession. Now, the priest proclaimed, with a shake of his head, modern art is all about the artist's inner darkness. 'Tracey Emin's "Bed",' he said, with no explanatory footnote, 'is a monument to social, personal, cultural and spiritual anarchy.' I looked around the church at the sleepy pensioners and colouring-book kids, the chubby housewives and spotty Goths, and I noticed they were all looking in different directions. One of the Down's Syndrome guys was peering over his shoulder, towards the back of the church; the other, however, seemed completely engrossed. How did the priest think the gig was going? Could he tell I was loving his stuff?

I often wonder, in church, what people are thinking. Those that look most bored might be experiencing internal rapture; others might be gazing intently at the priest but thinking about lunch. I still had, it being the morning of the last gig, my tour-head on. I was back at my recurring theme: how do you really know how it's going?

When I got in tonight, my first post-tour night, I watched the opening twenty minutes of my Birmingham DVD. It hasn't been edited yet; I just wanted to see how it looked. Despite the fact I've just done the show sixty-nine times, I found myself laughing out loud. I was alone so I wasn't embarrassed; little gestures and expressions I wasn't aware I did really made me hoot. I was right about that second-night gig: I was in really good form. But, when I took the DVD out of the machine, I realised I'd been watching the FIRST-night gig, the one I'd felt was too considered, too restrained, a little bit flat. I suppose, ultimately, my opinion is just one opinion, no more valid than another – perhaps less valid than those watching the show from the optimum position, out there in the dark.

When Adam drove us back from Harrogate, I told him I was thinking of buying Cath a mini. 'Which one?' he asked. Of course, I hadn't realised there were different types.

'Oh, one of the new ones,' I said.

'Oh, they're fun to drive,' he said enthusiastically. I asked him what that meant.

'Well,' he said, 'if you like driving . . .' and then went on to say something about acceleration and gripping the road.

'Do I like driving?' I asked myself, out loud. 'I don't really think of it as a thing to be liked or not liked. You might as well ask me if I like opening doors: it's just something I have to do to GET places.'

Adam laughed in disbelief. He said he often 'goes out for a drive' with no destination in mind – just for the love of it, just to drive. Then I laughed in disbelief. We talked about that advert on the telly for some car or other in which a bloke is trying to drive to Glasgow but the talking Sat Nav in his car insists on taking him an alternative route. Eventually the bloke arrives at one end of a long road, meandering into green hills. 'Enjoy,' says the Sat Nav.

'Every time I see that advert,' I told Adam, 'I always think, "enjoy what?"' Adam spluttered with delight. The conversation was turning into a sort of laugh-in-disbelief tennis match.

The tour had ended and we were returning to our respective natural states, the people we were before. We met in the middle, I suppose, but now we were truly going home. I was on my way to see, at the Royal Festival Hall that night, a 1924 silent film with a live orchestral accompaniment written by the bloke from Goldfrapp; and Adam was talking about cars. Soon we would come to that fork in the road, see the high-tech digital sign to Middle England and the weather-beaten marker-stone to Weirdo-Loner-Ville; we would both smile our home-again smiles and go our separate ways.

When he dropped me off outside my flat (the fork in the road was metaphorical) I clambered out of the Joke-Mobile, laden with boxes and bags. I looked at Adam and he looked at me and we hugged, our first hug of the tour. However, because of all my baggage, I couldn't really fulfil MY half of the hug. We struggled for a moment, then he put his arms around me and I lay my head on his shoulder. We stayed like that for a few seconds, and then I walked away. One of the boxes I carried was Adam's end-of-tour gift to me: the charcoal-grey overcoat from Selfridge's.

As I struggled to open my door, a neighbour walked past, a guy I speak to about once a year. 'Hello, Frank,' he said, 'you still not doing telly?'

'I've just come back from a sixty-nine-date stand-up tour,' I said.

'See you later,' he replied. I went inside. I laid down my bags and boxes and put the kettle on. While it boiled I took off my Kokopelli ring and put it back in the drawer. In that same drawer was a small envelope from Jenny, containing some keys I asked her to get cut. I've decided to ask Cath to move in. Manga-eyes, an hour-glass figure, Voltaire, Cranach, The Fall. I'd be an idiot to let that slip away.

I decided to go for a little walk, give the overcoat an airing. As I left the flat I got a text from Adam: the Joke-Mobile, during the course of the tour, did 13,000 miles. That's a lot of Radio Three.

I walked along the river to Victoria Tower Gardens, a little park next to the Houses of Parliament, where a sculpture by Auguste Rodin stands. It's called *The Burghers of Calais*. Apparently Calais was under siege and the attacking army said they'd let the people live if six leading dignitaries came out and died in their place. I stood admiring the sculpture; the six burghers, ready for execution. One frightened old man carried an enormous key and had a noose around his neck. I hoped it wasn't an omen for Cath moving in.

Just before I set off for that first gig in Leeds, nearly three months ago, I walked through this park and the burghers weren't there; only their empty plinth remained. It turned out they were away as part of a Rodin exhibition. I like the fact that, touring done, bright lights extinguished, the burghers and me are back home, safe and sound. Despite my resolution to not think about the end of the tour, I must admit I had been wondering, for some time, how it would feel when I hit that last note in the Osama song, onstage in Harrogate, and knew the job was done. As it was, I went to the C chord a couple of beats too early and completely fucked up the ending. The last moment of the last gig of the tour was a mistake. But that's OK; nothing's 100 per cent. I remember smiling to myself as I walked off into the wings. I suddenly saw the whole tour as a warm-up for the next one. Perhaps every tour, every gig, is exactly that.

APPENDIX (I)

WARM-UP AND TOUR DATES

16–21 July	Montreal Just For Laughs
26 July	Toronto Just for Laughs
13–27 August	Edinburgh Pleasance
9 September	Leeds City Varieties
10 September	Leeds City Varieties
12 September	Peterborough Broadway Theatre
13 September	Basildon Towngate Theatre
14 September	Hastings White Rock Theatre
15 September	Jersey Opera House
16 September	Tunbridge Wells Assembly Hall
17 September	Chelmsford Civic Theatre
18 September	Alban Arena
20 September	Aberdeen Music Hall
21 September	Dublin Vicar Street
22 September	Torquay Princess Theatre
23 September	Liverpool Royal Court
24 September	Buxton Opera House
25 September	Bolton Albert Halls
27 September	Hayes Beck Theatre
28 September	Leas Cliff Hall

29 September	Aldershot Princes Hall
30 September	Watford Palace Theatre
1 October	Cambridge Corn Exchange
3 October	Basingstoke Anvil
4 October	Bournemouth Pavillion
5 October	Dorking Halls
6 October	Reading Hexagon
7 October	Salford Lowry
8 October	Nottingham Playhouse
10 October	Blackburn King Georges Hall
11 October	Bedford Corn Exchange
12 October	Eastbourne Congress Theatre
13 October	Bradford St George's Hall
14 October	York Grand Opera House
16 October	Barnstaple Queen's Theatre
17 October	Chatham Central Theatre
18 October	Crawley Hawth
19 October	Skegness Embassy
20 October	Ipswich Corn Exchange
21 October	Southend Cliffs Pavilion
23 October	Oxford Playhouse
24 October	Wycombe Swan
25 October	Cheltenham Town Hall
26 October	Southampton Guildhall
27 October	North Wales Theatre
28 October	Newcastle Theatre Royal
30 October	Northampton Derngate
31 October	Kings Lynn Corn Exchange
1 November	Belfast Opera House
2 November	Salisbury City Hall

3 November	Preston Charter Theatre
4 November	Cardiff Wales Millenium Centre
6 November	Bristol Colston Halls
7 November	Portsmouth Guildhall
8 November	Plymouth Pavillion
9 November	Hammersmith Apollo
10 November	Edinburgh Festival Theatre
11 November	Sunderland Empire
13 November	Grimsby Auditorium
16 November	Brighton Dome
17 November	Doncaster Dome
18 November	London Lyric Theatre
19 November	Birmingham NIA
20 November	Birmingham NIA
21 November	Birmingham NIA
22 November	Glasgow Clyde Auditorium
26 November	Southport Theatre
27 November	Dundee Caird Hall
28 November	Hammersmith Apollo
29 November	Sheffield City Hall
30 November	Salford Lowry
2 December	Harrogate International Centre

APPENDIX (II)

REVIEWS

Frank has never read any of his reviews. Not a single one. However, as an accompaniment to his journals, he thought you might like to. Here is a selection for you to enjoy – the ones I think best illustrate his experiences, *On the Road*.

Mark Booth, Publisher, October 2008

The UK comedy guide
Chortle

Frank Skinner has chosen Montreal for his first major stand-up gigs in a decade – but his disappointing headlining set at the Britcom showcase last night brutally demonstrated that he's far from being fully gig-fit yet. Which much be something of a worry given his solo show – which also debuts at Just For Laughs – is just two weeks from Edinburgh and a subsequent high-profile UK tour.

He wasn't the only comic on the bill to struggle. Most did all right – no better, no worse – but as a showcase of all that's exciting in British comedy, much of that the night lacked va-va-voom, as the French-speakers here almost certainly don't say.

He didn't help things by making some fairly rudimentary mistakes. Coming on and boasting about how he's a huge star in the UK made him few friends. He immediately backtracked and said it was a lie. But then flip-flopped again, starting a routine about how he used his millionaire status to attract girls, dropping mentions of his wealth at every opportunity.

This isn't good, especially when you're Frank Skinner, a working-class everyman comic. We know his life isn't like that any more, but the arrogance didn't endear him.

Other routines died uncomfortable deaths, too, not least of which was when this 50-year-old comic told of how he went out with a 17-year-old. 'It's illegal here,' came one heckle which Skinner probably didn't hear. What grated was the matter-of-fact approach, not acknowledging that the situation was that unusual. Though the gags were self-deprecating, Skinner showed little embarrassment about the affair – nor did he make it boastful jokes about it, which could have worked in a bad-taste way. By presenting it as fairly normal, he again proved himself fatally out of step with the audience.

That said, he did produce a few corking gags, usually observations about topical events. His Paris Hilton line was a beauty, all the more so for completely sidestepping all the obvious gags about her wanton behaviour.

But he needs to find a lot more like it for his solo show to be a success, and time's not on his side. A comic of Skinner's standing shouldn't be skulking off stage apologising for his set at one of the most high-profile comedy festivals in the world so close to his much-vaunted comeback tour.

Reviewed by: Steve Bennett Montreal, July 18,2007

The UK comedy guide

Chortle

When Frank Skinner ill-advisedly chose the glaring spotlight of the Montreal comedy festival to launch his stand-up comeback after a decade away, the result was patchy, to say the least. A long way from being gig-fit, he just about held together a half-decent solo show, although it was way beneath his best, and virtually died in a club environment, where few would have known his pedigree.

But now, one Edinburgh run and 52 tour dates later, the assured comic on stage at the Hammersmith Apollo bears only a passing resemblance to that rusty figure, uncertain of where the laughs lay. Fun-time Frankie's got his mojo back – and is back on scintillating form.

Little material is left from that Quebec jaunt just over three months ago, save for a Heather Mill-McCartney routine, that starts with an astute, and little-made, observation on the sorry case, before lapsing into the inevitable bout of jokes about her missing leg.

For the most part, though, Skinner's back doing what he does best. Filth. And he's utterly disarming in delivering it.

When he talks about the stark realities of his sex life, it's not from some laddish braggadocio or some knee-jerk desire to be gratuitously crude for shock value alone. He simply abandons his ego and tackles his subject – and there really is only one subject – with a matter-of-fact honesty, sharing genuinely witty home truths that are easy to relate to, if slightly uncomfortable to bring up.

He might elicit the occasional pantomime shriek, of mock outrage as he describes in graphic detail some of his one-night-stand exploits, and just maybe the odd uncomfortable squirm of anticipation. But with his cheeky-chappy demeanour, he's so skilful at making the bad taste almost palatable, no one really can take umbrage. For all the talk of spunk, pi$s and paedophiles, he still comes across as little more than a harmlessly 'blue' comic, almost from another era.

Indeed, the only thing you might bristle at is a throwaway aside early in the night about sharing a dorm with a gay man that slips into a dated 'backs against the wall, lads' attitude; and even that's so quaint as not to be terribly offensive.

Skinner is one of those acts you suspect was always destined to be a comedian. His style is so natural and relaxed, that engaging 3,000 people comes as second nature. Plus he lives – or at least lived – the sort of reckless life that's sure to throw up a rich catalogue of embarrassing anecdotes ready to be shared with an eager audience.

But now he's turned 50 —though he doesn't look it and barely acts it – he's trying to take stock. He's on the pills now, given up the booze and the one-night stands, and the aging process provides an undercurrent to much of the material.
He even wants to settle down, and in a revealing out-of-character routine late in the second half starts agonising over the hidden meaning of a potential girlfriend's text message, until he's reduced to a quivering wreck, lying helpless with angst on the stage floor. For all his appeal to blokes, this shows another, dare we say more sensitive, side to the rakish Frank.

It's only a fleeting glimpse, though, for Skinner knows his demographic: the lads shouting encouragement from the stalls as if they were on the terraces. His appeal, though, is wider than that, His anecdotes are raucously hilarious, his charm palpable and his mischievous spirit as lively as ever. Welcome back, Frank.

Reviewed by: Steve Bennett Hammersmith Apollo, November 2007

EDINBURGH COMEDY

Frank Skinner
Pleasance Cabaret Bar
★★★☆☆

Mark Watson
Pleasance Courtyard
★★★★☆

Bruce Dessau

OUT with the old and in with the new? Not quite, but on last night's form one of our most naturally gifted storytellers has to get his act together, while one of our brightest new hopes revealed that he can deal with anything a crowd cares to throw at him.

Frank Skinner said at the outset of his smell-the-armpits, bar-room gig that he has not done stand-up for 10 years and at times during his intermittently hilarious and frequently gutter-crude set it showed.

The trademark dark jokes and easy banter were there, it was his usual in-the-zone momentum that was missing.

For a pub turn this was fine, as a warm-up for his imminent tour it lacked comedic consistency. At least the basics — the Heather Mills and sat-nav gags — were spot-on.

But Skinner was uncomfortably honest when 'fessing up about ageing. At 50 his tastes in pornography are becoming increasingly niche and the pills he pops make his urine luminous: "The toilet rug is like flying over Vegas."

He has clearly not lost it, maybe just mislaid it.

Mark Watson has done more stand-up in the last two days than Skinner has done in the last decade, having just completed a non-stop 24-hour gig.

The deceptively confident comic had every reason to be ragged, yet he was tack-sharp, mercilessly silencing a heckler intent on derailing him and justifying his status as everybody's Fringe darling.

The skinny 27-year-old's show is all about finding meaning in existence. Watson's preferred technique is providing his own internal sports-type commentary, whether watching someone miss a train or being propositioned by a stranger.

There were plenty of laughs, a few racy remarks, but the overall feeling was one of squeaky clean joy.

Looking for some comedy to take gran to? The choice of Watson is elementary.

● **Until 27 August.**
Information: 0131 226 0000.
www.edfringe.com.

Evening Standard, 12 November 2007

COMEDY
Frank Skinner

Hammersmith Apollo

★★★★☆

BRUCE DESSAU

IT IS NOT often that this critic is shocked by a comedy show but it happened twice at Frank Skinner's sell-out gig this weekend. Firstly there was the shock of how crude the Black Country bloke was. Secondly there was the shock of how astonishingly good he was compared to his lacklustre club gig at the Edinburgh Festival in August.

Comedians are often diminished by larger venues but Skinner, touring for the first time in a decade, was in his element. Utterly at ease, he might as well have been chatting to his chums at the football. Yet behind the casual delivery this was one of the most tightly structured stand-up performances I have ever seen, full of back-references, mock spontaneity and subtle pacing.

The material has evolved substantially since the summer. Some pertinent reflections on turning 50 remain — his gold tooth makes him look less bling, more fairground attendant — but two obnoxious routines, about his penchant for "granny porn" and his habit of chatting up women by referring to his wealth were absent, replaced by self-deprecating unquotable details of his bedroom etiquette.

Best and most uncharacteristic of all, however, was his closing tour de force, a spleen-venting confessional about obsessiveness, which ended with Skinner flat on the floor and the audience blown away. Not merely a comedy gig, a masterclass in how to turn pure filth into comedy gold.

■ Lyric Theatre, 18 November (0870 890 1107). Carling Apollo, 28 November (0870 606 3400). www.frankskinnerlive.com.

Times, 17 August 2007

Edinburgh Comedy

Frank Skinner

Pleasance Courtyard

★ ★ ★ ☆ ☆

DOMINIC MAXWELL

The anticipation is palpable. Here, in this small room seating fewer than 200 people, Frank Skinner is making his return to stand-up after ten years on the telly. He could have played a way bigger venue — indeed, come his autumn tour, he'll be doing exactly that all over the country. Can the brilliant Brummie reclaim his reputation as one of the best live comics of his generation?

Well, he's got some work to do. For the first 40 minutes of his set he's like his own warm-up man, playing off the crowd and local peculiarities in a skilful, affable way that nonetheless feels like a dereliction of duty in a one-hour show.

His real theme is turning 50 — "I don't want f***ing applause!" he chides, his new gold molar temporarily dazzling us — but whatever he might have to say on the subject, he's eking it out.

Skinner is still illuminatingly seedy. Masturbation — something he says he's supposed to be too old to do, let alone discuss — remains a key theme. "It used to be the icing on the cake," he says.

For the first 40 minutes of his set he's like his own warm-up man

"Now it is the cake."

But his vivid depiction of the "granny porn" he's taken to watching goes on for a good long while after he's made his point. And, as he acknowledges, starting a sentence with the words "One of the problems of being a millionaire . . ." is a sure way of earning our enmity. But he explores his exalted status so briefly that it doesn't justify raising the issue.

Skinner is too good a comic to do a truly shoddy show. Though he pads around the stage in a tentative way, his reactions are still fast, he threads ideas and motifs through his hour, and he ends on a definite up — plying the best Heather Mills material around in a town full of Heather Mills material.

It's a competent, sometimes colourful hour of stand-up comedy. But Skinner is circling round his subject. If he wants to tell us what it's like to be Frank Skinner and 50, he should get on and do it.

Box office: 0131-556 6550
Tour: www.frankskinnerlive.com

Times, 21 November 2007

Skinner is match-fit and tackling as dirty as ever

First night

Comedy
Frank Skinner
NIA, Birmingham
★★★★☆

Dominic Maxwell

Skinner puts on a good show, but the sex jokes grind on for too long

It's Monday night, it's Birmingham and Frank Skinner is talking dirty to 5,000 fans. And if the vivid details of Skinner's scattershot sex life don't grab you, maybe you didn't read the poster right.

"Warning," it says, "this show is not for the fainthearted."
Faintheart or not, I love a lot of Skinner's new show, a prototype of which he played in Edinburgh in August. Back then, Skinner wasn't quite match-fit, after ten years away from live comedy, concentrating on his chat shows and Fantasy Football League. Three months of touring later, a tentative joke-jabber has become a stand-up prize fighter. Slight, moisturised and big-browed, he looks like a cross between a choirboy and Ken Dodd. But he prowls the NIA stage with as much spunk as any of the rock gods that play here, his new gold tooth glinting out from the three megascreens high above the stage.

What your average rock god won't do, and what Skinner excels at doing, is debase himself. He tells jokes about paedophiles, Parkinson's disease, potentially predatory gays, David Baddiel's self-pleasuring techniques. But however laddish or gnarly some of his material, it's mostly made harmless by the way he implicates himself. He's feeling it. He's having nasty falls and forgetting things. Now that he's taking an over-50s multivitamin, his urine glows in the dark — "You should see my toilet, it's like flying over Vegas".

Skinner marshals his material brilliantly, interacting with the crowd or launching into set pieces as if it were all part of the same spontaneous thought process. He's one of the few comics who can play a room this big because, like Billy Connolly or Victoria Wood, his language is so evocative: "like a lizard's inner thigh," he says of his laugh lines. One man and a mike becomes a vivid visual experience.

But he's a bit too vivid sometimes. "I used to put myself about quite a bit, sexually," he says, before leading into an overlong exegesis of his shagging antics. When he's still mocking himself, it's funny: he wanted the woman to go home as soon as he'd "completed the act", he tells us, although maybe the women felt the same. "I don't know. I'm normally on the bus by then." But he gets lost in the nitty-gritty. There are more intimate details than the jokes can sustain; after five minutes, you've got the idea. After ten, the vision of Frank's bony bottom at work has burnt its way into your brain. Really, I could do without it, Frank.

The less blue material is told with the energy and sure sense of structure of a great comic. It's a good show. But if he would interruptus his tales of coitus a bit sooner, it could be a great one. *On tour. Next show tonight, Birmingham NIA. www.frankskinnerlive.com*

More reviews
times2, pages 14, 15

Daily Telegraph, 15 August 2007

Skinner's cracking comeback

EDINBURGH COMEDY
Dominic Cavendish

Frank Skinner
CABARET BAR, PLEASANCE

Frankly speaking: Skinner doesn't disappoint when it comes to bawdy humour

TEN years he's been away from stand-up, busy getting rich and (more) famous on TV, hosting his frisky chat shows for the BBC and ITV. Now Frank Skinner is back doing what he does best – standing in a roomful of people, microphone in hand, making them laugh. For the rest of the festival, he's playing to under 200 a night in the Cabaret Bar at the Pleasance – when he could, if he so chose, easily be packing them in at a venue 10 times that capacity.

Sentimental reasons have brought Skinner back to this low-ceilinged pit of a place. This was where, in the late '80s, he was first inspired to become "an alternative comedian". And it was here, more significantly still, in 1991, that he performed his first big one-man show, snatching the Perrier Award from under the noses of that year's equally hot contenders, Eddie Izzard and Jack Dee.

This isn't a particularly sentimental set, though. Skinner hit 50 in January and experienced what he genially terms "a two thirds of the way through my life" crisis. You might imagine that this landmark age would be the cue for a major bout of retrospection. But while Skinner has fun at his own expense – mocking the way he has slowed down, say, or his attempt to look under cred by installing a gold tooth – this ageing lad passes up the opportunity to show us a side to him we've not seen before.

Who's complaining, though, when – and this is what surely counts most – Skinner proves that in terms of delivery, style and audience rapport, there's considerable life in the old dog yet. Partly because of the warmth of that Brummie accent, no comic can match him for relaxed, grinning charm. It allows him to pitch in fast with his most risqué material – about pseudophiles – and leave you somehow feeling that no harm was intended, or done. As he compares the hyperactive kids of yesteryear with the obeser sort today – and deems the latter "easy pickings" – it's his ability to make you picture the caricatured contrast without dwelling on the grubbier implications of his theme that explains why he continues to exert such a popular appeal. Random childhood reminiscences dominate the hour, and Skinner remains a big kid at heart – recounting how he recently got a kick just walking around London using sat-nav to guide him.

Best known for his bawdy humour, he doesn't disappoint when it comes to the end of his set – unpicking the pleasures of watching "granny porn", one of the more preposterous consolations of bachelordom. "They all look so happy!" he says simply of the aged participants, to instant, affectionate laughter.

Skinner may no longer embody stand-up at its most young, thrusting or groundbreaking. I wished he would take longer detours down memory lane. But after such a considerable hiatus, only a curmudgeon would fail to be impressed by this cracking comeback.

Autumn tour details: www.frankskinnerlive.com

Old-school gags and fresh angst from Frank Skinner

Fabulous at 50 ...
Frank Skinner

Edinburgh Comedy

Frank Skinner
Pleasance Cabaret Bar
★★★☆☆

It's been a long time. Before Three Lions, before David Baddiel and Tara Palmer-Tomkinson, Frank Skinner was a brilliant natural stand-up who made the Edinburgh Fringe his own in the late 1980s and early 1990s. It has been 10 years since he starred here, and longer still, I'd guess, since he played a venue as small as the Pleasance Cabaret Bar. But the wilderness years (some call it TV stardom) haven't dulled Skinner's talent. The man is blessed with the gift of making people smile just by walking on stage and smiling himself.

Skinner's show is about turning 50, though he still has the mischievous glint of a scabby-kneed Brummie schoolboy. In this hour-long set, there's no concession to changing comedy fashions: this is meat-and-potatoes stand-up in which Skinner chats to the audience (his off-the-cuff stuff is as sharp as any in the business), reminisces about his childhood and frets about ageing. The pace is appropriately gentle for a man who seems to be confusing 50 with 90 – the running joke refers to the onset of dementia, and sees Skinner having to

Google words to see whether they exist, or whether he has made them up.

Half of the set plunders Skinner's (now distant) childhood, for memories of his first horse-riding lesson and an entertaining routine about the Beijing authorities torturing people by means of the Chinese burn. But the material here isn't as remarkable as Skinner's ability to calibrate it according to the crowd's response; he is constantly referring to us, bouncing off us, making sure we're involved. Which we usually are, particularly when he ratchets up the I'm-so-old shtick, worrying that the barber now offers to trim his ears, and that his new multivitamins are turning his wee fluorescent. At nighttime, "the toilet rug, it's like flying over Las Vegas".

Then there's the trademark vulgarity: Skinner appoints a moral referee from the crowd, to judge when he goes too far. There's no need: comedy has got cruder in his absence, and these paedophilia jokes won't frighten the horses. Likewise, the closing set-piece about "granny porn", which is cheap, obvious and raises a very British kind of titter.

All in all, it's a very welcome return for Skinner to what he does best and will hopefully keep doing – assuming he is not checking into an old folks' home any time soon.
Brian Logan
Until August 27. Box office: 0131-556 6550.

Birmingham Mail, 20 November 2007

Even at 50, Skinner's a winner

REVIEWS
FRANK SKINNER
National Indoor Arena

JUST in case anyone needed convincing, Frank Skinner, stand-up comic, is not for the faint-hearted.

Away from the comfy surroundings of Fantasy Football or his TV chat show, Skinner is something of an animal when it comes to the live stage.

You only have to ask Heather Mills after some fans were apparently upset at material relating to her during his recent show in her native Brighton - repeated last night.

Maybe it's down to the midlife crisis which saw the Oldbury-born star get a gold tooth on reaching 50 this year.

Whatever the reason, Skinner takes few prisoners during a frequently hilarious two-hour performance in front of a sell-out crowd.

Regular ventures into less tasteful topics include a prolonged and graphic description of one-night stands, while paedophiles and Islamic fundamentalists are also not off limits.

But Skinner, who warmed up for his first tour in 10 years with two shows at the Hare and Hounds pub in Kings Heath where it all began, is equally funny when dealing with subjects ranging from camp snoring and horse riding lessons to a Comic Relief trip to Africa.

Skinner returns to the NIA tonight and tomorrow.

VERDICT: ★★★★☆

TONY COLLINS

■ NATIONAL TOUR... Oldbury-born comedian Frank Skinner, pictured here at his Hare & Hounds warm-up gig.